2020
VISION

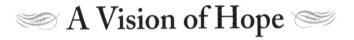 A Vision of Hope

Mary Lynch

BALBOA.PRESS
A DIVISION OF HAY HOUSE

Balboa Press books may be ordered through booksellers or by contacting:

Balboa Press
A Division of Hay House
1663 Liberty Drive
Bloomington, IN 47403
www.balboapress.co.uk
UK TFN: 0800 0148647 (Toll Free inside the UK)
UK Local: (02) 0369 56325 (+44 20 3695 6325 from outside the UK)

Because of the dynamic nature of the Internet, any web addresses or links contained in this book may have changed since publication and may no longer be valid. The views expressed in this work are solely those of the author and do not necessarily reflect the views of the publisher, and the publisher hereby disclaims any responsibility for them.

The author of this book does not dispense medical advice or prescribe the use of any technique as a form of treatment for physical, emotional, or medical problems without the advice of a physician, either directly or indirectly. The intent of the author is only to offer information of a general nature to help you in your quest for emotional and spiritual well-being. In the event you use any of the information in this book for yourself, which is your constitutional right, the author and the publisher assume no responsibility for your actions.

Any people depicted in stock imagery provided by Getty Images are models, and such images are being used for illustrative purposes only. Certain stock imagery © Getty Images.

Print information available on the last page.

ISBN: 978-1-9822-8661-3 (sc)
ISBN: 978-1-9822-8663-7 (hc)
ISBN: 978-1-9822-8662-0 (e)

Balboa Press rev. date: 11/17/2022

ABOUT THE AUTHOR

Mary Lynch was born near Lisnaskea, Co. Fermanagh, in 1959. At 18 years old, her life changed irretrievably after a female police officer pointed what Mary believed to be a loaded gun and pulled the trigger. The post-traumatic stress from this, together with the impact of the "Troubles" and her emerging facility to see and interact with people who had died, formed the background to what seemed an ordinary life.

After the Russian Roulette incident, Mary crossed the border to work as a hotel receptionist in Dublin before fleeing Ireland to work as a chambermaid in Munster, in Germany. In 1980 she emigrated to New York where she initially worked as a Nurse's Aid, before going to work in a Real Estate office.

In 1986 she settled with her husband in Castlerea, Co. Roscommon where she ran her own businesses.

She has two children, a daughter, Roisín, born in 1987 and a son, Jarlath, born in 1990.

This is her second book. Her first The Long Road Home was published in 2010 by Londubh Books. Mary then wrote a column for the Impartial Reporter from 2011-2013 (best weekly newspaper in Great Britain 2012). She now lives in Mayo.

To Love Means,

Loving The Unlovable.

To Forgive Means,

Forgiving The Unforgivable.

Faith Means,

Believing The Unbelievable.

Hope Means, Hoping When

Everything Seems Hopeless.

Taken from the plaque at Free Derry Corner in honour
of the late Bishop of Derry, Dr Edward Daly.

In Memory of
James J Lynch, Brendan Lynch,
Gary Lynch and
Piaras McElroy

PROLOGUE

In September 2007, when my youngest child went to college, I had time to cry me a river – that is, after telling my story to Gerry Ryan on his radio program. Behind the river came memories that lay deeper than those told on national radio. In January 2009 those memories spewed out in fourteen days, in a manuscript of 73,000 words, published the following year in my first book, *The Long Road Home*.

In the summer of 2009, after editing my first manuscript, I was drawn back to the desktop and wrote part one of this book which is similar to *The Long Road Home* but written in the third person. Starting before my conception, it tells the story of why I am here in an unemotional way. This balanced me, relieving me of the fear I had of putting my emotional story out into the world. I was asked to call it *Lessons She Learnt Along the Way*. I promptly filed it away unedited as I could not comprehend who was writing it: my guides, my higher power, my guardian angels! Later that summer, I had a spiritual experience that was so far past my realm of understanding that I told only a few people for fear I would be thought crazy, but I did write it down, then tried to block it.

In 2016, when I could no longer ignore this manuscript with my workaholism, I realised that I had to face it and the journey I chose to have on this Earth as walking against the tide was no longer sustainable. It was at this point I started writing part two which starts in the summer of 2009 where my first book had ended.

Part three starts in the summer of 2016 when Brexit forced me out of the North again and another spiritual experience took place, which I tried to make sense of by writing it down, again in the third person.

The book ends in 2020 when I put the three parts together and filed it away for my children to read when I had departed this life, then on the 6th May 2021, my youngest brother, Brendy, died. That day, I knew I needed to put this story out there to help not only my children but others to understand that death is a part of life and that we all move on to another realm when our work has been done. Should anyone find it hard to transcend, there are people like me who help them do so. They call us death walkers or psychopomps – the Greek word for 'a guide of the souls to the place of the dead'.

The epilogue brings the reader up to date with my life and my work.

In 2022, when finishing my final edit, I was encouraged by someone I had just met to meet up with a man called Ciaran, who is a shaman. He agreed to read my book and loved it. When he finished the epilogue, I received the email below, which to my surprise and delight validated my work.

Good morning, Mary

Hello from sunny France! And the heat isn't as bad as we thought it might be.

I've read through your Epilogue 2020 – 2022, and as with your other writing, it flows very well. The incident around the RUC woman was exceptionally powerful. And I'm glad you changed the paragraph relating to the bank. It conveys the injustice they've done to you more aptly.

Delighted too to see the story around Gordon unfolding. It brings the enormity of what happened to you in the RUC Station in Enniskillen into its proper healing perspective. I'm delighted he was happy with your inclusion of it.

It was somewhat strange for me to see me mentioned as 'Ciaran the shaman!' Why? Because I would never have described myself as that. I have been a shamanic practitioner for over twenty-five years, with seven years dedicated solely to Land of the Dead *transitions.* It is you who *is more appropriately described as a shaman than I am, because your calling has been so strong, powerful and internally challenging, where you have almost had no choice but to do the work of spirit in this specialised shamanic arena that is the Land of the Dead. It is I who honour you for your dedication and sheer commitment to a spiritual pathway which few would even dare to walk, where man's inhumanity to man beggars belief. It is astonishing the level of intense pain we inflict on others, not to mention the soul-destroying pain we inflict upon ourselves. Your pathway provides profound healing to all those who are stuck between the worlds, allowing them to transition on their own journey to the ever-unfolding 'yellow-brick road' of existence. Do not underestimate the significant importance and profound impact that your specialised dedication brings to so many people and their families that have been caught up in the horrific episodes of the human family.*

Yes too, to your comment that your healing journey is bringing you to internal peace … as it should be, and as it is. What a beautiful gift to have, to savour, to feel internally, to be. And just because your healing journey in relation to all of this is coming to an end, it doesn't mean to say that the enjoyment of peace is transitory too! It is not. Peace is with us always. It surrounds us. It is only when we begin to notice that it is there, through eyes cleansed of past pain, that we see clearly how beautiful this world is and how fortunate we are to live in heaven upon Earth.

Much love as always, Mary. You are an incredible soul who has walked her soul-path with honour and distinction.

Ciaran

PART 1

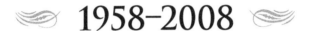 1958–2008

__Lessons she learnt along the way.__

'I have learnt silence from the talkative, tolerance from the intolerant and kindness from the unkind; yet strange, I am ungrateful to these teachers.'

– Khalil Gibran

CHAPTER 1

1958

Watching from the wings for a long time, the conditions were now perfect. After making all the plans and discussing with all involved it was an easy entry. It was her time, and for the next nine months she would reside in a warm comfortable place called a womb, being fed by her host, a woman who would be called her mother.

Mary was aware that this was not a planned pregnancy as there were very few of these in the country she had chosen. She had chosen a religion controlled by fanatics that considered themselves moderate and obedient to a God they believe in, but did not believe that a woman had the right to plan her family, so therefore were at the mercy of fate. But had these not been the circumstances at this time, she would not have had the opportunity to travel with her eleven siblings who were to be part of this life's journey.

Mary had chosen the part of the country that had other religious fanatics, that is, from another religion who considered her people second rate! This landmass was divided by an invisible line called a border. This line was constructed nearly forty years before her date of arrival, by the ancestors on the other side of the border and a government who ruled from across the water.

1

In their wisdom, they believed that this would work – that they could divide the religions, leaving members of her congregation in the minority and discriminated against.

The government that controlled her part of the country had laws that prohibited anyone from voting that didn't own property which excluded most of her religion and the poor of other religions (there were many religions on this planet, all believing they had the one and only true God!). This law also excluded most women, as few women had property in their name at that time. Had you more than one property you were entitled to more than one vote thus leaving both women and the poor of the male gender imprisoned in powerlessness and poverty with no release date. This law was limited to this part of Ireland under British rule, nowhere else on the British Isles!

On the other side of the border everyone had a vote by 1959, when Mary was born (including women over the age of twenty-one), but as the church controlled the government, and also the people from the pulpit (the stand where the priest dictated to his flock), their rights were severely limited too.

The fact that these inconsistencies led to outbursts of rebellion in both her land and throughout the world (where discrimination was rife) seemed to surprise those in power/control. The civil rights (equal rights for all) movement had started in the land of the free and the home of the brave before Mary arrived, but by the time she would reach the age of ten, her people would have followed suit.

This was a world controlled by the rich and powerful using whatever means possible to increase their wealth and power as others lived and died in poverty. To put it in a nutshell, it was a planet where the so-called enlightened believed that wealth and power were the answers to all problems, even though, funnily enough, they never seemed to be satisfied with what they had and died unable to bring anything with them!

Women's main function in the religion Mary had chosen was

to produce as many children as possible to enlarge its congregation, but these were the perfect conditions for this soul to learn its lessons. She had chosen well.

As Mary lay in the comfort of her mother's womb, she knew that when this woman was aware of her occupation, she would not be happy as she already had five children, all under the age of five! Knowing this, she would have been happy to stay in that warm comfortable environment, but nine months was the longest period one got to reside there. The time came for her to be born, and on a warm summer's day in 1959, she made her entry to not much fanfare.

The shock of detaching from her supply of food and warmth made her scream. The sound of her own voice made her scream louder. She may have found a sound to get another's attention but was instantly aware she would have to learn the language the others spoke to communicate – and like religions, there were many languages on this planet. For now, screaming was all she could do, and like love, this was a universal language.

In her first year on the planet, Mary didn't get much attention during the day as her mother was always busy, but at night as she lay in a cot at the bottom of the bed occupied by her mother and a man (who was called her father); she felt the love between them warm the room. It was without a doubt the next best place to the womb, but this too was short-lived as another child took her place less than fifteen months later. This time she was expelled to another cot which was on another floor level and seemed like a million miles away from her parents. She screamed again but to no avail. As her guides it gave us our first real opportunity to befriend her. We became what others called her imaginary friends.

Her entry into her religion was unusual as a man in a dress called a priest poured water over her head when she was just a few days old, to wash away her sins! How it figured she had already sinned was strange to us, but this church, like other churches, had comical ideas.

Mary was the name they gave her after her mother and the mother of their God. Mary, the mother of God, was adored by all in this religion and her picture hung in every house. She was a very important lady, but not quite as important as the men in this world or this religion. The pope (always a man, she was told, but there were censored rumours that said otherwise) was the head of this church. He lived in another country and was the closest person in the whole world to God, or so she was told.

Mary, the mother of God, was a special lady who conceived without sin, something our Mary learnt later from her prayers, even though she had no idea what conceived meant. Sins she understood very well from an early age, as everything seemed to be a sin.

The sins you committed had to be told to the priest as he was closer to God than his flock and would be able to forgive them. As you can imagine, Mary was very nervous at her first confession when she had seven years of sins to tell him!

Mary was told that God knew everything as he was always watching her, but for some strange reason, she still had to admit these sins to someone else to be forgiven. After that first confession she quickly learnt to just rhyme anything off on the first Friday of the month (the time when everyone divulged their innermost thoughts and secrets to the priest). She would sing the same sins every month: saying bad words, fighting with her brothers and sisters ... figuring out very quickly that she could really say anything as long as she remembered to leave telling lies to last as this last sin covered all the lies she had just told the priest!

At primary school, Mary learnt that if you died before you committed another sin you were then free to go straight to heaven. (Heaven was where special people went to be with this God.) The problem was that it was difficult not to commit another sin after leaving the confessional box (the box you went into to tell your sins), as even your thoughts could be sins and it was a long time to the next first Friday of the month (up to thirty-one days!). But if the priest got to you just before you died then you were okay, as he could clear your sins with the last rites and get you straight to heaven, so it was in your interest to keep in with this man (there were no women priests in this religion at this time and still aren't). We watched as he used this power to control his flock. If the priest didn't reach you in time you went to purgatory – if you were lucky.

Purgatory, Mary was told, was the place where you got a second chance. This was why it was so important to be nice to everyone when alive so that they would pray for you when you died to get you out of purgatory. When God heard all these prayers, he would take you to live with him and all those other special people.

Hell was where you went if you weren't so lucky. Hell was where really bad people went. It was down below (the earth, she imagined) and heaven was up above (in the sky, she assumed). There were flames in hell that burnt you all the time and the man who ran this place was called the Devil. Mary saw a picture of him once but it was not hanging in anyone's house. He was a horrible-looking man with dark eyes and she was afraid to ask who had seen him to know what he looked like, as she was told he could come in any guise (dressed as someone else so you always needed to be on your guard). The Devil was an evil man that was always trying to tempt you to sin and could even be disguised as a woman to tempt men, to do things that the church had not included in their rules and regulations.

God was everywhere, Mary was told again and again as a child. *If he is everywhere then he must be in everyone,* she thought. *And if he is in everyone then we are all part of him so we must all be one. We must all be connected, and if we were all connected, then why could we not all be good and nice and kind to each other?*

Ahhh … we thought, *the simple mind of a child who was not allowed to express her opinions.*

Later, when Mary found out what conceived without sin meant, she was even more confused. You had to have sex to conceive a child, but Mary, the mother of God, had a child without having sex and without being married! Sex was a sin unless a woman was married when she participated in this act to have a child. (Well, this was the case for a woman anyway, for some reason this didn't seem to be a sin for men!) *Maybe it was because men didn't carry the child,* she thought innocently.

All these rules and regulations got more and more confusing for Mary as she thought about them, then one day when she was about nine, her older brother (he was twelve) said in anger, 'I am not going back to confessions nor to the chapel.'

'Why?' she asked aghast.

'You know what religion is used for? It is used to control people by using fear … If you make people afraid of what will happen if they do certain things, then all you have to do is make rules and regulations to control them. Then, if you have a way to forgive them, like going to confessions, the control is increased.'

Mary looked at him horrified but knew deep down that they were the truest words she had ever heard.

Now that he had an audience he continued, 'You know the Protestants think they have the one and only true God too.'

'What are Protestants?'

'Have you not seen the other churches in town?' he asked.

Actually, Mary hadn't, but wasn't going to admit this because she knew he already thought she was stupid.

The next day she asked her friend Bernie, who was a year older and knew everything.

'Oh yes, they have churches. I will show you next time we go to the cinema in town.' Bernie's mother gave them money on a Saturday to see pictures moving on a big screen before there was a TV in their house.

Mary looked at one of the churches the following Saturday and realised that the reason she hadn't noticed it before was because it was much smaller than theirs, but there were a few of them, some looking just like a hall. She read on one bulletin board that they only went there once a month!

'That is because they are not as special as us,' said Bernie confidently, '"and they don't have as many children either, as God doesn't want as many of them around.'

'How do you know that?' Mary asked.

'Because Mammy works for them. She cleans their houses and there are only one or two children in their families.'

'Maybe we should pray for them?' asked Mary.

'Oh no. That is a sin. You can't pray for them.'

'Can we go inside their church to have a look?'

'No!' Bernie answered, horrified. 'You can't go in there; it is a sin, and they can't come in to our church either. God would know.'

A few days later, Bernie asked her mother if they could go with her to work. Mary couldn't believe the size of the house this family lived in, and Bernie was right, they didn't have big families. As they sat in the kitchen of the big house watching Bernie's mother work, she was reminded of a movie they had seen recently. The only difference was the mother and children in the movie had black faces.

That night, Mary prayed for these people called Protestants so that God would love them too as she couldn't believe that anyone as special as God didn't love them all equally.

Her brother's refusal to go back to the chapel or confessions caused ructions in their home so Mary decided it would be best to say nothing, to pray for everyone, do as she was asked but take it all with *a pinch of salt*. This was something her father always said. Something she couldn't explain but understood very well what he meant. Rebelling like her brother seemed only to cause trouble and we knew it wasn't her time to say anything just yet!

Later in life, when Mary found a God of her understanding, she wrote a poem which her father loved.

FIRST FRIDAY CONFESSIONS

First Friday confessions
Sunday Morning concessions
Religious obsessions
Men in dresses with no women to be found
In places of power on their Holy ground.

A God of Love I was sold,
With Terms and Conditions, I was told.
Until no more I could take, so walked away and took a chance,
With a God of Love, I could romance.

A God of Love I did find,
With no Terms or Conditions of any kind.
Only Love in her heart,
For me, For you, For all mankind.

CHAPTER 2

1969–1977

When Mary turned ten years old, the family got a TV – that is a box which showed moving pictures in their home. She was so excited that day she tried to start a fire in the cold sitting room with papers, but the only thing she managed to do was to set the chimney on fire. Thankfully this new addition to their home was put in the living room which was always warm and even warmer in the hot-press where she lay watching out through the space between its two doors, where only wee bodies like hers would fit. She would lie on the slatted shelf basking in the heat from the naked cylinder below as it warmed her to the very core.

The whole world was opened to Mary's family in their living room where they all watched this box together. There was news and movies and also series on the box – that is, stories told over weeks and years. Her favourite two series were, *Colditz*, which was about prisoners of war and their many attempts to escape, and *Land of the Giants*, a title that speaks for itself. *Colditz* was shown on a Friday night, and the first Friday confessions interrupted these impatiently awaited episodes. If they didn't get home for the start, they were all devastated, as this was long, long before there was any such thing as recording or playback. In *Land of the Giants*, which was shown on a Saturday afternoon, she saw herself as one of those tiny people that lived in a world of giants.

We watched with interest as these two series were to play out in her own life as two of her brothers were to become prisoners of war and there were many escape attempts from that prison. The giants who came into her life wore uniforms, carried guns and drove huge, armoured cars wielding as much, if not more, power than the giants on the TV.

On the six o'clock news in the late sixties, Mary watched people marching in their towns and cities for civil rights, watched as their houses were burned down because they were looking for equal rights for houses as well as votes, burnt by people with as little rights as those living in the houses they burned, but saw themselves as superior because of their religion. The army who had come from across the sea to protect her people started beating them on the streets. These men with uniforms and strange accents seemed to have the right to do whatever they wanted. *It is as if there is no God, or maybe they believe they are God,* thought Mary.

Before long, these soldiers were stationed in her town and they took some of her neighbours away to a concentration camp like *Colditz*.

'Why are people put into concentration camps when we don't have a war?' she asked her brother.

'In case they cause trouble. We may not have a war yet,' he continued, 'but this will probably start one. Probably what they want ... A war on their doorstep so they can train their soldiers.'

'Can't they train their soldiers at home?' Mary asked, wishing they would all go home where they belonged.

'Of course, they can and do. But if you create a war, you have a real-life situation, and then the soldiers will be better trained.'

'But why would anyone want a war?'

'Control. Fear. Fear will keep people from looking for their rights, and of course, a lot of money is made in wars.'

She looked at him, baffled.

'What kind of history are they teaching you ... let me guess, British economic and social history? You should go to the library and read books on history of their empire. *Divide and conquer* is their motto. All they have to do is divide the poor and have them fight each other, then bring in their soldiers and they have a war and control of the poor with fear of each other leaving neither with any rights ... You do know that we are second-class citizens ... Well, actually, you are a third-class citizen.'

'Why?' she asked, shocked.

'You are a Catholic and a female.'

'What's a female?'

'A girl, a woman. Men everywhere in the world have more rights than you. They are the bosses.'

Mary didn't ask anything more but what he said didn't seem right as their mother was certainly the boss in their house.

What Mary didn't understand then, but would eventually realise, was that she had chosen to be a member of a family of strong women. Her maternal grandmother had flown in the face of tradition when she married her grandfather in 1922, as not only was he believed to be of an inferior religion to hers (on the northern side of the border!), he was also much younger than her (something still considered unacceptable nearly a hundred years later, even though a man could always marry a woman of any age!). Her grandmother then changed her religion to her grandfather's and survived, even though she was ostracised at the time. Her paternal grandmother was part of a group of women who had their own cottage industry making lace, earning their own money which give them some freedom.

We watched as everyone's fear intensified in the late sixties north of the border. Soldiers were now walking around Mary's family's farm as if they owned it, and if this wasn't confusing enough for her young mind, she was then stopped on the road and asked her name and address by local farmers, neighbouring men who were now wearing uniforms and also carrying guns.

These men had got themselves a second job to protect everyone from people looking for jobs, a home of their own and therefore a vote. *How is this possible?* she thought. *Is everyone stupid, or blind?* But she asked no more questions as she could see that everyone, including the adults, were frightened.

In September 1970, eleven-year-old Mary went to the newly built secondary school in town, which her parents and all the congregation had to help pay for. It was a school for only her religion as their church leaders didn't want them mixing with other children of other religions. Even though she was taught to love her neighbour, it seemed to depend on their religion. Every morning as her bus passed the other school in their town she wondered, *why does a small town need two big schools? Would it not be better and cheaper if we all went to the same one?* A few parents did send their children to the other school but it didn't work very well, as the children there, in the majority, made the children in the minority's lives very difficult and the priests (from her religion) denounced the parents from the pulpit. This was, of course, one of the greatest ways of shaming them, and of course, shaming is controlling.

Mary's name, address and sex had categorised her up until that time. Now her school uniform added to this division.

Two years later, when she was to become a teenager, things changed again – this time dramatically.

At the beginning of that year, 1972, Mary had watched as people of all ages marched against internment without trial in one of their major cities. When the day was over, thirteen people lay dead on the streets (seven of them teenagers). As it was beamed on TVs around the world, she came to the conclusion (that of an innocent child) that this would stop everything, something would be done about the discrimination. Enough was enough. In her innocence, she couldn't believe that soldiers could shoot seven teenagers in full view of cameras and get away with it. Maybe the church tried to control them with fear, but surely her brother was wrong about governments. They would never do this, nor could she believe that any civilised nation that watched this atrocity would accept what had happened. Her illusion was shattered ten weeks later with the Widgery Report (Lord Chief Justice of England) who exonerated the soldiers that murdered fourteen people (another had died in the meantime) and later in life, one of these soldiers was honoured with an MBE for his service.

Mary quickly calculated on that day, the 18th of April (her brother's fourteenth birthday), that in two months she would become a teenager, therefore a legitimate target for this army. She also was aware that after this time teenagers were joining the IRA (Irish Republican Army, an illegal organisation who decided to take up arms to defend themselves).

Life as Mary knew it had changed again and any trust she had left in authority was completely shattered. She watched family and neighbours close down in this extraordinary situation that they were ill prepared for. She watched others prepare to fight back to survive, and even at this tender age she knew that she would kill if necessary for the survival of both herself and her family, even though she knew this wouldn't be in any organisation as she had already had enough of organisations. We were privy to the plans she made and they included using her father's shotgun to defend the family. There was no doubt in her mind that this was the only option left for her at the time.

By the end of 1972, 495 people were dead on her side of the border, including three of her neighbours. 'Killed by the army,' she heard the adults whisper.

'Why did they kill Michael, Andy and Louie?' she asked her brother.

'To make an example of them. To put even more fear in everyone else. Didn't I tell you before, the quickest way to control people is with fear?' he replied angrily, walking away.

After that year, Mary's home and family were her only sanctuary. She lay awake at night listening to stones crunch under the heavy boots of soldiers as they walked around their house at night. This sanctuary was taken from her a couple of years later when she was woken by the point of a gun. The army and armed police were now deemed to have more rights to their home than either her or her family as they entered it at any time day or night (usually five in the morning) with a piece of paper from the government which gave them permission.

The following day, an official from this government would arrive to assess the damage done so her parents could claim for the destruction of their house, but no compensation was offered or would ever be paid for the unseen damage done to the minds of the children within its walls.

What Mary was too young to understand was that she had to become an adult overnight, using whatever means possible to survive. That if she was lucky enough to reach adulthood, her teenage years would have to be lived at another time. She was later to understand this and eventually had to endure the emotions of a teenager in her forties, emotions suppressed when they should have been expressed, but at the time – in the seventies – she was lucky in the fact that the perimeters of this war finished about five miles from her home. She could cross this line through an armed checkpoint (the border) and have the freedom at the other side at weekends, socialising with these people who were free of war but burdened with their own lessons of control. Controlled in everything they did by a church, a control that was not quite as blatant on her side of the border where they had competition.

Control was certainly the name of the game wherever you lived on this planet that Mary was on and fear was its main weapon. Taking back control was a teenager's rite of passage, but she soon found that as she overcame one fear, there was always another to take its place, as there were many, many different fears used to control.

Finishing up at school, Mary had the opportunity to move on to college like her brother, but was very aware at this young age that this was not her direction. She had already decided that she wanted her lessons from life experiences, not from books written by others. She had thought nursing was the way for her, but it wasn't to be, and this was accepted.

As the war continued with a community even more divided, Mary had gotten used to living on red alert. By the age of seventeen she was listening carefully to her inner voice to survive, even though she was not aware at this time that this was the voice we used.

Six months working in a shop told her that this boring life was not for her, even though she had a romantic episode with a very handsome young man from the other side of the divide to distract her for a time. A relationship that would have been frowned upon had anyone known (but no-one knew as she was now adept at keeping secrets). A relationship that was the distraction she needed at the time but was far more important in the scheme of things than she could ever imagine. Her life's work was to be tied up with where that short romance would lead her, but she had a lot of living and learning to do before that was going to happen.

Mary had a plan for her life, a plan she chose and promptly forgot when she entered planet Earth. We were there to remind her when she was listening and help her to change direction (by whatever means necessary) when she wasn't. This she wouldn't understand for a long time, and it was to take her a lot longer to accept. This acceptance would finally give her the freedom that no-one could ever take from her – no religion, government or even an army and police force carrying guns!

When given the opportunity to move on to work as a hotel receptionist, Mary grasped it. She loved her new job, and all was well until the last week in 1977 when the hotel was bombed. As receptionist and the only person who saw the man bring in the bomb as luggage, she was questioned and answered what she was asked.

The following day, after the police connected Mary to her

brother who had taken up arms, she was picked up from outside the hotel and psychologically tortured to the point that her young mind froze unable to process the threats made on both her body and her family's lives, but the consequences of her surviving and telling what had happened didn't enter her mind. She believed this was the end of her short life, that these people in uniforms had the power to do as they wanted to her, and they believed it too, but in this unlikely place we were given the opportunity to show her our existence and what lay beyond the veil of the world she lived in. This happened when the trigger of the gun at her head was pulled and her soul rose from her body. Mary watched from above as the policewoman holding the gun realised immediately that the girl she thought she controlled no longer feared her. In that moment, Mary felt blissfully at one with the entire universe and had no problem letting go of the body that housed her – but it wasn't her time. Later, when she was dumped unceremoniously on the side of the road outside the hotel, she had to re-evaluate her life. Before morning light, she had blanked everything and had made plans to move on. She knew that the repercussions of her telling what had happened to her on a physical level would be enormous. What she had experienced on a spiritual level, well, that she didn't believe there was anyone she could tell!

For the first time in her life, Mary felt totally alone and bereft in the world, but this was the only place in which she was she going to find herself. All was in the order of things.

CHAPTER 3

1978–1979

We guided Mary across the border that had no barriers – only in the minds of people and states. Six months in the capital city was enough for her to know she could no longer stay in the country as memories kept surfacing and she trusted no-one to tell her story.

When we whispered to her that it was time to move again, she heard us. We needed her completely alone to reconnect with her, but she didn't want to go alone. We watched patiently knowing something she had yet to understand; you can't change the direction of another person's life. You may persuade people to go a different direction for a short time, but they have their own inner guide even if they are not aware of it and they will get back on track at the first available opportunity. The three others that she had convinced to go, dropped out one by one, but Mary knew she had to go: alone if necessary.

On Easter Tuesday morning, 1979, Mary stood on the side of the road outside a small village near to where she was born, hitching a lift. She had all her belongings in the small rucksack on her back and £100 in her pocket. She was leaving behind her family, friends and the only life she knew, going to a place where she had never been, a country where she didn't speak or even understand the language. Having taken a leap of faith, she now needed help. For the first time in her life, she was forced to openly ask us for it.

She spoke out loud, clear and directly to us, 'I know you want me out of here. I have done my part, now do yours.'

We contacted the first available lorry driver and asked his guide to ask him to stop. He did (we guides were all connected and brought people together when it was time for them to meet) and within minutes, Mary was on her way to Scotland, and with the help of this driver she got on another truck to Dover and was well on her way to West Germany. More important was the fact that she had acknowledged our presence and had witnessed our immediate response. In the future she would finally come to realise what she understood intuitively as a child – she was connected to everyone.

We now had her alone, and in this time, we were the only ones who spoke Mary's language fluently so she was forced to converse with us. Four months later she headed home with direct communication with us, reinstated for the first time in ten years. Unfortunately, this communication proved impossible to sustain when she returned. She let our relationship go from the depth she had reached us, but she never forgot it.

We knew this as we often listened to her tell the story of heading off to Germany alone. When others exclaimed how brave she was, Mary always replied, 'I wasn't brave, I was guided every step of the way.'

It was to be a long time before she asked again for help, apart from in business. It was like our relationship was changed to a business one, but we were pleased with any communication. We were only too aware of people finding their guides when they asked in a crisis, afraid to tell anyone about the help they got, afraid to be seen as different on this planet. The powers that be needed everyone to be the same to control them; the fear of standing out was overwhelming and had huge consequences.

On the way home from Germany in 1979, Mary was in a motorcycle accident in London. As she lay in the middle of the road drifting in and out of consciousness, she heard a voice in the distance ask, 'Is she dead?' and she wondered if this was her time.

Knowing she had no control in it, this time she neither feared living or dying. We heard her thoughts: *Why do I need to have an accident if it is not time for me to die?* We explained to her that sometimes it took an accident to change the direction of a person's life. We explained that we used whatever means necessary, even if it meant she was injured. In time she would learn that in other instances, a lot of guides would get together and lead a lot of people to their death at the same time, the time they had chosen, the plan they had made before entering this planet. We were their guides; we were not the creators of their journey. Our only purpose was to guide them back when they drifted off the path they had chosen, or to their death at the time they had chosen. The manner of the death didn't matter. If they didn't need to learn anything from suffering, then their death was instant.

A long time later in her life, in a tai chi class, her teacher told her that she had a long life ahead of her, that she had a lot of work to do on this earth. She had hated his arrogance and had replied, 'So, I can drive a car at any speed, and I am going to be safe?'

He had answered her very calmly saying, 'I didn't say you wouldn't be doing it from a wheelchair!'

In that moment, Mary understood that her body was her responsibility. How she kept it would make a difference. If she forced an issue, it didn't mean that it was time for her to go, it just meant she would be living under different circumstances, and of course, we would be forced to use those circumstances to take her back to her life lessons.

Flying home the day after the accident in 1979, she was met in Belfast by her father and brother. Back to a war which was called 'The Troubles'. A term that was used by the powers that be so that they could use wartime measures in troubled times. These special measures had included the use of internment without trial for her people. In time these special measures included Diplock courts (a court that had one judge and no jury and named after the Lord who had decided it was a good idea!). People were treated as prisoners of war until they reached the prison and then they were called criminals. These inconsistencies lead to even more violence, then some prisoners refused to wear prison garb and were left with only blankets to cover their naked bodies. This led to what was called the dirty protests, after the prisoners were beaten when they went to empty their commodes so stayed in their cells and threw it against the walls. All these inconsistencies finally led to the hunger strikes in 1981 that left ten men dead and kept the province in continual crisis.

We needed Mary home that day after the accident in London, and her first time on a plane was the quickest way to get her there. It was just before the weekend of the 27th of August. It was time for eighteen soldiers to move on – they were to die in Warrenpoint, Co. Down – and for a short period of time she and these soldiers would be alive and on the same landmass. These men which she was destined to meet again on a different level.

Her plans of remaining at home were quickly changed that weekend when the house was searched again, reminding her that even the contents of her drawers of underwear were considered items of national security!

A couple of weeks later, Mary went on a planned trip with her mother to Connecticut in the USA for three weeks. Four months later, she flew back to New York with a distant cousin and then moved on alone a few weeks later. In the interim, she had lived again in the so-called Free State (the other side of the border with nothing free in it, especially not the people). There, we created lots of situations to force the move to America, including getting her the money through a scheme called a disturbance allowance (this allowance was used by the British government to entice people from north to south of the border, her people, of course, as she doubted many from the other side of the divide were in any rush across this invisible line to a place where they would be in the minority!). This disturbance money she saved for the flight back to the United States, when flights were equivalent to nearly four months wages!

Situations we created were called either good or bad by earthlings, but they were neither good nor bad. They were just situations that changed a person's direction to what they had already planned. She was later to learn that all would flow if something was meant to be. This was to be one of the biggest shifts in her thinking. She had to rewire her thoughts from those of the society she was brought into. Thoughts from: *If it's worth getting it is worth fighting for.* To:

If the door is locked, it ain't your door. Really going with the flow was the name of the game – a game very few people played!

In years to come, Mary went to see a therapist when she was having a spiritual crisis. The woman asked Mary why she thought she had come to Earth and she replied without thinking. 'To learn to love myself.'

The woman replied with a smile, 'Well, you chose the perfect place. The middle child of twelve and into a war!' Twenty years later she called this woman again when she needed to tell someone what was happening in her life and she mentioned the word psychopomp, a word Mary had never heard before, another word that labelled people. A word that labelled some of the work she was doing.

This was indeed Mary's (and everyone's) greatest lesson. Until she learnt to love herself, she could not proceed with her real purpose on the Earth, as without love of the self, there could be no love for any other. The opposite of love is not hate, it's fear.

With love for the self, she would conquer fear. Without fear she could not be controlled. Without control she would be free.

With freedom she could do anything she wanted, including connecting to all the people on this plane and those who had left it and help on a spiritual level, finally understanding that helping another was helping herself, as they were all indeed one.

It was much later in life that she read and understood the quote from the philosopher, Khalil Gibran: *'I have learnt silence from the talkative, tolerance from the intolerant and kindness from the unkind; yet strange, I am ungrateful to these teachers.'*

CHAPTER 4

1980–1999

Within weeks of reaching New York, Mary had heard us clearly when we asked her to leave her cousins behind and moved in with someone else in this new and strange city. Her listening skills had been put to the test again and she passed with flying colours, but she was not content in the Big Apple. She didn't feel at home there, and after working day and night for nearly a year whilst also attending demonstrations outside the British Consulate for the hunger strike that had started at home, she headed back to her family home at Christmas. The home from where her eighteen-year-old brother had been removed and was now a prisoner at Her Majesty's pleasure, awaiting a trial. Guilty until proven innocent!

Two weeks later, Mary returned to the States determined to stay as she now had no doubt that she no longer belonged anywhere in the six counties of Ulster under British rule and didn't want to live in the free state. Back in NYC, we guided her to a yoga and meditation class. She loved it. In meditation we got her full attention for that time she was in class; it may only have been ten minutes a week, but it was a start. Within a year, we guided her to a young man who meditated every day and had been doing so for nearly ten years. This was the man she was going to marry, and Mary knew this the very first night she met him. She knew this as she was very aware, very aware but not very mature. She may have been a very streetwise twenty-two-year-old, but the traumas of her teenage years had left her an emotional child. She forced the marriage two years later. She was never under any doubt about this and had never a problem saying it. She was afraid of losing him, afraid that he wouldn't realise that it was meant to be but nothing needed to be forced. She was never going to lose him. How could she? He was to be the father of her children and these two souls had already chosen them as parents and were now waiting for the right conditions for their entry.

Mary often told this story to her daughter who arrived four years after the marriage, laughing at her ignorance and arrogance as she explained to her daughter Roisín that she may have been able to force the marriage, but couldn't force Roisín a day before her time. Like everyone else, her daughter had chosen her time and place of birth very carefully and no amount of pressure would alter that.

Married in 1983, Mary and her husband Marty worked in New York before returning home to Ireland in 1985. There, she continued her interest in real estate (from her job in New York) by buying their first property in Belfast. When the second property was purchased in the same city later that year, they were also negotiating the purchase of the family farm from Marty's mother. This property was the first they would buy on the southern side of the border.

Whilst both deals were going through, they decided to use this time to go back to the USA to work. Five months later, Marty returned from Florida and rented a house outside a wee village in Co. Roscommon which was eight miles from the farm in Co. Galway. Mary boarded a plane two weeks later and arrived the day before her brother Sean was shot, in April 1986 (when his comrade Seamus was shot dead. It was only in the writing of this fact did she realise that she needed to be back on the same landmass of not only the eighteen soldiers that were killed in Warrenpoint, but also Seamus passing on. Plus, the eight more equally brutal deaths that occurred a year later, which would lead to the first visions of healing she would see in 2009).

Going to live in the Free State for the third time, she believed that this was the time when she could open up about her experiences in her teenage years, but after the shooting of her brother, she was silenced again. Silenced in a place where no-one wanted to know as they were protecting themselves from a past that they had neither faced nor healed from.

This was another lesson Mary had to learn. People feared what others mirrored. Her past of war and violence reminded the people she now lived amongst of their not-too-distant past of a civil war, that had split families and left open, infected, unhealed wounds. Wounds that were now being carried from one generation to another. Unfortunately, those who reminded them of things they would rather forget were blamed. Attack seemed to be the main defence tactic on this planet. Whilst her fellow countrymen and women on the southern side of the border glorified their own past of war and violence; they had conveniently forgotten that it was this past which had created her peoples struggles. It was the nature of humans to blame others instead of dealing with their own issues. Ironically, this was what was perpetuating individual and world suffering. There could be no peace in the world until it was found in the self, and when Mary achieved this, nothing outside herself could or would affect her.

Mirroring by another person wasn't always a so-called bad thing. Sometimes when a person sang the praises of another, it was simply because they could not accept some of their own wonderful qualities/gifts that were being mirrored back at them.

For the next twenty years Mary would continue to attract the same type of people into her life. People who were mirroring herself, both her gifts and her wounds. To heal these wounds and accept these gifts, Mary would finally have to take the focus off everyone else. She too needed to stop the cycle of blaming to start healing.

We had guided her to a place within reach of her family of origin but outside of the warzone. The fact that parts of her soul were still in the places where she had been traumatised would have to be dealt with later. For now, all she could do was to chop wood and draw water. That is; concentrate on the day-to-day things she needed to do to survive. Mary did this to excess, giving her the reputation of being a wonderful worker when in fact she was a workaholic. This addiction would keep her memories at bay for the next ten years as her place of birth continued in turmoil.

In those years she went through the motions like everyone else, with advertising companies telling her what she needed to make her life complete and governments and churches trying to control her with fear. We watched as Mary and others were sleepwalking through their lives using their addictions to survive. Addictions that most weren't even aware of.

There were addictions to drink and drugs (which everyone seemed to be aware of before the addict!). These addictions were considered bad by society, but funnily enough prescription drugs were acceptable as the powers that be controlled the dosage and made money in the process. A work addiction like Mary's was also considered good, as in it, people were very productive. Others were addicted to helping people whilst they ignored their own basic needs – she later found that this was called co-dependency. There was also the addiction to food and sex, and the longer she lived the more things were added to this list. The thing was, it didn't matter what the addiction was, they were all simply an avoidance of the self.

In these years of her addiction to work, thankfully, she continued to meditate as she ran two successful businesses and had two beautiful children.

Mary asked for and took our guidance in business, never

questioning the direction we pointed her in, even when others did. Why would she question it as our guidance had always led her to so-called success on this planet, which was measured by finances. Mary realised what little success she had achieved with all the money she had made when in crisis, a time when she said to her doctor, 'I would give every penny I have to take the sickness out of my stomach for an hour!' At this time this was the only way we could stop her. It was now 1997, and there were talks of peace in the place she was born, and soon she would be in a safe place to unload the weight of her past and move on.

Medication was needed and given to her to stop the intensity of the memories that were forcing their way up from a well deep within her being. Mary didn't want to face what everyone else was trying to avoid, but in 1999, as the everyday fear for her family's lives was taken away, the burning lava from the volcano of the past was bubbling up looking to be dealt with immediately.

We watched as the medication only took the edge off the anxiety, knowing that she was heading for another addiction – this time one that someone else would control. She looked alive and well but inside she had died, unable to function with or without the drugs. She needed space and time to heal but neither were available to her. She had two young children and two businesses to run and no help to do either.

Society endorsed these chemical concoctions that she was given. These addictive substances where people could be back in the workforce as soon as possible as there was no time or space to heal naturally.

Governments had declared a war on drugs, which really was only a war on 'dealers' other than themselves. Representatives of these governments may not be dealing the drugs out of their own pockets, but countries were run on legitimate drug money as huge taxes were received into the country's coffers from pharmaceutical companies who, in turn, had huge power within these governments for their financial contributions.

At this time, Mary had been taking care of so-called psychiatric patients for ten years. Some of these people had been institutionalised for decades before she began boarding them out into the bottom level of their split-level bungalow. They were now her extended family who didn't fit into this controlled society for many reasons. Some had been surplus to requirements on farms and needed to be disposed of without actually killing them. Others did not fit into the perception of what was considered normal. Then there were the women who had a child that was not unlike the immaculate conception as no man seemed to be involved, but they were far from revered like the Virgin Mary! In this so-called 'sane' religious society, a lot of these women's fates laid either in institutions where they were drugged for the rest of their lives or they worked in laundries without any monetary reward after their children were taken off them. Either way it was a life sentence without parole and the only reason some of these men and women were released to Mary's home was that the government had found a cheaper way to house them.

Mary's extended family were controlled by substances that were changed at the whims of others. These others were people conditioned by the state educational system who were taught that this was the only way in a society which had neither the time or the resources to allow people to heal naturally, or indeed allow their differences. From constantly trying her best to reduce their drug intake, Mary was well aware of the difficulties in doing so. Knowing and understanding this system, she had no intentions of becoming another addict of prescription drugs nor another neglected vulnerable person in a crazy world.

This system she found easy to understand as she was brought into something similar, the only difference being that in her patch of the same country, the government could sanction and condone the killing of the people, including children, without fear as they believed they were answerable to no-one.

With this in mind she planned to get off all medication as soon as possible.

Six months later she crossed the border and got a supply of natural herbs to use; herbs that were banned on the side of the border where she lived as their value couldn't be evaluated – in other words, they were in competition with the pharmaceutical companies.

Mary was now starting her recovery naturally. She had no doubt it was going to be a long journey home but was well aware of the consequences if she didn't take this road, lucky in the fact that the people who she had cared for were now helping her as they understood her better than most. But she needed someone she could tell her story to, someone who she could trust and was willing to listen. It was coming close to the time to introduce Dave back into her life. A man she had journeyed with, in many other lives.

CHAPTER 5

1999–2002

In 1999, Mary was what was considered successful on the planet she lived on, as financial success was all that was considered. She had tried to mould her life into the so-called norm to fit into society's expectations of her by buying, renovating and renting properties in addition to taking care of her two children and her extended family of seven, but it wasn't working. Her life and her marriage were both falling apart as she could no longer sustain the level of work she was doing to achieve this success. We guided her to both marriage guidance and a tai chi class, both of which she started on the same day. The first session of marriage guidance had not gone well and she didn't want to go to tai chi that night. The only reason she went was to support her friend Maura who wanted a class and had found a teacher.

As Mary crossed the car park that evening, she waved to Maura and was introduced to Dave who was there with his teenaged son. The first thing that triggered her was Dave's English accent, but it wasn't only his accent that catapulted her back to her childhood of war but also the fact that he looked like a soldier. She followed him and Maura into the building vowing to herself that she would never go back.

When the class started, Mary was triggered even more when he stood arrogantly in front of them explaining how tai chi could help heal the body, mind and spirit. She had wanted to run out of the building and go home and hide under her quilt as flashbacks from her past were already overwhelming her and she certainly didn't want any more triggers. Her heart was beating so fast she thought everyone in the room must hear it. Inside we heard her scream, *I can't take any more of this.*

As she stood there, frozen, she watched as her soul left her body for the second time, watched as it went out to meet the soul of what she considered a foreign intruder. The hug that they gave each other was one you would give a long-lost friend. Was she hallucinating, she wondered, as she looked around to see if anyone else had noticed. Nobody seemed to and that included him.

In that moment we whispered, *He will help you and you will help him.* But she completely blanked this remark as Mary trusted no human being and if she ever did, she believed that it would never be someone with his background. Half an hour later, walking back to her car, we heard her thoughts scream again: *I'm not going back there.*

The next morning, she went to see her friend and said, 'I met a man last night, Teresa, and I know him even though I have never met him before.'

'How would you know him if you don't know him?' asked Teresa, surprised.

'I have no idea, and what is more, he represents everything I despise.'

'Are you going back next week?'

'No!' she replied immediately. 'Maura has got enough people for her class and no longer needs me.' But the following week, Mary's curiosity got the better of her and she went anyway. The feeling was still there. She was under no doubt that she knew him.

She continued to tell Teresa every week after her marriage counselling (which was going well) and the class (which wasn't) what was happening, and Teresa advised her to call Dave. She was shaking when she finally made the call and told him what she had told her friend after the first night.

'You better come down to see me,' he said.

The following day she entered his house, which he shared with his wife and two children, and took a seat at the far side of the kitchen.

'Explain to me what you saw.'

'The first night in class I knew I had met you somewhere before, it was like meeting an old friend, and I know it sounds crazy, but I saw my soul reach out to yours and hug you.'

'It's not crazy,' he replied. 'You and I have travelled many lives together.'

The relief flowed through her as he continued by talking about reincarnation. A concept that had never entered her mind as her church had taught her you lived, you died, you went to heaven, hell or purgatory. Amen.

'Did you know that the first time we met?' she asked.

'No,' he replied. 'But I knew in the first few weeks.'

Trust him, we whispered. *Talk to him,* we continued. But she never let on she heard us. She finished the conversation and got back to her life remembering that she had met other people she immediately felt a connection with, but not this close, and it frightened her.

Then one night when they were practising shiatsu in class, as Dave had been working on her he asked her to stay after the others had gone.

'What is wrong with you?' he asked.

'Wrong with me … Wrong with me?' she repeated, bitterly.

'Parts of you are stone cold,' he explained.

'People like you is what is wrong with me,' she said.

'People like me!'

'English men, British soldiers. I am from the North and my childhood was destroyed by people like you.'

He listened without any reaction and then said, 'If you ever want to talk about it, call me.'

She didn't answer. She walked out of the room and was sobbing uncontrollably when she reached the car and again, we read her thoughts: *If I ever tell anyone what happened to me it certainly won't be you.*

The flashbacks continued, and when he asked if she wanted to join a walking club that he had started, she said, 'No!'

'Why don't you go with them?' Teresa asked. 'It would do you good to get away for a break now and again ... You work too hard.'

'What if he brings a gun?' Mary asked.

'What do you mean?'

'I don't know what I mean ... I'm afraid of English men ... I suppose a part of me believes they all carry guns!'

But she did go a few weeks later and loved it from that very first day. She loved the fresh air, the wide-open spaces and the opportunity to talk to different people and tell stories – she was hooked, and every Sunday after, she was off to the mountains.

Talk to him, we whispered again and again but she ignored us as she went to different therapists for help.

A psychotherapist asked on her second visit, 'Do you know what you suffer from, Mary?'

'Depression, I was told.'

'No. You are suffering from post-traumatic stress.'

She laughed.

'Why do you laugh?' he asked.

'I have always known that, but I don't understand, why me? Why am I the only one in the family?'

'It is post with you. They are all still living in it,' he replied.

Mary felt like hugging him. Driving home that day she was so relieved that there was a name for her suffering, as on the planet she lived on everything had to have a name to be accepted.

She continued to walk every Sunday until foot and mouth hit the country, then the mountains were closed down for months.

The marriage guidance had worked for a while, but now, nearly a year later, everything was back to where it had been before. It was summer and her husband was away from first thing in the morning to last thing at night on the farm, whilst she was exhausted trying to keep everything else going. She thought a holiday might help, but it only made things worse.

When they arrived home on that Friday night in August 2001, there was a message on her phone to say the walking club were back in the mountains on the Sunday and she was delighted.

Mary drove to the cottage that they had recently purchased and she had renovated the following day (A place that was meant to be a holiday home for the family, but because it was bigger than they required, she divided it into two cottages, the bigger part becoming yet another business). That day she prepared it for guests who were arriving the following day. Arriving home later that evening there were six missed calls from different family members, which was highly unusual as even at the height of the conflict no-one made calls unless really necessary. *Someone is dead*, she thought, *Daddy is dead*. As she reached for the phone it rang.

'Did you hear about Gary?' her sister asked.

'Gary! What about Gary?'

'He was killed on his motorbike in New York this morning. A taxi driver hit him as he sat at a traffic light.'

Mary dropped the phone, sat on the floor in the hall and cried as if her heart had broken. The tears she could not release before flowed through her and wouldn't stop. The following day she went to the mountains as there was nothing else she could do until Gary's body was brought home. Before reaching home that evening, she had made two major decisions. The first one was to ask her husband for a separation and the second was to accept Gary back into her life from another level, as his spirit had been beside her the entire day in the mountains!

Tai chi had indeed made her physically, mentally and emotionally stronger, and the death of her nephew had given her the opportunity to grieve for everything she held in her body. This grief was acceptable in the society she was living in, but the fear of another breakdown petrified her. It was now time to tell her story, it was time to speak the words that she vowed never to utter.

We whispered, *Talk to Dave*, but again, she refused. She asked Marty if they could go back to marriage counselling. He said no, so she went alone to the same counsellor as before. He explained that he could not work with her alone regarding her marriage, but he would counsel her through her past if she wanted. She never returned because he too was English.

We tried to reach her in her meditations and even went as far as bringing her back to past lives where she knew Dave.

She told him about this.

'How did you know it was me?'

'The man had the same energy as you,' she replied and then asked, 'Do you remember what lives you met me in?'

'I don't need to remember,' he replied.

'No?' she answered. 'You have nothing to fear from me. I have everything to fear from you.'

As it was only three years after a fragile peace agreement, and she, who had not uttered a word to anyone about her experiences (including her husband or siblings), knew she never would unless with someone she trusted with her life.

As the end of the year approached, Mary was crying every opportunity she got, telling her children that it was about Gary but his death hadn't created any grief for her as she knew he was in the place that she had passed into twenty-five years before, and knew it was beautiful and he was free. Christmas arrived and as she attended mass in the local psychiatric unit with her parents and extended family, the visions of her being in a psychiatric hospital were flashed before her again and we finally got her attention. On New Year's Eve she called Dave and said, 'I need to talk. I feel like I am pregnant and about to deliver. What I do not know?'

'Come down this evening,' he replied.

Later that evening, sixteen months after she first met him, she sat in a room with Dave in his home and opened her mouth – and didn't stop talking for over an hour. He listened in silence as she blamed his countrymen for all of her problems.

When she finished, they sat in silence for what seemed an eternity before he said, 'You know, the soldiers were probably as afraid of you as you were of them. They were brainwashed into believing all of you carried guns. They believed that you would have shot them if you got a chance.'

'I would have,' she retorted immediately, admitting to him and herself that at the age of thirteen she had made a decision to kill if necessary, knowing that this was the greatest wound her heart was carrying: a decision made that couldn't be unmade. She had crossed a line that was a stain on her soul, her ticket to hell.

Driving home later she felt a tonne lighter and danced in the New Year without a care in the world, but by six the following morning the next memory was bubbling up to be dealt with and she had no choice but to go back and tell Dave the rest of her story. This no longer posed a problem. Mary now trusted him with her life as she had admitted her greatest sin, not to a priest looking for absolution but to an English man, who neither condemned or judged her.

'Why are you talking to him?' her husband asked.

'I need to tell someone what happened to me … I can tell you.'

He didn't answer so she continued to talk to Dave every opportunity she got. There was always time in the mountains or after class, but never on the phone. She didn't trust the phone as she was still paranoid about someone else listening.

As Mary finally opened up about her past, we knew that that the real healing had started, but her marriage of nineteen years had come to an end. Her husband was not equipped to deal with what she was going through, or what she needed to go through. She was in no doubt that the alternative to talking was a lifetime of prescription drugs and institutions. As this was not an option, it was time for her past to be faced. It was time for her to move on.

CHAPTER 6

When a memory surfaced in a flashback, Mary would feel it weigh her down until it could be spoken. If Dave wasn't around to speak to in person, she wouldn't tell anyone else, instead she would carry the burden until they met. Until it was verbalised, she found it difficult to eat or sleep. The relief afterwards was enormous – that is, until the next memory surfaced. She was now living one day at a time, dealing with one memory at a time.

Gary appeared in all her pain. *Why do you come to me, Gary?* she asked one morning on her daily walk.

Because I know if I help you, you will help the others, he replied through her thoughts. She assumed 'the others' were their immediate family as she was not yet reconnected to the child who knew that they were all one, that the entire population of the planet was her family.

She asked Dave, 'Why me. Why does Gary come to me? I was away most of his childhood and my sisters were much closer to him.'

'Because you are open to him. Our dead are all around us, but the majority of people are closed to them.'

One morning in the summer of 2002, as she walked the back lane behind her house making her way to the park, Gary appeared in her mind's eye and spoke to her as he always did.

Will you give Dad another message for me, Mary?

Of course, I will, Gary, she replied without uttering a word. *But you know I have tried to before. Why would he listen now?*

I know you haven't been sleeping nor eating, Gary said. *I know you need to tell Dave something and I know he is away with a group walking. I will get you to him today and then you will tell Dad how I did this, and he will listen.*

Dave is in Antrim, Gary, and doesn't have a mobile phone. I don't have anyone else's mobile number. How could I contact him, and you know I wouldn't tell him anything on the phone anyway?

I will get you to a place where you can meet up with him in person today and then you will tell Dad and give him the message.

If you get me to meet up with Dave today, it will be a miracle, Gary, and I will not have a problem telling your dad about the miracle or giving him your message.

As soon as Mary returned home from her walk, she started to do what all humans believed possible, control outcomes. This was learnt from the cradle: control and be controlled by whatever means possible. They really believed that their interference was going to make a difference, when in reality, it was nothing but a hindrance to us. Whilst she tried to help Gary get what he wanted so that she could get what she wanted, everything went wrong. This started when she suggested that they not go to Enniskillen as planned that day, as she believed that there was a better chance of her meeting this group in her hometown, but Roisín was not having it.

'You promised, Mammy, you promised we would go to Enniskillen today.'

'We can go tomorrow.'

'No! You promised we would go today!'

Mary finally relented. Off they set and Roisín insisted they take the back road to Enniskillen; again she relented to get a little peace. Unbelievably they got lost and ended up in Enniskillen an hour later than she had planned, leaving the chance of connection in her hometown with Dave impossible. She was devastated. *Another night without sleep,* was all that was on her mind as they entered the shopping centre. Half an hour later, her daughter declared there was nothing there that she wanted and then asked if they could now go to the town centre. So tired at this point, Mary nodded. Walking after Roisín through a shop in the centre of town fifteen minutes later, a voice from behind her asked, 'What are you doing here, Mary?'

Turning around, she faced a member of the walking group and replied in shock, 'What are you doing here?'

'Tom got us lost so we stopped here to eat.'

'We got lost too,' Mary replied. 'Where are the rest of the walking group?'

'In the restaurant next door.'

With her strength back she rounded up the kids and said, 'We are going to eat.'

Entering the restaurant, she saw Dave at a table against a wall surrounded by his wife and two friends.

No way am I going to interrupt this group, Gary, they are having a meal together.

Go say hello, we whispered.

As she stood by their table, Dave's wife got up and said, 'I'm going shopping.'

'I'm coming too,' replied her friend and as she rose; the only other man at the table proclaimed the same. Mary watched in amazement as the table was cleared in a matter of minutes.

'Can I talk to you for a moment?' she asked Dave, as she checked the children ordering food at a table close by.

'Sit down,' he said.

It took less than five minutes for her to tell him what had surfaced over the past few days when he was away, and in that time, no-one disturbed them.

She then returned to the children, ate right for the first time in days and had no doubt she would sleep that night, but before going to bed she would have to fulfil her end of the bargain and do what Gary had asked.

Later in the evening, when the children were settled in at her parents house, Mary went across the road to her brother where he was working in a bedroom of the new house he was building. She told him the story of what had happened that day and finished with Gary's message.

He didn't say a word, nor did she need him to. She was asked to deliver a message and had done as asked.

As Mary slept soundly later, we knew she had reached a place she could never come back from. Not only had she accepted that someone who had passed over was communicating with her, but she had shared it with another member of her family. Mary also saw a miracle happen before her eyes, realising that this couldn't have happened if they were not all connected, those in human form as well as those who had passed on.

Before the end of the same year, she went on holiday with her older sister and told her everything that had been happening. This sister would become her confidant in the years that followed when she watched things happening that no-one else seemed to be aware of.

She told Geraldine that just weeks after Gary had died in New York, she had sat in the hairdressers whilst they watched two planes gut the twin towers.

The hairdresser stared at the TV in shock. Mary told her sister she had said … 'Middle Eastern terrorists, armed and trained by America at some point in their existence. Mark my words that there will be new laws on international terrorism in the coming weeks.'

The hairdresser looked at her as if she were mad. She told Geraldine that she thought herself mad at that point too.

'I don't think you are mad,' her sister replied. 'But why you, why do you think you see all these things, how would you know those things?'

'I have no idea,' she replied. 'But life would be a lot easier if I didn't.'

As a child, Mary had watched state terror in Belfast and Derry on the TV before the murder of her father's cousin and his friend by the British Army in 1972. The local police force had spread rumours at the time that Michael had murdered his friend and then himself with a pitchfork, and this propaganda worked. It added an even greater rift between the already bitterly divided religious communities. It was to be six years before a soldier admitted to taking part in the killings. An admission made because he believed the infamous Yorkshire Ripper was one and the same man. He wasn't, but the murders were just as savage.

Before the end of 1972, she had understood and accepted what governments could and would do to achieve their own aims, which included the cover-up of the murder of innocent people if necessary.

Before the end of 2001, the USA Patriot Act was passed by the United States Congress and the Anti-terrorism, Crime and Security Act by the British Parliament – international terrorism laws were changed. The terrorists were blamed, we now had a war on terror to deflect the terrorist activities of governments throughout the world and no-one seemed to see the comedy in that, governments declaring a war on terror! Terror was now being used to bring even more fear into the hearts of the people to control them. Same old story only on a bigger scale. Nothing had changed.

Mary needed to be deprogrammed as the one she was on was also controlling, it had led to conspiracy theories and these too were another form of control. She needed only to attach herself to the universal energy, nothing else. In this place she would be aware of the connection she had with everyone and realise that all was in the order of things.

For the next five years, Mary continued to practice meditation, tai chi, walk alone through nature every day and with different groups of people in the mountains on Sundays. During this time, she also took care of her children, her extended family, renovated more properties and continued to watch the abuse inflicted on a planet that sustained them.

By the end of 2002, her ex-husband was settled into the house they owned next door and took the children every Sunday when she was walking and also on Wednesday nights. She was left with two days a week for herself and her memories.

The first thing that had surfaced after the separation was the threats on her and her family's lives. Also, the verbal sexual abuse she had received from the mouth of a policewoman when in the barracks in 1977 knowing she would be unable to verbalise this sexual abuse to Dave, we guided her to the rape crisis centre. A place where she would find refuge time and time again over the next twenty years as she came to terms with what happened to her and how these threats had affected her life and relationships.

The depth of fear in her was so deep she also needed another professional to help, so we guided her to an organisation aptly named 'Justice for the Forgotten'. An organisation formed in 1996 with the aim of campaigning for truth and justice for the forgotten victims of the Dublin/Monaghan bombings in May 1974, when thirty-four people died, the greatest loss of life in a single day of the Troubles. This group were also helping anyone living south of the border that had been traumatised in incidences during the conflict. Driving to her first appointment with a man who was trained to deal specifically with post-traumatic stress, Mary felt her unseen injuries were validated as the southern government were funding her sessions.

Halfway through her first session, the psychotherapist told her he didn't want to hear what happened to her, he wanted her to tell him how it was affecting every day of her life. The following week, as she talked, he asked where this feeling was lodged in her body. He then guided her to bring her attention to it and even though sceptical at first, she soon felt the release and relief of working with him.

On her third visit she said without thinking, 'Something in me trusts you.'

'Why do you say that?' he asked.

'Because there is a big jug in front of me and black stuff is pouring into it, and this only happens when I am alone or with someone I really trust.'

'And what do you do with the black stuff when the jug is full?' he asked.

'I bury it under a tree in my imagination as I don't want to leave it where it will poison anyone else.'

'How did you learn to do this?'

'I don't know,' she replied. 'One night when I couldn't cope with all I had to release this started happening on its own.'

'Did you ever read about the Native American Indians?' he asked.

'No?'

'This is one of the methods they use to heal,' he replied.

On those long dark nights of the soul when the memories could no longer be contained, we were there, guiding her in every way possible to heal, whispering different ways to release the poison stored in her body. She listened carefully and never questioned anything we asked of her. She was open and trusting so therefore had the entire knowledge of the universe at her disposal.

CHAPTER 7

One morning on her way to an appointment with Andy (her psychotherapist), Mary tuned into a national radio station. The presenter was speaking about the latest tiger kidnapping which had happened the previous night. (This was the time when the country she had chosen to live in was going through a boom period called the Celtic Tiger.) A bank manager had been kidnapped and whilst he was taken to the bank to hand over the money there, his wife and children were being held captive by gunmen.

Mary listened intently as the psychotherapist spelt out what would happen to the children if they were not given the right help. As he listed the symptoms, she mentally ticked off all the ones she was suffering from.

When the presenter stated, 'We have no experience of anything like this in this country,' she braked the car, pulled onto the side of the road and with a rage ripping through her body, called 11811 and asked to be put through to the Gerry Ryan show. A moment later she was speaking to his researcher.

'I am listening to Gerry speak to the psychotherapist and I just want to say, get those children help. I am driving to a psychotherapist as we speak, dealing with the same thing that happened to me over thirty-five years ago … in this country!'

'What happened to you? the researcher asked.

'I was held at gunpoint by the British Army and police in our home when I was fourteen years old, and I am only dealing with it now, and I have suffered most of the symptoms the psychotherapist has spoken about.'

She didn't expect another word to be said as there was little or no sympathy for the victims of state violence, so she was shocked when the researcher asked, 'Would you speak to Gerry?'

'I can't. I'm on my way to my appointment which is in five minutes.'

This, she stated, believing she had said all she needed to say and didn't want, expect or need any sympathy from this man that she had resented most of her life, as he had made comments about her people that were totally unacceptable to her.

'Would you speak to him at another time?' the researcher then asked, breaking through her thoughts.

'Yes,' Mary replied putting down the phone with no expectations of ever hearing from them again.

Two minutes later the phone rang and the researcher said, 'Gerry would like to speak to you now if you would speak to him?'

Speak, we whispered.

'Yes. Yes, I will,' she replied.

'Okay. Park your car. We are going into ads and we will call you back in three minutes.'

Quickly calculating that three minutes would get her to her appointment if she rushed, she rushed, parked the car and ran to Andy's door saying, 'I'm on the Gerry Ryan show and going to speak in a moment,' as he opened it.

'Go into the sitting room. I will listen in the kitchen,' he said. She rushed in, sat down and the phone rang as Andy brought her a glass of water.

Mary expected that she would be allowed to say just a few words so said, 'Get those children help. I am suffering from what they will face if they don't have immediate support.'

'Tell me what happened to you,' Gerry asked to her surprise.

So, she told him what happened that night, the first night the army entered her home. That first night when she had been woken up by the point of a gun. She told him how all the children were brought downstairs in their bare feet, then held for what seemed to be an eternity as their home was ransacked by the army and police. She told him how she had looked across the fields to the neighbour's house, watched as the lights of their home went on that winter's morning knowing they knew what was happening and there was nothing they could do. She told him that she believed that they were all going to be murdered and that neither her father nor her neighbours could protect them. When she finished speaking, she glanced at the clock on the mantelpiece in Andy's office to see that it was a few minutes to ten and knew the news headlines were coming up, but as she had said her piece, allowed her teenage self a voice and could only hope someone would get the children in question help.

'Mary,' Gerry said gently, breaking through her thoughts. 'I know you are missing out on your appointment, but I would be very grateful if you could wait until after the news headlines and talk to us some more, but I will understand if you want to go to your appointment.'

'I will wait,' she replied firmly, knowing that she had already reached this man on a level where he heard her.

After the news Gerry said, 'We have Mary on the line. She is in the waiting room of a psychotherapist as we speak and giving us a bird's-eye view of what it was like to live in the North in the seventies.'

For the next fifteen minutes she was allowed to tell her story on one of the most popular programs aired in the country. When the interview was over, Gerry thanked her and wished her well.

Driving home that day, she had no idea the impact that speaking out on national radio would have on her memories. This coupled with the fact that she had recently returned to the

North for her niece's wedding which had taken place in the hotel that had been bombed the night before the police had taken her into the barracks.

A few weeks later, she finished up with Andy. As he walked her to her car, she thanked him for all his help.

He replied, 'Thank you, Mary, you have taken me to the edge of my training. I doubt if you will ever need me again, but you know where I am if you do.'

As the summer of 2007 rolled on, Mary believed she was heading for another breakdown, understanding that she had taken everyone to the edge of their training. She was wide open and the flashbacks returned with an intensity she didn't believe anyone outside herself was equipped to handle. As her son got ready for college, she held the memories back with a promise to herself that they would be dealt with in September when he was gone.

As soon as her son moved, the floods of tears came again, this time she listened carefully to us as we directed her away from all her supports. Her friends, her businesses and tai chi which left her alone with no distractions (not advisable to most but Mary had already done this before). Totally alone, she asked us for help again and we sent it in the form of a group of enlightened souls which Henk later confirmed to be the white brotherhood.

What can I do with all these memories? she whispered in the middle of a long dark night of the soul, as they whirled around in her head with no exit point. Frame by frame they came, as if they had been captured on a video tape and were now being released in slow motion.

Write, we told her. *Write them out.*

'No. I can't,' she screamed, as this advice had immediately flashed back a memory of her brother running down the stairs when the army and police were ransacking their home saying, 'They are in your bedroom reading your diary, Mary!'

Enraged, she had rushed out the living room door, ran up the stairs where a nervous young soldier unlatched the trigger of his gun as she pushed past him into the bedroom that she shared with her sisters. She snapped her diary out of the hands of a policeman and screamed, 'That is mine. You cannot read it!'

He snapped it back and replied coldly, 'I can and I will, and there will be a lot more than me reading it before we are finished with it.' With that, the young soldier entered the bedroom and took her back downstairs at the point of his gun.

Mary dared not cry at the time; now she screamed as the fear she had held in her body for thirty years rose up with an intensity that she thought would choke her. The fear of what could be changed in her diary to incriminate her family or neighbours, leaving them with long prison sentences, left her frozen. When the diary was returned a week later, she threw it into the Rayburn cooker and silently vowed that she would never write a word again. Six years later, when she felt safer in New York, she did write short, bitter poems which she hid.

Write, we whispered again and again.

No! she replied to each request.

Mary had no excuse for crying this time, but as she was on her own from Sunday evening to Friday night, she let the tears flow. Behind them came deep and more disturbing memories. With no-one to tell these latest revelations to, she finally took her pen and wrote them in the middle of those dark winter nights on anything within her reach – backs of envelopes, art paper, even old official letters she had in a press beside her bed, and it never once entered her mind to buy a jotter to write as every day she believed there was nothing more to come.

CHAPTER 8

2008

B y the middle of 2008, Mary had most of her past taken out of her body and onto paper, writing at night after working with her brothers during the day, building a new home for herself. By the end of the same year when the entire world was heading into a financial crash, we guided her to a computer course, a skill we allowed her to believe she would need to get another job as a hotel receptionist. This was far from the reason she would need computer skills, but it wasn't time to reveal this to her yet. She was working on a need-to-know basis and she had already been told all she needed to know.

Back in a classroom for the first time in over thirty years, Mary found it wonderful to have company after spending so much time alone. Not only had she good company, but she was learning a new skill, believing that her past was dealt with and she was ready to move on with her life. This course had begun a week before she started because when she first applied, she had been told that it was full with a long waiting list. When she finally got an appointment to see the facilitator to check if there were any similar courses, the lady asked her what her first choice would be.

Mary replied with a smile, 'The computer course that started last week in Ballaghaderreen.'

'Okay! Could you start tomorrow, as a few people have dropped out?'

'Yes. Thanks. Great!'

'Leave me your bank details and I will start the paperwork.'

'You mean I get paid to do it?'

'Yes, everyone gets paid to do it and there is another Northern woman starting tomorrow morning too.'

Walking back across the road to the car in a daze, Mary couldn't believe what had just happened. Not only did she get the course she'd wanted, but was also going to get paid and have a fellow Northerner to make her feel at home. Driving home to the cold house that she could no longer afford to heat, she realised that she had to be on the right road as everything was falling into place. For the next few months, a pay cheque with enough money to keep the wolf from the door would drop into her account every week, as her only income at that time was from John, the one remaining member of her extended family living downstairs.

Parking her car before nine the following morning, a woman parked her car beside her. The first thing Mary noticed was the Northern number plate and smiled at the fact that they had both arrived at the same time. Introducing herself, they chatted all the way up the stairs to the classroom, by the time they reached it she knew that this woman was from the other side of the divide, but this no longer made any difference to her. At times like this both she and we knew how far she had come, how much she had let go. They got on very well together as Joan was a tonic and they laughed most the week until the Friday morning, when the teacher asked everyone to bring in their CVs.

Joan looked very worried when she approached Mary in the kitchen at lunch and said, 'I don't want to bring in my CV. I don't want anyone to know who I worked for.'

'Why?' asked Mary, laughing. 'Did you work for MI5?'

'No,' Joan answered. 'I worked for the police.' Explaining that she was a secretary in a police station in Belfast.

Mary froze, but as she was a professional at cutting herself off from her emotions, she replied calmly, 'Don't worry. No-one will take any notice of where you worked.'

No-one but me, she was thinking as she headed for the bathroom to compose herself.

Entering the classroom ten minutes later, Mary went directly to the teacher and asked if she could leave early as she wasn't feeling well. She drove her car home as if drunk, scraping the side of it on a narrow bridge outside the town having completely lost touch with both time and space. Reaching home, she immediately went to bed and hid under the quilt, shaking.

'You alright, Mam?' Jarlath asked later when he arrived home for the weekend.

'I must have come down with something,' she replied, knowing that there was no way she could act her way through this and could not tell him the truth as he had already seen too much of her pain.

Lying in bed the entire weekend, Mary couldn't believe that the year alone, facing so much, had left her feeling no better – in fact, she was paralysed with fear. When Jarlath was out training for football and working that weekend, she cried like she had never cried before and the fear of a return to medication was overwhelming. She decided she wasn't going back on the course, instead would go back into isolation.

Tell Joan, we whispered. She ignored us, but on Monday morning we watched as she dragged herself out of bed, got dressed and back into the classroom.

Arriving early, she went straight to Joan and told her what had happened.

'I am so very sorry,' Joan replied as she put her arms around Mary.

'It is not your fault, Joan,' Mary replied as she hugged her back. 'It is something I have to learn to live with.'

The week went on and the two women became even closer, whispering about their shared past.

By the following Sunday, Mary was back in the mountains, delighted that she had crossed a hurdle that she believed impossible. We were delighted too, but knew that she was about to face another person that very day that could knock her back again or leave her in a place of freedom, which would allow her to take a different direction in her life.

Mary always led walks from behind, keeping an eye on those who were struggling at the back, that day telling stories to an English man who had recently joined the group. This she found was a great way to keep their spirits up, and being a natural storyteller, was telling him the one about a woman in the class who wanted to borrow a tape recorder and had offered hers. 'It wasn't until I found it that I realised the tape of me talking to Gerry Ryan was still in it.'

The man interrupted her, 'What were you talking to Gerry about?'

'Post-traumatic stress. I suffer from it because of the Troubles.'

'So do I,' he replied.

Stopping in her tracks, Mary turned her body completely in his direction, looking him straight in the eye to ask, 'What happened to you?'

'I was a British soldier in Northern Ireland,' he replied.

We watched, wondering which of them looked the most startled; he who had made the statement and then turned a lighter shade of pale, or she who just heard it and had no reaction.

His eyes filled with tears as he tried to compose himself, she wanted to reach out to hug him but didn't, she had never before met anyone who admitted that they were suffering from this because of the war and was past caring who he was.

'I can't understand why I told you that,' he sobbed. 'I have never told anyone else. Some of my family don't even know that I was in the British army. I cannot sleep at night. I think it is my penance for the things I did there. I will never forgive myself.'

The rest of the group were way ahead taking no notice of what was happening between these two souls who were walking alone, completely at one with each other.

As they continued to talk, we listen with amazement as Mary said, 'You have to forgive yourself. You can't live like this. I now know that I have no problem forgiving you. It was a war. You were young and doing what you were ordered to do and this was part of your journey to learn whatever it is you need to learn.'

He turned from her and walked on in silence. She walked beside him and said no more.

Driving home that evening, Mary couldn't believe what had just happened or how she had dealt with it. How could she reach out to a man who was a member of the security forces who had traumatised her teenage years? A man who was aware and had admitted to the damage he knew he had done? A group she had held hatred in her heart for nearly forty years. A group of people she despised. It was a miracle. All the writing she had done had worked. She was free.

Sleeping soundly that night, we were aware that she had now reached a place of compassion for both herself and others, and was ready to use the skill she was acquiring in the computer class to tell her story.

The new year would give her an opportunity to take the next step on her journey if she chose to take it.

PART 2

 2009

CHAPTER 1

A NEW BEGINNING

At the beginning of 2009, Mary had reached a place where she accepted that some souls lived and died without recognising the love, help and support that was theirs for the asking. The problem being that it was coming from a so-called unacceptable source. That source being us, their guides. She had accepted Gary's presence from the moment he reached out to her, the 19th of August 2001. For the next seven years she had used every available means presented to her to heal, from finally taking a leap of faith and trusting us that talking to Dave would help. Also talking to and working with psychotherapists, kinesiologists, masseurs, herbalists, acupuncturists, a trauma expert and the wonderful women she met in the rape crisis centre.

The feelings and emotions of Mary's teenage years were finally faced in her early forties at the same time as her teenage children were going through theirs!

Her inner child who needed her attention, was getting it, and therefore no longer needed to act out in public. She had started to mature from the child that had been traumatised, nursed the wounds that were being triggered by other people and had come to accept that this was something only she could do.

First came the interview with Gerry Ryan, then her return to the hotel (which was the backdrop of her trauma) for her niece's wedding a few months later in 2007. After that came the death of another of her extended family that summer, followed by the loss of another when they moved on to a retirement home. All of this left only John, who was living in the bottom of her house. When Jarlath left for college in September that same year, she listened to and took our guidance to remove herself from all her other supports and distractions, leaving her alone with us for the second time in her life. Once again, we were the only ones who spoke a language that Mary had come to understand, after letting go and trusting that we would be there with her on those long dark nights of the soul. In that winter she finally found the courage to write the hurt, anger and bitterness out of her body and go back to do a course that would be needed in her future.

Before the end of 2008 the world hit a recession which wiped out the financial security that had taken her thirty years of hard work to accumulate.

Mary was now in Limbo (a place that was no longer used in the religion she was brought up in, but a name she still used for that in-between place that we called the void).

Getting ready for Christmas 2008, she started by cleaning the house to welcome her children and parents for the holidays; a house which had been neglected for three months as she did her computer course. After finishing the living area two days before Christmas, she reached her bedroom late afternoon. As it housed the only double bed in her home, she started preparing it for her parents. Clearing the locker at the side of the bed, she came across all the pieces of paper she had written on over the year and had stuffed into its drawers.

As she stared at them, we whispered, *Burn them.*

No! she replied immediately, utterly shocked at the request.

We asked again. She didn't reply, instead went to the hall closet, took out her jacket and headed out the door for a walk.

As we continued to ask her to burn everything, she continued to refuse, repeating the words, *I can't. I need my children to know what happened to me.*

Arriving back at the house an hour later, she sat down and went into a meditation where we mentioned it again. We watched as she rose from her chair and took everything she had written out of the lockers and lay them on the bed. Then, she sat down to read them.

There is no need to read anything, we whispered. *Burn them!*

As if in a trance, Mary walked out of the bedroom and into the sitting room looking for a matchbox or a lighter that worked (as Jarlath was a smoker at the time) but could find neither, even amongst the collection he kept in his bedroom for some reason. She then proceeded to rip up every piece of paper and threw the scraps into the empty grate in the fireplace without reading a word. Returning from her walk on Christmas Eve, she saw smoke coming from the chimney. Her parents had arrived and her father had started the fire which was now burning her angry and bitter past.

On the first day of January 2009, Mary headed north with Roisín to spend a couple of nights with her parents, siblings, their partners and some of the next generation, coming back home on the third. On Sunday the fourth, she went walking with friends. On the morning of the fifth, she got out of her bed and into the kitchen to find the mess left from the night before and heard us say loud and clear, *Turn on the radio.*

Okay. I will listen to Gerry Ryan; he will cheer me up. He will blank all the thoughts about the financial crash and what I do now. What if I can't pay the mortgage? What if I can't pay the college fees, what if, what if? The what-ifs that had been churning in her mind for weeks now. We saw the disappointment on her face when Gerry wasn't presenting the show that morning. As she reached over to turn it off the lady presenter said, 'If you ever thought of writing a book, stay tuned. We have one of the country's best-known authors to tell you how.'

You can write a book, we whispered, and she remembered the last words Joan said to her when the computer class was over, two weeks before.

'I will type that book for you when you write it.' And they both had laughed.

She hesitated, but only for a moment, before getting a pen and a piece of paper to write the magic formula which was: 2,000 words a chapter, 100,000 words a book. Mary smiled and was reaching to turn the radio off for the second time when she heard the author speak the words that we wanted her to hear, 'It took me six weeks to write the first 2,000 words.'

Mary walked out of the kitchen, leaving all the dishes in the sink, and turned on the old desktop in the guest bedroom which she had turned into a wee sitting room as she couldn't afford to heat the big one.

Two hours later Mary had written 2,000 words when Roisín burst into the room and said, 'Mam, I need to be at the train station in ten minutes, will you please bring me?'

Rising from her chair and putting a coat on over her pyjamas, she followed her daughter to the car. On the way to the train station she said, 'I have started to write a book, Rois.'

'That's great, Mam, will you pick me up at six?'

Before leaving for the station at six, Mary had not only cleaned the entire house, she had also written 2,000 more words and believed us when we told her that the book would be published.

Two weeks later Mary had finished the story of her life thus far, and only then did she have time to be frightened of the words that had poured out of her at the speed of lightning as she used her typing skills learnt in secondary school. A skill never used before, words that had been waiting a lifetime to be released on a computer she had only recently mastered.

With the manuscript which told the unfolding of her life,

Mary had reached a true understanding that this was a part of her journey, that the people who forced her from her home, her country and her family were there to facilitate this journey and in her near fifty years of living on this planet she had done the same for others. She had come to understand that most humans in power in both religions and governments operated from a place of unconsciousness, believing that they had the power to do anything whilst ignoring all the signs that they certainly had not.

She was now not only communicating with us, but also with Gary who had passed on, and was aware of another man who had tried to contact her from the other side of the veil. She knew and accepted that she had been here before, that this life was her university, a place where she came to study her chosen lessons and that if she did not pass the test, we would have no choice but to create the conditions for her to repeat them. She understood that when her work was done, she would return to the energy from where she came and be with all those who passed before her.

The conditions were now perfect for her to change direction again. She had surrendered to win, understanding that all was as it was meant to be and that nothing needed to change except her perception.

CHAPTER 2

Her manuscript needed to be edited, so Mary called her cousin Deirdre's husband, Brian, as he wrote for a magazine, believing she had done her part and now only had to hand it over to someone else to finish. She thought Brian would find someone to do this for her – that is, if he didn't want to do it himself, but she was in for a rude awakening.

He listened to her and then said calmly pronouncing each word as if she was a child, 'Mary, the first draft is never the last draft, but you can't have a last draft without a first draft!'

'Okay,' she replied, seething, but knowing exactly what he meant.

When she put down the phone, we whispered, *You can do this yourself. You can edit.*

Going directly to her computer, she opened up page one and knew immediately that this was something no one else could do, as not only would they not understand what she wanted to say, but the fact was that even spellcheck found it difficult to decipher most of her words.

Six weeks later, the 73,000 words had been expanded to 84,000. Every night during this period she had called her youngest sister Gertie and read the latest edited chapter, then sent the changes to her email address where she could access it from anyone's computer. On St Patrick's Day, two copies of the edited version were printed, then one taken to her friend Marita's – asking her at the door if there was any drink in the house.

'I can't believe you are asking for a drink in the afternoon, Mary … You, who rarely drinks.'

'I need a drink, Marita. I have written and printed my truth, and I am now frightened what will happen to it.'

Marita looked her straight in the eye and asked, 'Did you tell the truth about your brothers?'

'Yes, in the first page.'

'Did you tell the truth about your age?'

'Yes, in the first line.'

After a sip of wine (as that is all that was needed to bring her down), Mary left the copy with her friend and went home and read the other copy, trying to get into her friend's mind and figure out what she would think (something she continued to do as she allowed others to read it).

Then one morning we guided Mary back to her desktop to write the first part of this second book as we dictated it to her. She smiled at the idea that someone else was telling a different version of her life but it also frightened her, so she filed it away and told no-one.

As others were reading the hard copy of her first manuscript, she continued to edit and research things she had written about. A few things came up that triggered her, other things puzzled her. One thing that had done both was about a young policeman that had been shot dead not far from her home one weekend in 1977, when she had been away. She didn't understand why this one particular person was on her mind but did remember that this incident had put an end to a relationship she was in at the time. After pondering for some time, she finally googled the RUC (Royal Ulster Constabulary) official website to check out details about him as she knew of nowhere else to look.

Her fingers trembled as she typed in the name of the website as the RUC were the people she feared most and trusted least. The only information found was his name and that he was eighteen years old when shot dead.

Same age as I was at the time, was the only thing that crossed her mind and then she looked again at the date of his death and realised that he was shot six months before she was taken into a police barracks. *Could there be a connection with this policeman's death and my treatment at the hands of his comrades?* she wondered.

Whilst walking in the mountains with her brother a week later, she brought up the young policeman's name and age and her brother said, 'Yes, he was the youngest policeman killed at that time. Probably the youngest ever. He had just finished his training.'

Trained in the barracks I was taken into! she realised immediately.

'I wasn't at home that weekend. I was in Castlederg with a boy I was going out with,' she said, trying to blank her last thought.

'Did you know that the policeman was from Castlederg?' her brother asked.

'No!' she replied, shocked.

'You should check out a book called *Lost Lives* if you want to find out any more about him. In fact, you will find out about anyone killed in the war. It's a big expensive book but you can get it in the library.'

'Thanks,' she replied and changed the subject as her heart pounded, overwhelmed with all this information and all the coincidences.

Driving home later that day she realised that the boy she had been going out with at the time and staying in his family home that weekend, was the same age as both her and the young policeman. In fact, these two young men must have known each other. They must have gone to school together as they were of the same religion. A different religion from hers!

Later that evening, in the safety of her home, she went into her meditation and back to the memories of that Sunday in 1977 when he had been shot. She had filed it away at the time as she wasn't able to either speak about it or deal with its consequences. Now, over thirty years later, she knew she needed to reopen the file.

She had been sitting that Sunday afternoon watching a movie with her boyfriend and his family when the movie had been interrupted with a newsflash of the shooting. There was nothing unusual about this at the time, but she had immediately recognised the address.

Knowing it was within a couple of miles of her home, she knew that their house would be raided immediately. No-one made any comment about the newsflash that day as they all continued to watch the movie, but Mary had sat there frozen, no longer able to concentrate on anything.

Her boyfriend moved across the sea to work a few weeks later and wrote asking her to join him. She could remember him so clearly, or did she imagine that he was the image of the very handsome singer David Essex?

Getting out of her chair that day in 2009, she took down all her old photographs and sat on the floor of her bedroom and went through them, looking for the photo that he had given to her at the time. As she searched through her albums, the memories flooded back as if this had all happened the day before. She even remembered his address in England, even though she couldn't remember what city he was in, nor could she remember if she had written back to him.

She doubted if she had ever written back as she had not the words to explain to him why she couldn't go. As she looked at his picture, she knew now that they could never have been together for many reasons – and yes, she thought, as she smiled at the picture in her hands, he was the image of David Essex.

Shocked with all these coincidences she decided to tell no-one, not even her sister, whom she always confided in. She needed more information and to process all of this herself first, so she went to the local library to look for the book her brother had mentioned.

'Do you want to take it out?' the librarian asked.

'No!' she replied, shocked. 'I only need to check something,' she continued as she had already decided that she didn't want this book in her home. She believed that she had already enough to deal with without the names, ages and circumstances of every lost life in the war.

Very little details were given about the policeman or any of the casualties (she didn't like the word victim as this word would include her and give her power to the perpetrator), but she understood why it had been written. This book was a recognition of the many lives that had been lived before they were lost.

Whilst there, she found herself checking out the details of other deaths, especially Seamus McElwaine's who was shot dead in 1986. He had been with her brother who was also shot at that time by the SAS (known as the assassination squad), but her brother had survived. We whispered another name and she checked him out as well. He too was a friend of her brother's, another man that had a shocking brutal death. She had never met either of these young men, but she had felt the spirit of one of them around her shortly after her nephew Gary was killed in 2001.

Even though she had never met her brother's friend Jim, she knew it was him immediately that day in the park. She completely ignoring him then, but did tell Dave at tai chi that night.

'What do you think he wants?' she had asked.

'He knows you are open to Gary, and he is looking for help.'

'Help from me? What kind of help could I give him, I can't even help myself?'

'Ask him!'

'I will not. It is taking all my strength to keep my body and soul together. I am not able to help anyone else. Gary and I help each other.'

One morning, shortly after getting the information in the library in 2009, she went out for her usual walk in the countryside, now walking four and sometimes six miles a day alone as she processed all that was happening. This particular morning, Mary had just reached where the loop started when a young man appeared beside her, and she immediately knew who he was even though there was no-one there!

He spoke to her through her thoughts as Gary always did. He was asking for her help. She couldn't believe it and was so nervous she burst out laughing. It was the young policeman.

She ignored him. *How dare he ask me for help,* she thought, walking faster, hoping to shake him off, feeling the rage rise in her as he continued beside her in silence. She continued to ignore him until she could no longer stand the silence.

'Why would I want to help you and what help do you want?' she asked sharply.

He didn't get a chance to answer as she continued, 'You know that my whole life changed because of you, that I was tortured because of you, that I lost my family, my friends and had to leave the country because of you ... You know you were so much luckier than me ... You got to die. I had to live with what your comrades did to me; I had to carry the wounds everywhere I went. I still carry them.' As the tears flowed down her face she continued, 'Do you have any idea how many times I wished that I had died that day, that I wouldn't have had to go through all of this? Now you dare ask me for help. Her entire body was shaking as she crossed the railway line to continue the walk.'

I was to die; you were to live, he replied softly.

Allowing the tears to continue, she kept on walking the deserted back roads outside the small town where she had hidden herself and her past for over twenty-five years and he continued walking beside her.

Anger rose from her chest up into her throat as she started to talk again, talking about all the little details that she had locked away and told no-one. He listened in silence as she unburdened herself of the secrets she had been carrying.

We watched with interest, wondering what she would do next. Would she ignore him after saying her piece or had she reached a place where she would do what she could to help him? Had she really understood that this was both of their journeys and there was nothing either could have done to change anything? Had she reached a place where she would actually help someone who she considered the enemy?

When she got back to where she had first encountered him, Mary stopped for a moment before saying, 'I will help you if I can but I have no idea how.'

Without a word, he disappeared.

Immediately she started to ask questions of people who she thought might understand, starting with Dave.

'He is probably stuck and needs help to move on,' he said.

'And how do I do that?'

'I have no idea. I have never done it, but you will find the right person to help when the time is right.'

She asked others she thought might know, but no-one did, so she left it and said no more.

Then one morning shortly after, her sister called and said, 'Mary, I need to tell you something, a friend of mine needs help and I know you understand this stuff. My friend's daughter's boyfriend was driving through Armagh the other night and got lost. He knew the road well but was drawn down a different road and couldn't stop. He got to a corner and there was a cross at the side of the road and a man was standing at the cross. He slowed down but the man started running. He drove slowly behind him but hit him. The man came through the windscreen of the car but the windscreen wasn't broken and he wasn't in the car! He was completely distraught. Still is. My friend said she would have found this hard to believe but this young fella doesn't drink! They checked the cross and found the young man's picture who had been killed there but it wasn't him. A few weeks later, her daughter and him were watching the news and it was the thirtieth anniversary of the of the eighteen British soldiers killed at Warrenpoint. They showed their photos, and he recognised one of them as the man he had seen. They don't know what to do. What do you think he wants?'

'To be moved on, I guess,' Mary said and then told her sister about the policeman.

This latest revelation renewed her efforts to find someone to help the policeman as she was delighted that she wasn't the only one who experienced these things. When she found someone to help, she would give their name to her sister's friends so that everyone could find peace, including herself.

CHAPTER 3

O ne Sunday morning later in the summer of 2009, as Mary was heading to join a group to go walking, she was forced to pull the car to the side of the road as her heart started thumping. Her breathing became erratic and her body started to shake. Mary thought this was an anxiety attack and as this always preceded a flashback; she believed she would have no choice but to go home, or at least stay in the car until it passed. Either way she would miss the walk.

It's okay. Go ahead, we whispered.

She hesitated but only for a moment, then drove on, trusting that we were there for her. By the time she reached the town she had pushed it down. She drove to the square, parked the car and got out with a smile on her face as if nothing had happened, thinking, *I could be an award-winning actress,* as she crossed the road to meet the other walkers. Thankfully there were only a few walking that day. One of them was new. His name was Henk; he was Dutch but had been living in the country for thirty years. He had recently moved to the area and had just joined the local walking club. She felt drawn to him and they chatted like old friends. He was a herbalist and as they walked and talked, she asked lots of questions that he was able to answer. Instinctively trusting him, she started telling him about the people in white she often saw around her, especially at night when she was facing things that couldn't be faced alone. She had asked others too about these beings, including Dave, but no-one knew anything about them. As soon as she mentioned them to Henk, he said, 'The white brotherhood.'

'How do you know about them and who are they?' she asked, excited that someone else had come across them, and even though she trusted them with her life, there were times she did think she was going mad.

'They are a group of enlightened souls that come to help anyone who asks them.'

'I don't remember asking.'

'You must have asked them for help at some point as they don't ever come unless asked. They can help you with anything and everything. If I have a problem with my accounts, I ask them. If I need help to treat someone, I ask them. They have a knowledge way beyond our understanding of anything.'

'I once asked them why they were all men when I knew they were following me on my walk,' Mary said. 'And they replied, "we are neither male nor female".'

'They are neither,' confirmed Henk.

She walked the fifteen miles without a bother that day, relieving her of the confusion she had about things that happened to her. It was as if he was sent to answer her questions, she thought (which, of course, he was). She had forgotten all about the policeman and soldier when he said that he also worked in energy efficiency. As she needed help with upgrading her holiday cottage and had very little money to do so, she listened carefully.

He explained that there was a grant she would be entitled to, and he would be delighted to check out the cottage for her and rate it for energy efficiency as he was qualified to do this too. Driving home that evening she was so happy. She smiled as she passed the point where she had stopped that morning, believing she would have to go home, not realising until weeks later that she had stopped at the road that led into Henk's house!

They had planned to meet the following weekend at her cottage in County Mayo and he was going to have a look at it to see what needed to be done. She, in return, was going to cook him dinner and bring him for a walk in the Ox Mountains.

The following Saturday she was already at the cottage when he arrived. They looked around and he told her exactly what she needed to do to get a better rating with the least amount of work and what the grant would cover.

They then headed into the mountains. It was only when they got to the first peak and sat down did she think of the soldier, but had forgotten all about the policeman. She told him her sister's story and he said, 'He needs help to move on.'

'I know that! I have asked lots of people who I thought would know but no-one seems to know how to do this.'

'I have done this before and will be glad to help,' he replied.

She couldn't believe her ears, but then said, 'I don't really know anything about the soldier but a policeman has asked me for help and I think I better sort him out first and then tell my sister.'

'No problem. We can do it after dinner.'

'You mean this evening? No way! I am not ready ... I need a day or two to get my head around this.'

After dinner Henk went home and Mary drove to the parking place at the top of the mountain to watch the sunset and meditate in the car. She had barely closed her eyes when she found herself at the scene of the policeman's shooting which had taken place thirty-two years before. Frightened, she opened her eyes and said out loud, 'No, I am not able for this alone and too tired to do it now.' She was adamant and everything stopped. She went home and straight to bed and dreamt about the policeman – dreamt that she was back at the scene of the shooting again. She refused to wake up even when he was really distressed, but she spoke to him gently in her dream saying, 'I'm still too tired, I will leave part of me with you and you will be okay until morning. I promise I will call Henk in the morning.'

She woke at six. It was dark. Henk had told her to call any time but it would have to wait as she had no mobile coverage in the cottage. She sat up in the bed, closed her eyes to do a meditation and was immediately back at the scene of the shooting again with no idea what she was meant to do next. Knowing she couldn't stop this again, she did what felt natural. She held the young man in her arms as he cried and then her nephew Gary arrived. *Great,* she thought, *Gary will know where to take him,* but then her uncle appeared. He who had been dead over twenty years!

'What are you doing here, Uncle Johnny?' she asked.

He looked at her as if she was still a child, a look that said *don't question me.* She replied with a look that said *I am no longer a child. I asked you a question and I want an answer.* He answered abruptly like he always had, 'I am here because I was there!'

She knew by the look on his face that this answer was not up for discussion, and as everything was happening so fast, she didn't ask. Instead, she watched as the young policeman went off between her uncle and her nephew, but he looked back at her with an expression on his face that she could easily read. She replied thinking, *It's okay, you will be fine. They will take you home.*

She said it with confidence but couldn't help herself questioning her uncle again as this was going to be the end of this for her and she wanted to make sure it was done right. 'You will take care of him, won't you, Uncle Johnny?'

'Why wouldn't I?' he replied sharply and just as abruptly as before. 'Wasn't he the same age as my son?'

At that, they all disappeared and she lay down under the quilt, exhausted. Later, she got dressed and crossed the road outside the cottage to the car where she had coverage on her phone. She called her youngest sister first, as she was in their home the day of the shooting and there was a question Mary knew she could answer.

After telling her what had happened, she asked, 'What would

Uncle Johnny have meant when he said he was here because he was there?'

'He was the first on the scene of the shooting,' Gertie replied immediately.

She didn't need to ask anything else. Uncle Johnny's son, her first cousin, was the same age as her therefore the same age as the young policeman.

She then called Henk and told him all that happened.

'Well done,' he said, delighted.

'I don't know if I did it right.'

'There is no right way. You just create a space and allow it to happen, that is all you can do.'

At home later she called her other sister to tell her everything so that she could tell her friend as Henk had said he would help the others with the soldier if they wished, but her sister was working nights. Immediately Mary knew it would be a few days before they would get to talk but it could wait as she needed time to process all of this.

That evening she decided to go back to the scene of the shooting in her meditation to check if everything had been cleared. There was no-one there. Happy that all was done and dusted, she went to bed early and slept like a log.

CHAPTER 4

The next morning Mary woke up delighted that she was now free to get on with her life having done as she was asked and, in the process, realised that by releasing someone else she too had been released.

Smiling, she sat up in her bed, closed her eyes to do her meditation and immediately found herself in a room with Gary, the policeman, Dave (her tai chi teacher) and her uncle, and before she could ask what they wanted, she watched others come in and take their seats around an oval table.

Seamus, who had been shot dead when her brother was badly wounded, had been the first to arrive, then about twenty other people (some she knew others she didn't), including her brother Noel (Gary's father). The last two to arrive were her parents; they took the last two seats on the bottom right of the table just before the doors of the room closed. She opened her eyes, petrified to stay there as she had no idea what was going to happen next and couldn't face any more.

Shaking, she called Henk and told him what had happened.

'I have never worked with anything like this before,' he said, 'but you must be open to this and other people are coming to you.'

'But they are not all dead people!'

'No,' he answered but with no explanation. 'I will be honoured to help you with this, Mary.'

'I'm not doing any more. I am not able for this.'

'It wouldn't have been asked of you if you were not able for it. Ask the white brotherhood for help.'

Feeling a little bit better she got off the phone and sat down to talk to whoever was listening, to explain that she was not able for this.

She was told that they would not leave her for a moment throughout it. She didn't know about her being able for any more but did know that she had never been left alone for a moment when awake night after night, petrified when the flashbacks came one after another in the long winter nights of 2007/08.

We reminded her of the first time they had surrounded her with a white light that filled her with love and peace, a light that stayed with her for as long as needed and returned when necessary.

Mary decided to talk to her friend Ann who she knew wouldn't understand but would listen. Ann wrote down the names of everyone in the room that Mary knew as she called them out. Some she just described as having a uniform on. She knew all the different uniforms that they were wearing, and none of them gave her any comfort as they were the different security forces that had terrorised her teenage years. At home later, she realised that this was a group of people that would never have consented to share the same space in any situation in their past.

As the children were with their father for the night, we guided her to the cottage in Foxford again, stopping in to see Henk on the way.

'You can stay here if you want,' he said, and even though it was tempting, she was aware that she needed to be alone to finish this. When leaving, Henk said he would keep the phone by his bedside that night.

'Thanks,' she said with relief as at this point, she didn't care if she needed to cross the road in the dark to call him, even if it was the middle of the night.

She decided not to call Dave as she had stopped going to his tai chi class but continued to practice at home. She wasn't surprised that he was one of the people who had entered the room that morning as he had often told her if she ever needed help to reach out to him, on a soul level, if necessary.

What surprised her this time was that she actually didn't look for his help, but he was there. In fact, she had called no-one in; her choice would have been Henk and her sister but she had not been given a choice.

Have I really created this place as Henk had said for whatever was going to happen, and do I really only need to watch without interfering? she thought as she drove to the cottage. Going into a meditation later to see if anything had changed, she noted that nothing or no-one had budged an inch. It was as if they were all frozen in time.

The following morning in her meditation, some of the people at the table got up and started to change seats. Dave was the first to move and take the seat at the bottom of the table opposite her. Nobody seemed to have any objections to this but we could feel her irritation as she imagined that he would want to take over. Before she could think another thought, the next move was by her brother's comrade, Seamus. He moved to the centre on the left side of the table and Gary moved to the right with his father moving beside him. Then, as she watched in amazement, an energy moved from her to Dave, an energy so strong it nearly took her breath away. It then moved from Seamus to Gary and as she looked from the top of the table she saw that this energy made the sign of a cross.

Before she could wonder any more about any of this, another man arrived as the table disappeared. He stood within the oval shape in front of Dave, facing her, and she knew immediately it was the soldier her sister had told her about. He asked permission to come into the room and take the seventeen others killed with him that day. We felt her overwhelming fear of what was coming next as the people she knew were now going to be outnumbered by people in uniforms and believed that she couldn't allow this to happen, so, we connected her to the white light that surrounded the entire group which then connected to the sign of the cross. At that moment she knew, as she did on those long winter nights, that all she had to do was let go and trust. She said nothing to the soldier – there was no need to. He read it from her heart; it was okay. They could all come in. They all moved in silence and sat on the floor in the centre of the original group as the space expanded to accommodate them. Nothing was said by anyone as this mixture of energies just froze. She had seen enough. She now found it easy to open her eyes and leave everything as it was (as it was meant to be).

She then rushed across the road to call Henk thinking they may be outnumbered, but at least no-one was carrying guns.

'This is wonderful,' he said when she told him what had happened.

'What if there are more to come?' she asked.

'There may be more. Am I in there?'

'No, but I did see you and my sister on the outside as if you were watching.'

'Take a rest, Mary, eat well and let it go for now and call me anytime you need to. Day or night!'

She headed home again and checked in later that evening – nothing had changed, nothing was being said, but she could see that the energy inside was being balanced by the energy outside. She felt that they were all safe, including herself.

The next morning, as soon as she closed her eyes in her meditation, her brother's other comrade, Jim, the man that had followed her in the park years before, was standing in front of the soldier, irritated. Looking directly at her asking with his heart to be allowed in and bring his seven comrades and a civilian that were killed that day. He knew from her heart that she was delighted to see him. She watched as everything expanded again to accommodate them – the oval shape, the cross and the white energy outside – and for the next few days she watched as all the energies moved through each other as if they were one. She watched as Seamus and the soldier worked together with any difficulties that arose in the group. All the pain from the traumatic deaths of these two groups of people flowed through everything and everyone, and the energy from outside stayed constant.

During this time Mary was full of energy, fascinated at what was happening, until a couple of days later when she was asked to leave. She reported this to Henk, and for the following two days she could see nothing at all, only an oval shape of light.

Then one evening, when she was driving to the cottage in Foxford, it opened. She could see it all without closing an eye, as if she was now in two worlds at one time (which she was). They were all mingling and there was music and her brother's friend Jim asked her to dance.

She was driving, he had been dead for twenty-two years, but they danced as everybody watched and it was as real to her as the world she was living in. She loved to dance, and Jim was a great dancer, and as they waltzed around the floor he sang into her ear. She could feel the lightness in his body and knew he had been unburdened of all that he had been carrying. He was free.

'If I had known you when I was alive,' he whispered.

'I wouldn't have had anything to do with you,' she replied, laughing. 'You were everything I didn't want. I had no intentions of spending my life going to prisons or graveyards to visit any other men. I already had two brothers to visit in prison.'

He too laughed as they continue to dance.

By the time she got to Foxford the dance was over and he said to her, 'If you ever need any of us, we will be together and will be there for you.'

'Thanks, but it's okay,' she replied, surprised at how sharp her voice was. 'I have people helping me.'

As she said this, we again flashed the night in 1977 when she was held in a police station, the night that we first made ourselves known to her. That night when the trigger of a gun was pulled at her head and she thought she was going to die, she saw the light and passed through it and didn't want to return. That night in '77 she realised that there was only a fine veil between this world and the next, and the next one was beautiful. Now, thirty-two years later in 2009, she understood why she could pass through it again without a problem. She was living in two worlds!

CHAPTER 5

We knew very well Mary wouldn't be satisfied; there would be questions. She would want to know what was going on. What went on? What was the reason for all of this? She needed an explanation that would prove to herself and others that she wasn't crazy, and we understood, she was in human form, and humans needed explanations for everything.

She called Dave and told him the story.

'I have been in bed all week drained. Now I know why.'

'Sorry.'

'No problem,' he replied. 'Now be careful ... you are going to be exhausted.'

'I have never felt better in my life. I will be grand.' But secretly thinking, *Why does he think he knows everything?* For the next three days, she was exhausted and spent most of the time in bed – but she never told him this.

Exhausted as she was, she was still able to use the phone, so she called her sister who knew both of her brother's comrades – had known both since she was a child, had met them after Mary had left home.

Mary asked, 'Was Jim a good dancer?'

'The best.'

'Singer?'

'Great.'

'Charmer?'

'The women loved him.'

Mary smiled and thought, *That is him summed up.*

'And Seamus?'

'He was gorgeous, and I was mad about him. Not that he said much but I adored him from afar.'

Smiling, she hung up the phone. After a few days rest she was back to herself and back to work finishing off a few things with her brother at the new house she was building beside the cottage and had a few questions that only he could answer. She also knew this was not going to be an easy conversation to initiate as he never ever again mentioned what she had told him years before (about his son Gary being around her).

After breakfast the following morning she asked, 'Do you ever dream about Gary?'

'No,' he replied sharply.

'Never?'

'Hardly ever.'

'When was the last time you dreamt of him?'

He hesitated for a moment and then said, 'Last week.'

'What did you dream?'

'I dreamt that I was in a room with him.'

This, she took for a sign, and so she told him the story of what had happened to her the previous week.

He didn't say a word but he did listen.

When she had finished, she had to ask him something she was trying to figure out. What was the common denominator? Why would these two groups of people who were enemies in life come together to help each other after their deaths? She finally came up with something that made sense to her, so she asked, 'Were the eighteen soldiers killed in Warrenpoint the biggest loss of life the British army had in one day in the North?'

'Probably,' he replied. 'Yes,' he continued.

'And Loughgall the biggest loss of life for the IRA?'

'Yes.'

'One last question.'

He narrowed his eyes, but before he could refuse, she asked, 'What was Seamus McElwaine like?'

Immediately, her brother's face lit up and he replied without a thought, 'The local curate ... Ahhh, you know what I mean.'

She knew exactly what he meant. When in that room he had an energy that she had never encountered before. Like he was a holy man. A man who understood and was comfortable with why he had lived and why he had died.

Her brother moved from the breakfast table and went back to work. She followed him and neither of them ever mentioned the subject again. She didn't need it to be mentioned as she now had a reasonable explanation. His replies had made it acceptable for her even though she had no idea why it had happened, nor the changes it was going to make to her future.

She wrote down everything that had happened and added it to what we had already dictated to her a few months previous then called Henk and asked if he would store it all on his computer as she wanted it out of her sight but in a safe place, knowing both pieces were very important because we told her so!

'No problem. Send it on to me.' Then he added, 'You know there will be other people who will come to you now that you are open.'

'No there will not be!' she replied immediately. 'I have just closed down again. This time for good. I have done my bit. I will never do this again.'

As we listened, we said nothing as this was her choice, and even though she had made other plans before she entered this planet, she had free will. The choice was hers to do as she wanted. We were her guides, not her controllers, but we flashed another memory into her mind from the late nineties when she had what the society she lived in called a breakdown. We called it a breakthrough. She was on medication that she didn't want to take. Her marriage was on the rocks. She was finding it very difficult to focus on her business or cope with her children. She had visions of herself in a psychiatric hospital, alone and afraid.

That day whilst on her daily walk she had knelt on the narrow back road, looked up to the sky and said out loud, 'I need help. I think my marriage is over and I will let it go if necessary. I am no longer capable of running my business and I will let it go too. If you think my children are better off without me I will let them go with their father but if I can keep only one thing, please, please, please, let me keep my children.'

That must have been the day Henk had spoken about, she thought. *The day that I asked for help.*

She then called her sister and told her everything, before blanking it, wanting to return to society's version of normal as soon as possible.

CHAPTER 6

We wondered how Mary planned to go back to normal as this experience would not be something that could be easily forgotten, but as her friends were giving her good reviews of her first manuscript, she focused on the task at hand. As she continued to put it out into the world, she carefully chose the ones allowed to read it before she could even think about it going anywhere near the people who would be her harshest critics: her family of origin.

The local doctor, who had first-hand knowledge of Mary's issues, passed her house a few days later and stopped for a chat. 'What are you at this weather, Mary?' he asked.

'I have just written a book,' she replied, then told him what it was about.

'You should send it to our local paper,' he said. 'The editor is from the town.' She smiled, knowing we were talking through him and did as asked.

The editor replied: *Hi Mary, read the part of the book you sent me and think it is a fascinating story. I have forwarded it to a publisher to see what they think with a view of it being published. In any event, I think it is a story that should be told. Christina.*

This not only shocked but frightened her as someone she didn't know was going to judge her – and she had lost control.

The following week she took the manuscript to her parents' house in a plastic bag to give to her sister, who had heard it chapter by chapter as it was being edited, then requested the entire manuscript to read. Mary was delighted as everyone in the family knew it was written but no-one else had asked to read it, believing, like most people, that it would never see the light of day!

She had just placed the bag at her feet under the kitchen table when she heard her mother ask, 'What's in the bag?'

Surprised that she had even noticed, Mary replied, 'It's my book. Gertie wants to read it.' She continued nervously in case her mother thought it was going to be forced upon her.

'Can I read it?'

Never expecting this question, Mary replied as calmly as she could, 'Sure! You can give it to Gertie when you are finished.'

She excused herself and went to the bathroom. Looking in the mirror, she saw a face as white as a ghost. What would her mother think, she wondered, as there were things written in the manuscript that only Gertie knew about. Sitting on the side of the bath, she composed herself before going back to the kitchen where a different conversation had started. She then spent a lovely evening with her parents without the book being mentioned again.

The next morning, as Mary walked up the corridor with her bags to leave, she peeked into her parents' bedroom, and there on her mother's locker, was the unopened plastic bag with the manuscript in it. She was delighted; it didn't matter if it was never read, it had been acknowledged and accepted, and that was more than she had ever imagined possible.

A few mornings later, her mother called to say they were coming down, and Mary knew in her heart her mother had read the manuscript, as she was not only an avid reader but rarely made surprise visits.

Running around the house to get the bedroom ready, her heart was thumping knowing that her mother was the boss in their family. If it was accepted by her, it would be accepted by everyone without question. Two hours later, they arrived and went directly into the kitchen.

'Put the kettle on, Josie, for a couple of hot whiskies,' her mother said to her father. (An unheard-of request by her mother at this time of the morning.)

As he was making them, her mother sat down at the kitchen table opposite Mary. 'Is this what happened to you?' she asked, as she pushed the manuscript across the table.

In that moment, as she replied 'yes', we flashed into her mind all the times her parents had entered this house to help her, when she couldn't help herself.

'Peter said he can't believe it,' her mother then stated, as her father continued at the countertop with his back to them.

'I don't blame him,' Mary replied. 'I can hardly believe it myself. I had to blank everything … What else could I do? Who could I tell? I wanted to tell Doctor Ferzell as I knew and liked her, she used to let us swim in the pool at the back of her house. I started by telling the doctor that I had a pain in my back, expecting her to ask what happened to me but she said, "A pain in your back at eighteen! What do you want me to do? Call Burnhouse?"' Burnhouse, her parents knew, was the number you called when you wanted an animal put down.

'Dr Ferzell would never have said that,' her mother said.

'No, she wouldn't,' agreed her father as he put the two hot whiskies on the table. 'But Dr Henry would and often did.'

As her dad spoke these words, we flashed the moment when she stood at the door of Dr Ferzell's house, realising as she stood there that this woman was not their registered doctor, so she walked to the other side of town to a doctor that she had never met as they were never brought to doctors as children.

Her mother's voice broke into Mary's thoughts again as she said, 'You know you have a case against the police?'

'I know, but I will never take it. They nearly destroyed me once. I won't allow it to happen again. I will not go there … Did you finish the book?' Mary then asked to change the subject, as her father sat opposite her with tears in his eyes.

'Yes,' her mother replied.

'What did you think of it?' Mary asked boldly.

'It's very good ... I only wish I had been reading it about someone else!'

That was it. The subject was closed and we could see the relief in Mary's entire body as she relaxed with a cup of tea. The book had been read and accepted. Nothing else mattered to her, not even the fact that the first few chapters had been read and refused by the first publisher to see it, in fact, she was relieved. She wasn't ready, nor was her manuscript. The next day her parents left and her brother Peter called.

'You need a good publisher. Caitriona knows an author who goes into her classroom to read to the children. I have met her too and I think you should send it to her.'

'I will send it to anyone now. Who is she?'

'Her name is Morgan Llewellyn. She is American but lives in Dublin. She is a historic fiction writer. She has written over thirty books. About five of them about the Troubles spanning over a hundred years. I will get in touch with her somehow. A friend of mine is a friend of hers. I will ask Leo,' he continued as if talking to himself.

That was settled. Peter put down the phone and Mary started to make plans. She knew she needed to move fast as we had been whispering to her to have it professionally edited. We had mentioned a man's name to her a few times, but she had ignored us. Now she decided she would have to go see him, at once. She drove the five miles that afternoon to the shop he was running since he retired, a man known to her in his profession as a social worker as he had interactions with one of her extended family. She had read and loved one of the books his son had published, and knew we were guiding her to his editor. Entering the little shop on a main road in the middle of nowhere, a bell rang and Kevin appeared from a door behind the counter.

'Hi, Mary. How are you?'

'Great,' she replied, then rushed the following words out of her mouth, words she had been reciting since she put down the phone from her brother. 'I have written a book and I was wondering if you could ask your son if he has an editor I could use, as I have no idea where to find one?'

'Good for you,' Kevin replied before disappearing back through the door he had just entered. A few minutes later he came out with an address book and wrote down his son's numbers, wishing her luck as he handed them over.

She drove off but stopped at the first gap in the road and called the mobile number, leaving a message when it wasn't answered. Driving into Roscommon town ten minutes later, her phone rang and she explained to Kevin Junior who she was and where she got the number.

'I have a great editor,' he said. 'The very best. Have you a pen?' Mary was ready with the pen and took the name and number.

'You finished a book?' the woman said when she answered the phone a minute later. 'Well done. Do you know how many people start books but never finish them? Many. Hmmm, I will text you my email address, you will send me the manuscript and I will get back to you. Okay?'

'Okay.'

Putting down the phone, Mary lay back in the seat of the car and thought, *Now the complete manuscript is going out there to someone who doesn't know me.* But deep down she didn't care anymore. That night, her story was sent out into the universe.

Two days later she got an email that read: *Have read the first twenty chapters. I can't believe I am from the same country as you. Reared a hundred miles away. I am around the same age as you and I have no idea what you are talking about. Call me?*

As Mary rang the number, we read her thoughts. *How would*

you know about people like me when we are never given a chance to tell our stories?

'We need to meet up,' Eileen said when she answered the phone. 'You need to trust me if I am to edit this for you. I will have lots of questions I will need answered. I can meet you halfway between Castlerea and Galway?'

'No need for you to drive anywhere. I will gladly come to the city. Just tell me where and when.'

The following Tuesday morning, they met in a coffee shop. They shook hands and before she sat down, Mary asked, 'Did you finish the book?'

'Yes.'

'What did you think of it?'

'This is the type of book they make movies of,' Eileen replied.

'So, you think it will get published?'

'Not many books are published, but I believe this one will be.'

Half an hour later, they had agreed on how they would proceed, and Mary went home knowing that the journey to publication had just begun. In the meantime, Peter had got in touch with Leo, who had got in touch with Morgan, who was very busy at that time but had agreed to read the book.

CHAPTER 7

June 18th, Mary's fiftieth birthday, was celebrated in her brother Noel's house. Already feeling overexposed and overwhelmed, she hadn't wanted a party but went along with it knowing she would have to face them all eventually. Her sister-in-law, Jenny, had made a beautiful cake with an open book carved out with icing on top – on the first page she had written the first words of her book: *It was the first day of my fiftieth year.* The words that we had whispered to her that morning when she faced a blank page, the moment she knew that she was being guided to write then continued, *I had driven with my daughter the eighty miles of back roads from the west and crossed the border as it was getting dark.*

As the family chatted around her that day she sat quietly, she was nervous, and before leaving they presented her with a gift of a brand-new laptop to replace the old second-hand desktop that she had written the two manuscripts on, but Mary didn't want any more changes so when home, this new-fangled object was left in its box in the corner of the sitting room.

Winter rolled in, and finally in November she got a time and a number to call Morgan Llewelyn. But there was a problem, Roisín was coming from college that evening and needed to be picked up in the next town at around the same time as the call was to be made. All would be well if the bus arrived on time …

It didn't. When the phone call was made five minutes late, she was aware from the tone of the author's voice that she was not impressed.

'I'm so sorry for calling late,' Mary said and then explained what had happened.

Morgan listened, then laughed, 'I understand. Our children must always be taken care of.' She then proceeded to tell Mary all about her son. Mary listened with interest, so grateful she had put her daughter first even if it meant she could have missed this wonderful opportunity. We had told her the first day that she started writing that the book was going to be published but hadn't given her any idea how this was going to happen.

Morgan finished by saying, 'Put the manuscript on a CD as I am not into emails. I will get back to you when I get time to read it, but I must tell you, I have been writing since the seventies and it has never been more difficult to get a book published.'

'Thank you.'

By the following afternoon, Mary had the professionally edited manuscript on a CD and in the post.

Christmas arrived without a word from Morgan. She was disappointed and her patience was wearing thin. Her editor, Eileen, had sent her manuscript to a few publishing houses but had received no replies. This didn't bother her as she believed that the publisher had already been chosen and her latest lesson was patience.

2010 rolled in with still no word from Morgan. Then, one morning when she was on the phone to a friend, a beep indicated that someone was trying to get through. After her call, she listened to a voice message from Morgan that said, *'I have finished your book, Mary, and I think it is wonderful. I'm going out now, call me at six and we will decide where you need to go from here.'*

Mary called her sisters from her mobile and played the message on the home phone so that they could hear it, for she feared that she had imagined it. Then she played it to her brother Peter and friends and kept listening to it herself all day. At the dot of six, Morgan was called and repeated, 'It is a wonderful book, Mary. Now we need to get it published. I think you should contact ...' and named the same publishing house that had been mentioned to Mary before by Danny, a friend of her brothers.

Danny, who was a published author, had said if you ever get it edited, call this woman. He named her and the same publishing house Morgan had just mentioned. Danny had continued by saying, 'She meditates too.' And Mary had no doubt that he thought this was the only reason she might consider it.

Morgan broke through her thoughts saying, 'You need to choose 500 words to send to the publisher with an email of three short paragraphs. Two hundred words or less to outline who you are, what the book is about and why you wrote it.'

Mary had drifted off again as she thought ... *500 words.*

'Five hundred words!' she then spoke aloud.

'Would you like me to re-read the book and choose these words?' asked Morgan.

'Yes please! If you don't mind ... If it's not too much trouble!'

'No trouble at all. I will be delighted to. Now, you spend the weekend writing the cover letter and I will spend it re-reading your book. I will call you Sunday evening.'

Straightaway, Mary sat down at the computer and wrote the letter, then spent the rest of the weekend editing it.

'It's more difficult than writing the book,' she told her friend. 'Every time I passed the computer, I would change a word here and there until finally on Sunday morning, I knew the letter was finished.' Her parents had come down for the weekend and left on Sunday evening, and she waited by the phone, and even though it never rang, she knew in her heart that this was not a problem and so she went to bed and slept soundly.

The next day, she had a missed call and checked her messages to find that Morgan had called on the Sunday when she was on the street waving goodbye to her parents and had left a message for her to call back Monday evening at six.

'Okay,' said Morgan as soon as she answered the phone. 'I have chosen the 500 words which starts with, *The first of us were born in 1954 ...* And ends with ... *that was when I planned on how I could save the family when the army came to our house.* When I read those 500 words a chill went through me that didn't leave until I had the book finished. Now read me what you have written.' Mary did as asked and Morgan said, 'Perfect, I couldn't have done it better myself. Now put the letter and words together and email them to the publisher, the woman Danny recommended.'

'Thank you. I will let you know if I hear anything.'

'Please do,' replied Morgan before hanging up.

Mary was so nervous that she was all fingers and thumbs, and it took hours to get it together and press send, not expecting a reply in a hurry (as she had learnt a little patience). But at 9:15 the following morning there was an email from the publisher to say they were interested. Ecstatic, Mary's first thought was to start planning her move to the cottage as she didn't want to launch the book in the town where she had hidden herself and her past for twenty-five years, afraid of the reception she might get. But as much as she wanted to hide again, this was not as it was meant to be.

The following month, on the 27th February (her ex-husband Marty's birthday), Mary headed off on her walk without her mobile phone so as not to be disturbed – returning hours later to four missed calls. One from Marty, one from Roisín, one from Kate (Jarlath's girlfriend) and one from a number she didn't recognise. Putting all thoughts on hold after the first one which was ... *something has happened to Jarlath,* she called Marty.

'You heard about Jarlath?' he said.

'No,' she answered, holding her breath.

'He was in a car accident. The car is written off, but he walked away without too many problems. I think he may have broken bones in his hand. I was driving behind him and saw it all. When I got out of the Jeep and ran across to the car – it was the longest run of my life. When I got there the three of them were climbing out of the car windows.'

Getting off the phone, Mary sat down and cried as she heard us whisper, *He is going to be fine. He is going nowhere yet and neither are you.*

Driving to the hospital to see him half an hour later, she stopped at the scene of the accident with instructions from Jarlath to try and find his phone that was lost. Crossing the field to where the wrecked car lay, she met one of his friends who said, 'Ja was lucky, Mary.'

Smiling she thought: *He wasn't lucky, Nathan. It wasn't his time.* Knowing that after this accident launching the book in the town would no longer pose a problem, she was under no doubt that she could face anything after this.

After the initial email from the editors which said that they were bringing it up at a meeting at the end of the month, Mary emailed twice and had two replies, but neither satisfied her and impatience set in again. Then, her friend Anne called to say that a friend of hers was having a book launched in Westport, and she thought Mary should go. In fact, she was told by the angels to tell Mary that she should go! Mary sighed in despair as she hated being told what to do and even more so by reminding her that there was something else out there, guiding her through other people when she wasn't listening.

'No. I'm not going,' she replied, annoyed. 'She probably self-published anyway.'

Her friend mentioned it another few times but to no avail, even when she told her that the book was not being self-published.

'No, I am not going. I have a publisher.'

At this time, Mary was taking her friend Georgina's dog for a walk most days, as the dog wanted to walk but her friend didn't. As Foxy never gave the friends a chance to speak until he was exercised, the following day when she returned from the walk, she told Georgina what Anne had said.

'Why don't you go? It would do you good to get out and might be fun. And who knows, maybe she is right. Maybe her angels are guiding you too!'

'I'm exhausted, too exhausted to drive,' Mary replied.

'Then go on the train.'

'Yes, I suppose I could do that.'

The day of the book launch Anne met her at the train station, and later that evening they went to the venue.

The first thing she noticed was a friend who walked with her in the mountains sitting at the bar.

'What are you doing here, Tom?' she asked.

'I know the author. What are you doing here?'

'I have written a book and am wondering if the publisher will be here.'

They chatted until the author got up to speak, followed by the publisher who finished by saying, 'If there is anyone out there who has a non-fiction book written, come see me.'

Mary had no doubt she was talking to her, so without a thought she got off her high stool, walked across the room and waited in line.

'I have a book written,' Mary said after introducing herself.

'What is it about?' the publisher asked.

'It is about me.'

'What about you ... What is the book about?'

'It is about growing up in the North in the seventies and then living in the west. It is about how the Troubles affected me and how I dealt with it.'

'Are you from Belfast?' the woman asked.

'No! Why ... do you think there was only a war in Belfast?'

'Yes!'

'Well, I am from Fermanagh and there was a war there too,' she replied with a tone as sharp as the publishers.

'What have you done with the manuscript?'

'I have sent it to a publisher and they have accepted it but they are sitting on it.'

'Who is the publisher?'

When Mary mentioned the name, the lady said, 'I used to work for them but moved out on my own when they closed their Dublin office. Write to them and ask again what is happening, and if you need any help with anything call me.' And with that she handed Mary a card and moved on to the next person waiting in line.

On the Monday morning, Mary wrote another email to the publisher. But before she sent it, she called Jo (the publisher she had met two nights before).

'Too sharp,' Jo replied, and then told her what to write instead.

By the end of the week, she had the same reply as before and was totally frustrated so called Jo again who said, 'Send the manuscript to me. I will give you an answer by Monday night as I have to go somewhere tomorrow and won't get to it until Sunday.'

Mary sent it immediately and then started to clean the house with a vengeance that continued over the weekend. Before Monday came around, she took the time to contact Danny (her brother's friend) again.

She had called him first when she started writing as she felt she needed to talk to an author, and he listened as she explained that she couldn't stop writing, that sometimes she was writing 5,000 words a day.

He told her that wasn't possible to write 5,000 words a day, that he was lucky to get a few paragraphs written in that time. Then he asked her if she was naming people by their correct names and when she replied yes, he said, 'You can't do that. I have changed names and people still recognise themselves and cross the street when they see me.' Getting off the phone that day, Mary decided to stop writing as she had no idea how to slow down the pace, nor how to write and change the names at the same time and even if she could, people would recognise themselves anyway. *What was the point in writing at all?* she thought, heading to bed early. Waking in the middle of the night, she followed our guidance back to the computer and back to her writing, thankfully she had neglected to turn the heater off and the room was warm! That day she wrote 8,000 words whilst continuing to use real names!

Danny was called again after editing the first few chapters and asked if he would read it. He emailed her back and told her that nobody wanted to read what she had written on the first page which was:

> *As I drove with Roisín, who was sleeping like she was unconscious (she had partied in Galway with her friends the whole night before), the realisation that I was at home filled every cell in my body. The warmth and love that flowed through me was the most wonderful feeling I have ever had.*
>
> *It was not because I had crossed the border to where I was born, nor even the fact that it was so peaceful in the car listening to Lyric FM. It was because, in my heart I had found a peace that I knew would travel with me wherever I was to journey for the rest of my time on this Earth; a peace that I had been seeking for nearly forty years; a peace that no land, nobody or nothing could give me; a peace that I had finally found in myself.*

You may well ask why she continued to call him, but Mary knew he meant well and was trying to help, trying to make her understand that few of the books that are written are published.

Contacting Danny that night in 2010, she explained that two publishers now had the manuscript. He replied, 'I have worked with both, and if you want my advice give it to Jo, if she will take it … She is the best editor in the country.' He then finished by saying, 'And don't expect to make money out of writing. I have written eight books and haven't made any.'

Putting the phone down that evening, Mary did what her mother had often told her to do. She never let on she heard him.

Mary wasn't writing to make money. She was writing because she was guided to. She never told him this but was very grateful to have him on the other end of the phone. He who knew the difficulties every writer faced, told her exactly what he thought (something she did for others when they contacted her in the future), but she did what felt right for her and never did change the first page of the book. The best review she got highlighted the same paragraph as Danny but for different reasons – the reviewer loved it! Danny (his real name) really was trying to help but was operating from a different mindset to her!

As she continued cleaning that Monday morning waiting for Jo's call, she had decided that she was going to take one piece of advice Danny had given her. She would let Jo publish it if she wanted to.

CHAPTER 8

By Monday afternoon, Mary was so nervous and the house was so clean, that she decided to head back to Anne's by train to keep her busy. They walked and talked all day and went to sleep at ten with no word from Jo, but in her heart, she knew all was well. The next morning, an email from Jo which had been written at 10:15 the night before read: *Give me until tomorrow evening as I want to finish it. I will be in touch by evening.*

Not able to stand the tension and needing to keep moving to distract herself, Mary got back on the train and headed home in the early afternoon. Getting into the car to get some groceries that evening, Jo called and said, 'Okay, we will need to get together to do some more editing and it will have to be on the shelves for the autumn.'

Listening in disbelief, Mary asked in shock, 'Are you going to publish it?'

'Yes. Sorry it took an extra day but I wanted my sister who is a psychotherapist to read it.'

After that, everything started to happen so fast that Mary's head was spinning, so grateful that she had listened to us and done all the extra work we had suggested, like allowing people to read what she had written about them. This meant she was well able to keep up with the publisher who worked as fast and intensely as herself.

Driving home from Dublin with her copy of the contract a few days later, she thought, *This is really happening. I am going to have my book published, and Danny was right about another thing. I need to get in touch with all the people I have named in the book who aren't aware of it and change the name if asked.*

'Whatever you write is fine with me,' her oldest brother said when she contacted him. 'I will read it when it is published. You might be better to copy the statement I made after I was shot. You will find it under Seamus McElwaine in *Lost Lives*. I made this statement at the time of the shooting, if it's not exactly the same it will be pointed out.'

Mary had already sent it to the rest of the family who wanted to know what was said about them and all were okay with it. The ex-British soldier was then contacted and told what she had written, explaining that not only his name but also the circumstances of the meeting had been changed. His and another Englishman (who was paranoid as he was barely mentioned) were to be the only names she was to change in the entire book. The ex-soldier thanked her but said he didn't want to read it, that he wouldn't be able to read it.

Then there was a man in New York that Mary had dated for a while. She doubted he would ever come across the book, but this man had questioned her about her life in the Troubles from the first night she met him on a train in the Bronx, knowing this book would answer all the questions that she wasn't able to thirty years before. Googling his name, she found he was still working for NBC sports in Manhattan.

'Are you the Kevin Monaghan who lived in the Bronx with Shay Kelly in the early eighties?' she asked when she was put through to his extension.

'No! But if you hold the line, I will put you through to the other Kevin Monaghan working here.'

An answering machine asked her to leave a message. 'If you are the Kevin Monaghan who lived in the Bronx with Shay Kelly in the early eighties, this is Mary Lynch, and I have written a book which is being published and you are mentioned in it. Call or email me.'

After leaving her details, Mary headed directly out the door for her daily walk. She returned to two missed called and an email which said: *Yes, I am the Kevin Monaghan who lived with Shay Kelly in the Bronx in the eighties. How the hell are you, Mary Lynch? Please call me.*

They chatted about everything and everybody as if they had spoken only the day before, and he said, 'Send me the piece about me and I will read the book when it is published.'

The next morning, he replied with instructions of what needed editing, then told her the reason he was so interested in the Troubles. He had been working in a summer camp for children of the Troubles in the seventies with Liam Neeson (the actor) in Ballymena.

Mary had told Marty that she had written the book, but he didn't ask to read it as he too believed it was going nowhere. Then one evening Roisín said, 'Daddy wants to read the book and he won't like what you wrote about him.'

'Why?'

'I don't know, but he won't like it.'

She put the manuscript in a large brown envelope and slipped it through the letter box of his house next door, with a note that read, *This book was not written to hurt anyone, Marty, and especially not you. If there is anything in it that you want removed just tell me and I will remove it.*

He handed it back a couple of weeks later and wished her luck with it without asking for anything to be either changed or removed.

With everyone contacted, Mary relaxed until the 15th of June 2010, when the news headlines showed David Cameron, the newly elected British Prime Minister of Great Britain, apologising to the people of Derry for Bloody Sunday, for the murder of the fourteen people that day.

Listening to his words, Mary broke out in a cold sweat, then started shaking uncontrollably, realising only then the impact that day had on her thirty-eight years after the incident. Crying until exhausted, she picked up a pen and wrote five short lines that expressed how her life had changed that year.

1972

Adolescences beckoned with great expectation,
innocence of youth, expectations of the innocent.
365 days. 495 deaths later it ended.
With the loss of that innocence,
and the death of those expectations.

Then, like a woman possessed, Mary wrote another chapter for the book before crying herself to sleep. The following morning, we guided her to the library to get all the information needed to verify what she had just written. A few days later the new chapter was sent to Jo with the simple message: *Chapter 12 A. The Blame Game. The game we all play when we don't want to look at ourselves.*

A few minutes later her reply read: *You mean Chapter 13. It had better be good as I am about to finish the final edit.*

The chapter was added and a few days later Mary drove to Dublin, this time to go through the final edit.

'We will contact Gerry Ryan about going on his show,' Jo said a few weeks later.

'Great, I was thinking the same thing. I have no doubt he will take me back on. I doubt that anyone else in RTE will, I don't tell the story they want to hear.'

A few weeks after that, Mary's chances of getting on national radio were shattered when Gerry was found dead in his apartment in Dublin.

* * *

The night before meeting Jo, she stayed with her brother in Dublin. After a long conversation about their childhood, she went to bed, where her head and the room started to spin, immediately realising with horror that she had vertigo – and having experienced it often enough to know that it was going to totally disable her, she laid back on the bed and prayed, 'Please, please help me, please let me sleep.'

The room was still spinning as she fell asleep, and in the morning, it was gone.

Later that afternoon, after the final edit was complete, she headed out of Dublin knowing all she could do was done. Now all she had to do was wait for the first copies to be printed then face the town for the launch of the book which was in a couple of weeks.

Driving to her parents' home to meet her brother who was bringing the first copies from Dublin for the family and local media, she pulled into a lay-by overlooking a lake to do a meditation. Closing her eyes, we reminded her of the time when she was watching an episode of her favourite program, *Sex and the City*, the episode where Carrie was going to get the first copy of her first book. *Who would ever have thought that I could or would write a book?* she thought, smiling, *Who other than myself trusted that it was going to be published?* After the meditation, we flashed her another memory. It was of her watching Carrie sitting in her apartment writing her column every week. At that time, we had whispered to her that she would write a column.

'Not a column,' she said out loud as she drove on. 'A book!'

Driving in the narrow road to her parents' house, Mary was apprehensive; the first thing she had to face when she picked up the book was her own face on the cover.

We had told her that this was what was going to be, so she hunted down a picture of herself in 1977, sent it to the publisher, who then sent it to the designer. It came back and she emailed it to Eileen her editor, who replied: *No! A picture of you today, happy and free.*

Mary replied: *I couldn't do that.*

Why not? Others have no problem doing it. If they can, why can't you?

Mary wasn't sure of that but pulled out the pictures that her brother had taken for publicity. Paddy had always been a good photographer, and as he had been home from London to visit at around that time, he had offered his services.

Twenty pictures had been taken when he said, 'That's enough.'

'If I was eighteen and a model, there would have been thousands taken of me for one shot,' Mary replied.

'I know,' he answered with a grin. 'I have delivered those photographs as a courier in London, but you are not a model and you are not eighteen.'

Mary had picked the best one of them and sent it to Jo for the new cover and liked it, but to have to look at it on every book was another thing. An hour later, with the book in her hand, the reality that she now had to face the publicity sunk in.

Her sister, Ruth, a local county councillor, had called a few days before to ask if she could email the editors of the local papers in the North, asking if they would like to review it. One was the nationalist paper who was once owned by her English teacher's family. The other, a unionist paper which she had never read.

'Okay,' she replied reluctantly, accepting that she had no choice but to face exposure in her home county.

An answer came straight back from the editor of *The Impartial Reporter*, the unionist paper.

Ruth had written: *Denzil, my sister Mary has written a book about being brought up in the Troubles and the effects of it on her. Would you like to do a review on it?*

He had replied: *Sure would, Ruth, tell her to call me?*

In their telephone conversation, Denzil told her to bring the book to him. He would read it and then call her to ask questions.

We read Mary's thoughts loud and clear. *If you read the book, you won't have to ask me any questions!*

The morning after receiving the first copies, she brought a book to his home as requested, grateful that he wasn't there, very happy to leave it with his wife. With the other delivered to the *Fermanagh Herald* offices, she headed home later that day to get ready for the launch which was to take place the following week on the ninth anniversary of 9/11.

The morning of the launch, Mary went for a walk to get away from her mother who was fussing with nerves, making her even more nervous than she already was, stressing over the conversation she had with Jo about how long she would speak at the launch. 'No longer that five minutes,' Jo had said, and Mary wondered what she could possibly say for five minutes. Continuing down the familiar country roads, the fear in her was palpable. She approached an old dog that she petted every day, but he growled, then jumped up and bit her. In that moment she knew that if the dog could sense her fear, then so would everyone else. Shaking it off, she headed back, reminding herself on the way that this was only a couple of hours and that after this night she would have the freedom to move out of town to her cottage in the next county for a new life.

Later, sitting at the door of the venue with her sisters, wondering if anyone would show up, people trickled in slowly – but within an hour the place was packed. Speaking for less than three minutes, Mary then danced the rest of the night to relieve herself of the stress of twenty-one months from when the first sentence of the book was written. The launch went very well with not only all her family in the country showing up, but also Morgan Llewellyn and a huge number of the townspeople to support her.

CHAPTER 9

The editor of *The Impartial Reporter* never did call her to ask questions about the book, but he did have a review in the paper the day before the launch.

Ruth had called to say it was in.

'Send it to me, please,' Mary answered, and we watched her tremble as she read it. This was not only her first review but the most important one for her, that is, after her mother's. She didn't really care what anyone else had to say; this review was coming from what would have been called the other side of the divide. If this editor accepted what she had written then she felt that she had succeeded in writing her story without bitterness or anger, a story that could be read by all communities. After she finished reading his review, Mary emailed him saying: *Thank you for reading the entire book, Denzil, and understanding it so well.*

He replied: *Thank you, Mary, I think your book is brilliant.*

There were other reviews, and they were all good but no other really mattered. Mary knew she had reached a place that she never dreamt possible; the child in her had finally found a voice in the place where she was born.

The week following the launch, she was on the local radio station, which she thoroughly enjoyed and had no problem talking for twenty minutes. It was as if there was no-one else in the world,

only her and the presenter. Not unlike when on the air with
Gerry Ryan; like talking to a friend, the man who knew how to
put her at ease and at the same time ask the questions he wanted
answered.

A few days later Jo called and asked, 'Would you go on TV?'

'Yes!' Mary replied.

'Great, could you be in Dublin tomorrow? The producer is
going to call you in the next hour.'

My God, she thought. *That is fast, what am I going to wear?*
Having heard that there are some colours that didn't look good
on TV.

Wondering where she had heard this, we whispered, *Watch
the program.*

Going directly to her new laptop (which had finally been put
to use after the old desktop refused to write another word), she
noticed that the seats in the studio were red, that the man being
interviewed had a royal blue jumper on and it looked stunning
with the red. She rushed to her wardrobe where she had a pinafore
the very same colour (rushing as if it was going to disappear if
she didn't get to it before someone else!). She then located a blue
short cardigan to match and a pair of boots bought in London
years before when visiting the city with her daughter. Everything
she needed was in her wardrobe as if they were just waiting to be
brought together for this outing (which they were), reminding her
that when she connected to the universe, everything was in her
grasp. Later at Marita's house, we guided her eyes to the kitchen
window where a pair of blue earrings lay, the exact same colour
as her outfit.

Chris, who had done her make-up for the publicity
photographs and the launch, worked her magic again early next
morning. Then off to Dublin Mary went, picking up Roisín on
the way to the studio.

Waiting around for two hours gave her a chance to get her
bearings before being brought onto the set. During this time one

of the presenters came to talk to her, telling her that his father was from the North, giving her the reassurance needed for the interview.

As she passed the producer on the way to the set, she asked, 'Do you edit?'

'Not unless the roof falls in,' he replied, laughing.

On the way to the red settee, we read her thoughts. *This is my one opportunity to speak my truth on the only TV station that will allow me tell my story, even if they sensationalise it the day before by using the words … At the age of twelve, Mary knew she would kill.*

'That was a bit dramatic,' her sister-in-law had said.

'Maybe, but it is the truth,' Mary had replied.

The other interviewer was a woman who immediately asked her what most people would have considered an awkward question about her brother that had been shot, but Mary didn't flinch. She was open, honest and straight to the point, no longer hiding anything.

When it was over, she was surprised when the woman said, 'Well done. You did well, Mary.'

Walking off the set, the producer who was standing with her daughter beamed and said, 'Great interview.'

At Jo's home the next day when it was broadcast, they watched it together. The TV was so big she thought she looked awful, but later when she replayed it on her laptop, she realised that everything she had worn looked absolutely perfect and she couldn't have spoken any better. Later that evening, after Foxy had his walk, she asked Georgina if she would have believed her if she didn't know her.

'Yes. You were quick to answer and avoided nothing that was asked. The truth never changes, Mary. The truth will be the truth in twenty-five years. A lie changes every time you tell it. You have never changed your story.'

Three days later, she was asked onto another radio station. Mary had no doubt this was going to be a very different experience from the first one. The interviewer had a real problem with her background, with her being allowed to tell a story that didn't match his narrative. Her brother said this man would make it difficult for her if she ever had to face him, but Mary didn't care. She had got the thumbs up from a paper that she didn't think would even give her a review. A man who wanted to promote the only story he had been fed and she had been sure he wouldn't intimidate her – but he did.

Walking into the studio that autumn morning, the first thing she noticed was that the interviewer was sitting on a seat at a much higher level than hers, giving him an immediate advantage. He was on his own territory, which was another advantage to him, plus the fact that he was an expert at this. When he started to talk there was a chill in the room and she lost all her confidence, but as he was fond of the sound of his own voice and believed he had all the advantages, his ego got the better of him. He rambled on and on, giving Mary ample time to collect herself. She used it wisely. She connected to us.

Finally, he welcomed her and asked her a question about the book which made it obvious that he hadn't taken the time to read it, so she had her second advantage (us being her first). He then tried to blame her parents by using words to insinuate that they were the ones who changed the direction of their children's lives. As Mary rejected these accusations, she knew he wasn't listening, he was already thinking of another way to change her version of her life to his. This gave her a third advantage, an opportunity to say all the things she wanted to say. She talked about what it was like to be a child in a war. How Bloody Sunday and the events of 1972, especially the murder of her neighbours and cousin, changed her family's life forever, speaking in a calm, clear, concise way.

Knowing he was getting nowhere with his line of questioning he said, 'I can't—I cannot believe that a female RUC officer put a gun to your head. I just cannot believe it.'

Mary looked up at him and replied, 'But she did.'

He then tried another approach, as Mary watched the clock behind his head ticking away. He had told her that she had fifteen minutes and now it had been over twenty. He finally looked down at her and said from his heart, 'Do you expect me to understand – me, who was born and brought up in a small town in the west of the country?'

'No,' she replied. 'How could you?'

Knowing and openly acknowledging he was way over time, he then started another approach, and Mary spoke to him in a way she rarely used. She spoke without opening her mouth, spoke like she did to those who had passed on, spoke directly to his soul.

Do you really believe that you can intimidate me in a radio station studio with thousands listening, when I couldn't be intimidated in a police barracks when no-one even knew I was there? They had the power to kill me if they wanted. I knew that then, and I know now that you don't. I am open, honest and being guided as are you. The difference is I am no longer blinded with bitterness nor blame. It was as it was, and I accept that. Now, can you please do the same?

Whether he was conscious of what was happening or not didn't matter, he was aware enough to wrap up the interview and wish her well.

Walking down the narrow metal stairs to the lobby, Mary's legs were shaking, but her heart was full of gratitude for the guidance she had received. After this, she knew that she would be able for any interview, and from her heart, she thanked him.

Her friend Ann was waiting in the lobby. As they were heading out the door, the receptionist called Mary over and said, 'A woman called when you were on air and asked me to give you her number. She said she's related to one of the murdered men that you spoke about.'

Walking to the car, Mary told Ann what had just happened in the studio and they laughed so much it released the tension in her body which had been frozen for twenty-five minutes before calling the number she had been given, and before the conversation was finished, had made an arrangement to meet the woman the following Saturday.

Aware that Mary had bolted some doors which she may never enter again, we now could only work with the doors that were open to us. Unlike humans, we would never try to unlock doors that were not available to us as this never worked. Maybe sometime in the future she would be ready. Maybe not, only time would tell, and the choice would always be hers, but if not, she would be back facing the difficult task of walking against the tide.

CHAPTER 10

The Saturday morning after this radio interview was spent with the woman who had left her number with the receptionist. The two women had a lovely day together, but what really interested Mary was a story she had been told, a story which she repeated to her friends the following day as they walked part of the Suck Valley Way. That evening, she opened up the laptop and wrote the story, calling the woman in question afterwards to read it to her.

'That is it! That is exactly how it happened, but if you ever publish it, please don't use my name ... My father told me never to tell anyone and I promised him I wouldn't.'

'It's a beautiful story and I'm sure your father wouldn't mind it being told. I doubt if I will ever be publishing it, but if I am I will tell you and I won't mention your name.' as, *Why would she think I would publish it?* was running through her mind.

Calling in to see some friends a few days later, Sean told her another story which was written as soon as she arrived back home.

After reading it later that evening to him and his partner he said, 'How did you know all that, Mary? I didn't tell you all that. You were only in the house for twenty minutes.'

She smiled, thinking how much people told her without

realising it and how easy it was to fill in the blanks. Getting up to leave, Sean said, 'If you ever publish it—'

'—Yes, I know. I won't use your real name.'

'No, Mary, if you ever publish it, please use my real name, it is a story that I always wanted to tell.'

Within a month, lots of stories that she had been told over the years were written, delighted with the diversion from the events of the summer as we reminded her of another piece of advice that Danny had given. *Think of your stories like children. They are very precious. Write them, then file them away for use at another time.* We also reminded her of the advice Morgan Llewellyn had given her after asking how she remembers things so well.

'I think it is because I'm always telling stories'. Mary replied

'Most writers are afraid to tell others the stories they heard in case they will write them. If you tell the story', Morgan continued, 'it will never be forgotten. Keep telling stories and you will always have plenty of material to write with.'

'I will,' Mary had replied politely at the time, wondering why this woman would think she would ever write again, not understanding what both Danny and Morgan already knew, she had caught the bug. That is, until one morning in December when we whispered, *Call Denzil and tell him about your stories, ask him if he would be interested in publishing them in* The Impartial Reporter. We did this using the same tone of voice as we had when we asked her to write the book. Recognising it, she called no-one for advice, knowing instinctively that this was going to happen.

'Who's calling?' the receptionist asked.

'Mary Lynch.'

A moment later a voice asked, 'What can I do for you, Mary?'

'Denzil, I have been writing short stories about other people's lives, true stories, and I was wondering if you would be interested in publishing them?'

'Yes,' he replied.

'Okay … but you will want to read them.'

'Yes, of course, I want to read them, but I am interested in publishing them.'

Then he started to explain that he had a new format for the paper, and as she listened, she hadn't the heart to tell him that she had never read this paper, that in the past the paper he now was the editor of wouldn't have been allowed to darken the door of their home when they were children.

'Okay,' she said when he had finished talking. 'I will edit a couple of stories and send them to you and see what you think.'

'Great. I look forward to reading them.'

Attempting to edit them as perfectly as Denzil had said they would need to be for publication, she failed miserably, so Jo was called for help.

'I will teach you to edit over the Christmas,' Jo said.

Mary went to bed with a heavy heart, already feeling like a failure.

When she woke, we whispered, *Call Denzil and ask if you could read a story to him.* She didn't hesitate, and he took the call immediately.

'Denzil, I have to be honest with you, I don't know how to edit but my publisher said she would teach me over the Christmas break. I don't want to waste your time or mine so I wondered if I could read you a story to see what you think?'

'Okay, read me a story!'

When she finished reading the story about Sean, he said, 'Mary, that's a brilliant story and it doesn't need to be edited.'

Laughing with relief she replied without thinking, 'I read it the way it should be, Denzil, not the way it is.' Realising in that moment that this was how we had guided her to edit her book. When reading to her sister every night she corrected the mistakes, all that was needed now was someone to listen to her stories.

CHAPTER 11

At the end of 2010, the weather hit its lowest temperatures in decades, bringing the country to a gridlock and stopping her parents from coming to her home for Christmas for the first time in eight years. This gave Mary time to get her stories ready for her column for the start of the new year. She felt like Carrie in *Sex and the City*, and even thought she wouldn't be writing for a New York publication, she was writing for the paper she would have chosen over any other in the world.

Taking out her stories from where she had them filed on her laptop, Mary was delighted to introduce them to an audience that would have been inaccessible to her at any other time in her life. An audience who would watch her like a hawk. There would be no room for mistakes and the only way this was going to happen was for her to be completely at one with us, just as she was when writing her first book.

Recently Mary had written a short story for another book, so decided that this would be the best story to introduce herself. It was about her family, sharing what it was like to be one of twelve children, the perfect story to introduce her to those who didn't already know who she was.

Nervously, she sent it in the following Monday morning.

Having no access to the paper, she asked Ruth to confirm that it was in the following Thursday.

Ruth called and confirmed.

'Which page?' Mary asked.

'What difference does that make?' Ruth enquired.

'Which page?' she repeated. 'What is on the page opposite?'

'It's near the middle of the paper, and Denzil's column is in the opposite page. Does it matter?'

'No,' she lied, adding, 'can you send the two pages to me?'

Looking at the two pages, she noticed Denzil had put the heading of her column in a green frame and his was in red. She smiled, knowing all was well. She was in the perfect page under the perfect colour.

Her second column was about the weather and how it had grounded the country to a halt over Christmas and New Year. How wonderful it was to watch people help each other after nature had brought them to a standstill. Nature that people had been using and abusing. She named this column: 'Where did we all go so wrong?'

A local school teacher agreed to proofread for her and all was well as Mary kept the articles neutral, until her brother ran for election which coincided with the twenty-fifth anniversary of the time he was shot. This article she called 'Quarter Century turn', and in it wrote about the changes the past twenty-five years had brought. Denzil had no objections. Others did though, and they wrote in letters to voice them; these were printed but that was it. The following week, the elections held on May 5th coincided with the thirtieth anniversary of Bobby Sands' death on hunger strike in 1981. As Bobby Sands had been voted in and died, an MP for Fermanagh/South Tyrone (the catchment area for the paper), she believed this was a good reason to write about this tragic time in their history. This column was named, 'Where were you on the 5th of May, 1981?' In it she told the story of how she got on a plane in New York, heading to the West Coast of America, trying to run away from it all again. Not knowing at the time that her teenage brother Kevin was in solitary confinement in Crumlin Road Goal using the words: *This was a time when you needed a riot squad to take a teenager out of a shower in a prison for listening to a radio, before putting him into solitary confinement for a week.*

More complaints, but nothing worth worrying about yet. She was getting more confident, but never stepped over the line in the sand that we drew for her, knowing when she did that writer's block would set in. She immediately retreated, knowing and accepting that her every word was being guided as well as being watched.

Changing the subject for the reader, Mary wrote stories about all kinds of things. One was about after her marriage broke up. One of the many stories she had told her sister; how she was treated as a separated woman in the part of the country that had only recently voted in divorce (the start of the end of the church's grip on this side of the border). Geraldine had replied laughing at that time, 'You should be writing a column called "The adventures of a separated woman."' Which seemed far-fetched at the time, but here she was with her own column and the freedom to write about whatever she wanted, so she wrote one of these stories and named it 'The adventures of a separated woman'.

After the first column in January 2011, Mary was back making plans to move to the cottage, but that had to be delayed again as she not only needed to make arrangements to accommodate John, the only remaining member of her extended family, but she also needed an income to live on. So again, we needed to put a halt to her gallop (another saying of her mother's).

When Mary and Roisín had gone down to check if the weather had done any damage to the cottage, they found that the two showers had been destroyed by the frost – which was the least amount of damage we could use to stop her. Her tiny income was already stretched to the limit and there were no funds to replace anything. Driving home from Foxford that day, Mary was bitterly disappointed knowing she had no choice but to surrender. Back home in Castlerea she found an email from a man who had written: *Hi Mary, my name is Gerry, and I am from Belfast. I have just finished your book and I want to talk to you. I too was brought up in the Troubles and would like to come to meet you as soon as possible to talk about my experiences and how it has affected my life. Please call me on ...* and he had left his mobile number.

Mary had already received a lot of emails from people who had read the book, people who had been traumatised by different events, but all with the same results. This one shocked her, not only because this man was from Belfast, but he was admitting that the Troubles had caused him problems and no civilian had ever admitted this to her before, as most were unaware of it! Also, deep down, she too (as well as her publisher) believed that the city people had a worse time than they had in the country, that she had no right to write about her experiences. It was the reason she snapped at Jo when she first asked if she was from Belfast.

After replying: *Thank you, Gerry, for your email, call me on ... and we can arrange for you to visit sometime.* Mary headed out the door for a walk to clear her head of the latest two issues that had arisen (not understanding at the time that they were connected and that they would both be resolved together).

When she got back there were two missed calls from his number and another email message that said: *Please call me back, I have the car full of petrol and would like to come to see you tomorrow.*

As she finished reading his message, her phone rang – it was Gerry.

'I'm busy all day tomorrow, she said over the phone. This was true, but she also needed time to ground herself before she met this man.

'If you can book me into a local bed and breakfast, I will stay tomorrow night and see you the following day,' he said.

His persistence made her more curious, and this curiosity got the better of her so she asked, 'Where did you get my book?'

'My girlfriend's father heard you on the radio and bought the book, then gave it her and she gave it to me and told me I should read it. I did before Christmas, but I didn't want to bother you over the holidays. I understood what you have written, as I have gone through similar things to you.'

'Okay, come here after six tomorrow evening, I will have time to talk with you then and I will book you a bed and breakfast with a woman that I know.' Then she added, 'I can leave you some dinner if you want?'

'Great! I look forward to meeting you and I would be delighted to have dinner with you,' he replied.

'Are you mad?' Marita said when Mary told her about Gerry. 'You don't know this man; he could be anyone. He could be a madman!'

'Well, I'm probably considered a madwoman, so we might get on well,' Mary replied.

The next evening at the dot of six, the doorbell rang, and Gerry came in. After dinner they sat in front of the fire and talked about their experiences for hours, then, when leaving he said, 'I know you go for a walk first thing every morning, I will be back to go with you if that is okay as I know you know someone who can help me.'

Shocked, Mary replied, 'How do you know?'

'I read your book,' he replied 'I know you walk every day and I know you have been to many therapists and I need help.'

'How would I know which one to send you to?' And then without thinking added, 'I think you would prefer to talk to a woman.'

'I would.'

And out of her mouth came words that we put there, 'I know a woman who may be able to help you but, I don't remember her name and don't have her number.'

'You will find it,' he replied with a big smile and left.

As she got ready for bed, Mary wondered where this number

could be found when she couldn't even remember her name. The following morning, she found the woman in question's card sitting on the countertop in the kitchen!

When Gerry arrived, she handed it to him and said, 'This must be the woman you're to go to.'

We watched, knowing that Mary had totally let go and we knew she was already aware that this man was in her life for a reason.

As they walked, the therapist was called and an appointment was made for two weeks later.

'Can I come to see you after my appointment with her?' Gerry asked as he was leaving her house later.

'Yes, and you can stay here if you want. No point in you paying for bed and breakfast when I have plenty of rooms.'

'Thank you very much. I would like that, and we could go down to see that cottage of yours in Foxford. I may be able to help you fix it up and get it ready for you to start taking people like me there.'

'Thanks for the offer, Gerry, but I have no money. I can't afford to pay you.'

'I don't want any money from you. Just feed me and keep me ... You are a good cook.'

'But ... I don't have any money for materials either!'

'I will use the materials you already have at the new house to do the work. There has to be lots of stuff left around there.'

'That would be great,' Mary replied, excitedly knowing he was right. 'Okay, I will bring you down when you are back here in two weeks.'

Two weeks later they stayed the weekend at the cottage and whilst she painted, he started making doors for the kitchen shelves and made plans to build in presses in the bedrooms.

'You will need two new showers,' he said at dinner on the Saturday evening. 'And you could also do with a stove, it's freezing in here.'

'I know, but as I said I have no money.'

They left on the Sunday evening with a lot done, but with a lot more to do.

'I'll be back again in two weeks,' he said when leaving and she was delighted.

During this time other people were emailing her with their stories. One was a woman who was abused as a child and asked if she could come down and stay in the cottage in Foxford. Mary emailed back: *Unfortunately not, as I can't really bring anyone there until I get showers and a stove and I have no money to buy either.*

The woman replied: *I am running a marathon for charity in two weeks, and I will give my money to you for the showers and there may be enough left for a stove.*

Mary: *You can't. I am not a charity.*

The woman answered: *I can and I will. The money is collected for people who are supporting others and that includes you, so I am giving it to you.*

Gerry was delighted. When the money came through there was enough for the two showers and a cheap stove. Both of which were promptly installed by Gerry.

CHAPTER 12

I n the spring of 2011, all was ready for the move to the cottage, but Mary still had to find a solution for John who had been living in her home for nearly twenty years; John, who they all thought of as family. It was not only the income from his keep which made her hesitant to let him go, even though this was her only source of revenue, but also the fact that the health board would probably put him into independent living (their latest buzz word), and this she knew would be disastrous for him. John was an alcoholic; left without family support he would drink again and there was no way she could let that happen. From the first day John had arrived in her home he had helped her, he washed the dishes, swept the floors and kept an eye on the rest of her extended family in the area, which was an enormous help to Mary. During the day, he worked in the gardens belonging to the health board until arthritis set in, then he worked inside. In all the time he was living in her house, he only went back on the drink a couple of times (usually when she was on holidays) but with dire consequences. Thinking long and hard about what to do, she finally turned it over to us and we whispered, *What about the flat in Marty's house next door?*

'Thank you. That's a brilliant idea,' she spoke out loud but knew that she would need to convince a few people before she could even mention it to John. Her first call was to his brother, who was next of kin. After explaining the situation to Martin, she finished by saying, 'If Marty rented the place to me and I put John there, he would be safe and I will make sure he has everything he needs during the week and bring him and Jacinta their dinners at the weekend.' (Jacinta was John's friend who had been coming to visit every evening and during the daytime at the weekend for the previous ten years.)

'Sounds good to me,' Martin replied. 'If you have any problems with the health board let me know and I will come down and talk to them.'

'Thanks,' Mary replied, neglecting to mention the fact that she had no intentions of telling the health board about anything until it was all sorted. With his brother onboard, Marty was the next person who needed convincing.

'I have a proposition for you,' she said when he opened his door later that evening.

'What?' he asked as he stepped aside to let her in.

'You know I want to move to the cottage, and I can't just go and leave John. I was thinking that if he moved into your empty flat, we could take care of him between us'

'I don't know. What would I have to do?'

'Nothing really, just give him the flat and I will pay you out of the money I get from the health board. You know him, and you know he will be a good tenant. I will do everything else. He hasn't drank for years and I know he will not drink in your house. He will be safe with you and you with him.'

'Let me think about it.'

The next day he called and said, 'Okay, I will give it a try.'

'Great,' she replied. Two down, one to go.

John was the last person to ask as there was no use in mentioning anything to him if she had nothing to offer. He hesitated, Jacinta didn't.

'Can we see it now?' she asked.

'Of course,' replied Mary and took them over.

Jacinta loved it. John said nothing.

'Will I still be able to come here every evening?' Jacinta then asked.

'I can't see why not.'

'And weekends?'

'Yes, and I will have your dinners here in the fridge on a Friday and you can heat them in the microwave when it suits you.'

'And … if I wanted to stay over would Marty let me?' she asked as she glanced at the double bed.

'I think you better ask John that before I ask Marty,' Mary replied and they all laughed.

John came around to the idea but her move was delayed again to make sure he settled in okay and to be there for Jarlath's twenty-first birthday party which was at the end of April.

For this special occasion a column was written called, 'Cutting the umbilical cord … again.' In it, Mary explained that as she had no money, the only thing that she could give Jarlath was the house for the summer and his freedom, quickly realising that by giving Jarlath his freedom, she found her own.

A few weeks before her fifty-second birthday, Mary packed her car and moved counties, driving the forty-mile journey, crying all the way but happy in the knowledge that this was finally the right time for everyone involved. Jarlath had the house to himself for the summer. Marty had a good tenant. John and Jacinta had a lovely place and she finally got to move on.

Arriving at the cottage an hour later she dumped her bags in the hall, sat in the middle of the sitting room floor and wrote an article about the move, which was her first one in twenty-three years, then wrote about the twenty places she had lived in before that.

CHAPTER 13

For the following month Mary felt as free as a bird, feeling like the teenager that she had never been allowed to be, a teenager without a care in the world. Her only problem was the new laptop, it had been giving her trouble so she found someone to fix it.

The computer guy called her one evening to say that the hard drive was gone.

'What's a hard drive?'

'Storage.'

'And can it be fixed?'

'No. It needs to be replaced.'

'Okay, replace it.'

A couple of days later he called to say it was ready to be picked up. On the way she called her friend Anne and said, 'The hard drive on my laptop has been replaced.'

'What's a hard drive?'

Mary explained and then added, 'I feel like something changing in me too. A lot already has, but something else.'

'I know what you mean,' Anne replied. 'Something on the outside is changing because something on the inside already has.'

'That's it. That's exactly it.'

With her laptop back she started to write her column that evening, laughing out loud as she wrote about her sister Ruth, her friend Pat and their kids who had come to stay for the weekend. (This was not a normal weekend; it was the 12th of July bank holiday weekend north of the border, and everyone was looking to get away from the Orange Order Parades that were in full swing.) She wrote about Jarlath too, who had chosen this particular weekend to come and visit with no real understanding or sympathy for those bailing out of the six counties and taking his place. She too was annoyed with what was happening but delighted to get it off her chest with black humour. The column that week was about her hike in the mountains with her niece, nephew and Ruth's friend's daughter and the negotiations that took place on the way up regarding who would get which bars of chocolate she had in her rucksack. Finishing up by telling how the negotiations concluded, before asking if a trip into the mountains with a few bars of chocolate might help those negotiating the marching routes in the North. Then, the following words were written on the page: *So, as men in bowler hats march on Irish soil, carrying British flags, celebrating the victory of a Dutch man, the British government once again pay the price of a week of violence and destruction. And the Irish government once again rake in the revenue of their best week in tourism.*

Reading back over what she had written, she was about to delete it when we whispered, *Leave it, it's okay.*

No way. They will have all the ammunition they need to get rid of me. I love writing this column and don't want to give it up.

Leave it, we repeated.

After meditating on it the follow morning, she heard us repeat, *Leave it in.*

With a sinking heart she emailed the column, believing that this was the end of her writing in the paper but consoled herself all week with the thought that Denzil would edit it if he thought it would cause a problem, not knowing at the time that Denzil too had taken the week off!

It was printed without a word being changed, then he emailed her: *Mary, I have had five letters complaining about your column.* She didn't know what to say so replied: *Could I read them?*

She read them and knew this was serious, as one was written by the leader of a political party, another one by the head of the Orange Order and three more scathing letters which were anonymous.

Not wanting to cause any more problems for Denzil she wrote back: *Thank you for allowing me to write in your paper for six months, Denzil. I loved it. Just let me go.*

He replied: *Even if I wanted to let you go Mary – which I don't – no-one will tell me how to run my paper. I just hope there are people out there who will support you.*

Mary: *Me too. I will apologise and explain in next week's column that I didn't write it to hurt anyone,* which she did under the heading: 'The truth hurts so let's just all accept that and move on.'

She did apologise and offered to meet the men who wrote the letters as she had no doubt they were all men even though three of them were both nameless and faceless.

Mary wrote: *I will meet you anywhere. You will recognise me as not only do I stand behind every word I write but my picture is in the paper every week.*

The week dragged as she thought. *Will anyone support me? Will there be more letters written against me?*

In the meantime, the issue was picked up by a national paper. This article included a picture of her which was placed between a picture of her brother (the politician) and the other politician (who had written the letter) under the heading: 'Editor refuses to censor Republican columnist'. We watched her laugh at the idea that everyone seems to consider her a Republican, except Republicans! Then, when she thought it couldn't get any worse, *BBC Northern Ireland* requested an interview between Denzil and the politician involved to discuss the issue on air, this never happened as the politician refused to face Denzil who had accepted the invitation.

Ruth scanned the paper the following Thursday morning and sent it to her. There were seven letters in support of her and nothing had been changed in the article she had written that week. In fact, nothing was ever changed or edited in anything she wrote. She had written a column about her friend who was abused by a priest in the west of the country, which was then published in a local western paper (at the behest of her friend) and it was edited to bits. She couldn't believe it, so called Denzil to ask, 'Why do you never edit anything I write?'

'Because if I did, I might as well write it myself, Mary.'

This made perfect sense to her, and even though her words triggered things in others, that was never because she was being vindictive, but because the truth really did hurt. This column was giving her the opportunity to say things that a case against the police would never have allowed, and she had no doubt that they were some of the people who wrote in against her. She now had a voice that no amount of money could pay for, and she used it but never abused it – a voice not only for herself but for others too.

This new-found strength gave Mary the courage to write her most difficult article, about attending the rape crisis centre, written in the third person and called 'The question of verbal abuse', which delved into the question of verbal sexual abuse which she suffered from the mouth of a police officer, deciding to admit it was about herself to any family member who asked – anyone except her parents. The only person to ask was her father. In fact, he asked twice. Who is the woman you wrote about in your letter this week? (That is what he called her column.) On both occasions she replied that the woman didn't want anyone to know who she was but was under no doubt that he knew it was her. She felt like Judas as she denied herself, but there was no way she could tell her parents what had happened to her in that cell as she still hadn't found the strength to face it herself.

Changing the content of her column from the Northern issues, Mary wrote about other people's issues: her children, the state of the country. But when Martin McGuiness ran for president in the Republic, she wrote 'The race to the park', laughing the entire time it was being written, watching politicians and journalists south of the border running scared of a man who now had a voice, a man who was now joint leader of the Northern government, a man who was called a terrorist in his past. Ruth called to say she thought it was her best piece!

Continuing on the same theme, 'The picture of changing times' told the story of the picture she had drawn of Martin McGuiness and Gerry Adams, a picture taken on the night of the Good Friday Agreement, as these two men had sat disillusioned on the steps of Stormont. The story continued by telling how she had used this drawing to bring her background to the forefront in the small town where she had hidden her past by displaying the drawing at the local agriculture show, not expecting or receiving a prize (as she had before) as the subject matter wasn't to their taste. Reaching up to take it down after the show had closed, a man with an English accent asked if she would sell it. Shocked with this request, she took his number (declining to give hers). The story continued that evening as she was bringing the picture to another exhibition. Stopped by the Garda (Southern Police) for speeding, they cautioned her and were waving her on when the picture was spotted on the back seat, which cost her a speeding ticket! Entering the next venue with the framed picture under her arm she continued the column by telling how the owner of the premises approached her and asked if she had drawn it. 'Yes,' she had answered defiantly to this man who she knew well.

'Would you sell it to me, I would like to hang it in my restaurant?'

Reeling with shock again, she named a price and he put his hand it his pocket and produced the money. A week later she drew the picture again for the man with the English accent and forgot all about it. The story continued the following year when she was in with the bank manager looking for yet another loan for yet another property. Entering his office that afternoon and before she could sit down, he said, 'You draw, don't you, Mary?'

'Yes,' she replied, wondering how he knew this.

'Would you draw a picture for the local hospice?'

Laughing, she told him the story of the picture in question and was shocked again when he asked, 'Would you draw that one again for us and … could you get it signed?'

'I will draw it for you, Chris, but can't promise that I can get them to sign it as I don't know or have never met either of these men, but I will ask my brother.' The picture was drawn, signed and to her delight it earned £750 for the hospice at an auction in Dublin at the end of 1999! This is where her story ended in the paper, but not in her future, as she had no idea what a huge impact one of these men was going to have on her future.

In all of her writings she never did cross the line we had set for her, knowing that she was walking a tightrope, one slip and she would fall. Mary believed the issue on the 12th of July 2011 was the fall, but instead it gave her the confidence she needed by showing her not only were we guiding her every word, but also that the editor of the paper was supporting her. He was one of the few people she ever met that truly believed in freedom of the press.

CHAPTER 14

Whilst all this was going on, Mary was still going to monthly meetings with her new-found group of people who were helping each other with mental health issues. After meeting one of them at her book launch, she explained to them how in the spring of 2012 she had moved and had a spare room for anyone who needed to get away from it all, and another room for someone who could come and help her. She didn't have to wait long before someone was in crisis and others came to help.

One night, when sitting beside the new stove with Dara who had helped start this group, we listened, amazed, as she told him in detail what had happened with the souls that had passed on in 2009. She knew Dara would understand at some level as he had named some of the techniques she had mentioned in her book, techniques used for healing herself, like soul retrieval, a phrase she had never heard before.

When finished, she asked, 'Do you think I am crazy, Dara?'

'You don't present yourself as a crazy person, Mary,' he replied.

Her friend laughed when she told him this and continued by saying that it was Dara's nice way of saying you are crazy, but she knew it wasn't what he meant, thinking, *Who would make up this story, and if I did why don't I want to write it as fiction?*

We were happy that she had spoken about it but that was it.

Back she went to trying to save everyone else (those who were still alive), even when they weren't asking for help.

One day when Gerry was visiting, he said, 'I was just thinking, Mary, I can help you to decorate that house you have for sale in Belfast so that you can get it sold, pay the banks and finish the new house.'

'That's a brilliant idea, Gerry,' she replied. 'I can't afford to pay you but I will be able to when the house is sold.'

'Okay. We have a deal. You come up and stay with Teresa and me when you are ready and we will get started.'

The following week they began. Knowing he was a perfectionist, she did as she was told as she had in the cottage and watched the terrace house being transformed. Gerry woke her at 5:30 every morning and they worked ten hours a day. Seven days later, it looked so good Mary wanted to keep it, but she knew that she couldn't afford to. It was time to let it go.

Two days later it sold, and she was back to a building that she had started five years earlier before she ran out of money when the recession set in. A place (buildings and writing) where she felt totally at one with the universe (and us!) as she went with the flow. Listening and taking direction as it was given, rarely questioning anything as she watched everything fall into place.

*   *   *

Mary's original idea in 2007 had been to sell the cottage and live in the new house she was building around the corner. This was her human plan; her soul had different ideas. With the sale of the cottage, she had visions of living mortgage free, continuing to do what she was already doing but on a bigger scale. That is, doing for others what she hadn't learnt to do for herself!

The recession of 2008 had put a halt to her idea overnight. Now she had the money to finish the new house and get back to her original idea and there was nothing we could do, only watch her go down a road that was not part of her journey as we looked for ways to get her back on track.

After paying off the bank, her parents, her brother and Gerry, she left the remaining money aside to finish the new house but nothing for herself, continuing to believe that her function on Earth was to support everyone. Still feeling worthless because someone tried to kill her!

The house in Belfast had been the first property Mary had bought with Marty in 1985 in the middle of a recession. He had wanted to buy in Galway city but when she pointed out that they could buy in a city north of the border at half the price and twice the rent, he relented. They then bought another house in the same city, whilst they were negotiating the purchase of the family farm from Marty's mother with the money earned and saved in the US. The second house needed a mortgage and Mary negotiated all the dealings for this as Marty dealt with the purchase of the farm. This second house in the city was not a property we had guided her to. It wasn't meant to be and was sold within a couple of years, creating a lot of hassle but taught her to listen more carefully.

The family home was the next purchase. Marty was the one who spotted it in 1987, but again Mary negotiated, pregnant with Roisín and looking to settle. The house was more expensive than they could afford, but in a recession, it was a buyers' market. 'We still can't afford it,' Marty had said at the time after she had negotiated a third off the price as the interest rates were nearly 20%.

'If we buy, Marty, I will earn enough in it to pay the mortgage,' Mary said with confidence, even though she had no idea how this was going to happen. But she was enjoying herself listening to us and had heard us loud and clear when we told her to buy their first real home together.

When her brother-in-law Paddy asked, smiling, 'How long are you planning to stay here?' (as he had watched her and Marty move seven times in their four years together) she had answered with the same humour.

'A stick of gelignite won't move me again, Paddy, until I have my children reared.' Something that was said in jest but knowing that this would come to pass, which it did!

The house was a split-level bungalow which had three small flats in the basement with no planning permission. We whispered, *Get planning permission,* even though her solicitor had said, 'Don't worry, I know all your neighbours; you will have no problem.' But she followed our instruction and also heard us say, *Rent to the elderly.* We watched as she planned to set it up in a way where she could charge a little extra and help the elderly in the flats. Semi-independent living, she planned to call it – actually, she was open to doing anything in this space as going back to the States or north of the border was no longer an option.

Having had enough of New York, she was delighted to be back in Ireland in 1985, south of the border where she believed she would be happy – not understanding at the time that happiness is a state of mind. The following year, after working for the winter in Florida, they arrived home again, the day before her brother was shot by the SAS.

When her parents came to visit shortly after, she brought them to mass in the next town where her father spotted a man from his childhood in the North, whom he had played football with. Mary knew no-one else in the area, so Paddy and his family became her friends and family. In 1988, when she was painting their new home, Paddy's wife Freda took care of Roisín. Paddy would drive the infant to Mary to be breastfed when she was hungry, then wait patiently in the car and take her back to his wife when she was fed. Mary would then get back to the mountain of work that needed to be done to make the house habitable as Marty farmed.

When Paddy suggested she apply to the health board to board out psychiatric patients, Mary didn't hesitate, aware of the fact that we were talking though him. Knowing this, she had no fear, their backgrounds didn't interest her as she was prepared to do what we asked to get what she wanted. That was, to be a stay-at-home mother and make a living in that home.

At that time, applications were made directly to the person running this new scheme, so Paddy took her out to meet Jimmy, another connection that had been made through football. Jimmy informed them that all the patients had been boarded out and she accepted this. When her eighteen-year-old sister Gertie, who was helping her paint at the time asked, 'What if you can't get anyone to rent this space?'

Mary had looked at her as if she was blind, thinking, *can she not see how obvious it is, can she not see how everything is falling into place even if I had to borrow the first month's mortgage from Mam and Dad!*

Gertie continued bravely by asking, 'But what if no-one comes?'

Mary didn't answer this either, she just looked at her little sister and smiled thinking, *Ye of little faith.*

Paddy, who had been dealing with cancer for some time before Mary met him, died shortly after. Sitting at his wake, she wondered how she would manage without him. He was her rock; he was one of her own, he knew her background, he was her friend. Arriving home that night Marty shouted outside the front door, 'Jimmy Finnegan is on the phone again!'

'Who is Jimmy Finnegan?' she whispered as she came into the house.

'The man from the health board!'

She steadied herself, took the phone and listened as Jimmy asked, 'Would you take two people we want to board out?'

'Could I meet them first?' she enquired.

'Yes, and we would like to see where you plan on putting them.'

The following day, before Paddy's funeral, he and the head

psychiatrist in the county arrived and passed the place which was now looking great after months of renovations.

The day after Paddy's funeral, Mary met Michael and another Jimmy and took them home with her. They moved in with an elderly man that had answered her advertisement in the local paper. Within a few months, Jimmy (from the health board) had sent her another two people and she was earning enough money not only to pay the mortgage, but also to start renovating the part of the house they were living in with no doubt that Paddy was still helping her from the other side of the veil.

CHAPTER 15

I n the short time Mary had known Paddy, he had introduced
her to another man called Gerry who ran his own workshop
on the other side of town. Gerry helped her with anything that
involved wood in the renovations of their house and guided her
to tradesmen he trusted with everything else. When she could
do a job herself, he loaned her all the tools necessary and became
the friend she lost in Paddy. When her son Jarlath was born a
couple of years later, he was one of the first to congratulate her.
When his daughter Laura was born four years after, Mary brought
Roisín and Jarlath out to meet her and bring the child a present.
What none of them knew at this time, was her son Jarlath and his
daughter Laura had already chosen to spend time together in this
life, and years later, would live in this first house that Gerry had
helped Mary to renovate – but that's another story!

After the renovations were finished, Marty and Mary decided
they would get another mortgage and buy another property. She
suggested Galway where he originally wanted but he said, 'What
about the house next-door when it comes up for sale?'

Mary didn't wait for it to come up for sale, instead she followed
our guidance and wrote to the owner who was living in South
America and asked if she would sell the empty house, and if so,
how much she would want for it. The reply was positive, and the

price was fair so a third mortgage was secured. She then oversaw the renovations with the idea of taking in more elderly people. This didn't work as she was far too busy to extend her already large family, so more renovations divided the house into two flats which she rented out. This house was to become Marty's home after they separated, and the extra flat was where John would spend the remainder of his life when Mary moved to the cottage!

With all their properties rented, Marty noticed a building in the town that was up for sale – a shop with a flat above. Mary was in her glory again as she negotiated another mortgage, purchased the property, then added site manager to her job description as she oversaw the men who ripped the inside out – and helped them do it. It was then renovated from scratch with the help of both her brother and Gerry, working with her again when needed. When they were finished, they had another two more flats and a shop to rent, which she did.

The next property they purchased together was the cottage in Mayo, which was to be their holiday home; a place to retreat to as their marriage was in trouble. Mary had believed the marriage could be saved if they had more time together, not knowing at the time that their futures were not with each other. This cottage was to be her future home.

Marty had mentioned Westport as a place to buy that time, but Mary pointed out that it was too expensive and far too commercialised. North Mayo was cheaper, quieter and Inishcrone beach was the destination she had in mind that first and only day they looked. She drove, following the directions Marty gave her, without question, delighted that he had agreed to come, delighted that they had a day together. We guided them up and down back roads until they finally got to Inishcrone where she quickly changed her mind, as not only were the properties expensive but the place was too busy and they were looking for peace and quiet.

Taking Marty's direction again after lunch, wondering where

they would be guided to next, she drove from Attymass heading into the Ox Mountains.

'Take the right,' Marty said at the T-junction. Then, 'Take the next left.' And again she did as she was told, driving down a narrow, twisted road that felt like they were going into a rabbit hole. As she navigated the car carefully, they came to another bad corner, and there on the left was the most beautiful lake with the Ox Mountains as a backdrop.

'We were on this road this morning,' Marty said as they reached a fork on the road. 'Take the right,' he instructed, and there on the left, was the cottage for sale. They both got out of the car and looked around at the breath-taking scenery.

'This is it,' Mary said.

As Marty looked around, Mary rang the doorbell of the small bungalow on the fork of the road.

'Sorry to bother you, but do you know who owns the cottage down the road?' she asked.

'We do,' the woman replied. 'But you better call the auctioneer.'

'Thanks. We will, but is there any chance we could see it whilst we are here as I have no idea when we can come back?'

'Okay,' the woman replied and got her a key.

As they walked through the three-roomed cottage, Mary was under no doubt that they had found what they were looking for. Marty agreed.

With another building to renovate and the belief that her marriage could be saved, Mary got to work on the negotiations – which are always complex but this one more so, as the cottage came on its own but there was a byre (cowshed) beside it, and we guided her to buy this too. With no space for a septic tank, she had no choice but to buy the field across the road. They also bought the piece of land at the back of the house, which would bring her property up to the fork in the road which was overlooking the Ox Mountains – and there was a hayshed, part of which would become Roisín's home/office twenty years later when she had nowhere else to go in the pandemic and couldn't stay with her mother as she had become a carer for her parents!

Mary Ellen (the woman selling the cottage), helped her find a builder as her brothers were busy at the time. This local builder (another Gerry) gave her a price on the job after plans were drawn which would extend the cottage over to the byre and include it in the building. All was well until her brother Noel looked at the plans and said, 'You won't be able to put a roof on that extension between the two buildings. It is too narrow.' Another brother, and her sister's partner, said the same thing, but as the builder hadn't mentioned a problem, she hoped against hope that they were all wrong.

Gerry called a couple of days into the job and said, 'I can't put a roof on the extension between the two buildings. It's too narrow. We will have to build an extra five feet out the back to do this.'

'Is it possible to do it, and if so what will it cost?'

He came back with a figure and the reassurance that as it was to the back of the building and within the dimensions of an extension; it could be done without further planning permission. 'Okay,' she replied, even though she was now over budget but trusted that the money would come.

Cash in your investments, we whispered. She checked them out and found that they were worth a lot more than she had believed.

A few days later Gerry called again, 'You better come down; we have another problem.'

Mary calmly drove the forty miles, then listened as Gerry explained that now that he had the five foot extra at the back and a huge attic, she could actually have another bedroom in the attic.

'Not without a bathroom,' she replied, 'as it would be too far to the one downstairs.'

A few days later he gave her a price.

'Go ahead, I will find the money somewhere.'

'I wish I could run my personal life the way I run a business,'

Mary told a friend the next morning as they went for a walk. *You could if you listened*, we whispered.

The original plan for a three-bedroom cottage was now so big that she had enough space to make it into two cottages. *One can be rented as a holiday home and we can use the other one for ourselves*, she thought, but by the time it was finished their marriage was in tatters.

With no money left for a holiday that year, she asked her sister if they could have their holiday home in Donegal for a week, grasping at straws as she tried to think of another way to get her marriage back on track as marriage guidance had only worked for a while.

She thought back to all the holidays they had taken before and all the wonderful times they had as a family: they had travelled all over Ireland, Wales, England, France, Jersey and Scotland (which wasn't the best as she wasn't well at the time). They had even gone for three weeks to the States, which they all loved.

Before they headed home from Donegal at the end of the week, Mary realised that there was nothing more she could do. She had tried everything, and nothing had worked. In despair, she handed it over to us, allowing us to guide her in a relationship for the first time in her life.

When they arrived home on that Friday night in August 2001, this was the day that she got the call about the walking club being allowed back on the mountains after the outbreak of foot and mouth, and next day her nephew was killed on a motorcycle in New York.

Six months later, Marty moved to the house next door, but it took some time to reach an agreement on the division of their properties – finally agreeing that Marty would get the farm and the house he was now living in. Mary would get the house in Belfast, the cottage that she had renovated, plus the family home where she ran her business. The sticking point was the building in town, which she believed should be hers as she wanted to use the income from it to pay for their children's education. We whispered that there was another way, but she didn't listen. Instead, she dug her heels in and completely ignored us for a year. Finally letting go and trusting us, giving us an opportunity to show how little we could do when she blocked us out and how quickly we worked when allowed, we whispered again, *Give Marty half the building.*

Her solicitor who was on sick leave at the time did not agree, but Mary insisted. 'Give him half and he can pay half of all college fees etc. I don't know why I was taking all the responsibility for the children.' (*Control,* we could have told her, but said nothing!)

This was agreed and all was settled so they decided to sell the building, pay off the loan and split the profits, but the auctioneer dragged his feet for months (which was in the order of things). The weekend before it was to go up for sale, Mary was walking in the mountains with her friend who was talking about an investment property she and her husband had just bought. Mary listened with no real interest of going down that route again, but driving home later we whispered, *Buy Marty out and keep the building.*

Shocked, she wondered why, as the building had now been lying idle for over a year and needed money spent on it. Money that she didn't have. But that didn't stop her walking next door that evening and telling Marty she wanted to buy him out.

'You are mad. It's not even rented. Where will you get the money?'

'Maybe I am mad, but I have always gone with my gut (the name she called us), and my gut tells me to buy it. I will give you half of what the auctioneer has put on it. Think about it, and I will get back to you tomorrow evening.'

'Why would you buy it, Mammy?' Jarlath asked.

She repeated what she had said to his father, not understanding at the time that her children were learning from her actions, not her words. The next evening Marty asked for more money than the auctioneer had priced it at.

Give him the extra money, we whispered.

'Okay,' she replied without a thought.

As she walked back to her home that evening, she wondered how she would convince the bank to give her the money. This had never deterred her before, but this was her first time doing it alone!

Later that evening as she was making pizza for the children, the phone rang.

'Is that Mary Geraghty?' a woman asked.

Not any longer, she thought.

'Yes,' she replied, as she hadn't changed her name and had no intentions of doing so whilst her children were still at school – they'd had enough change already.

'Do you own the old ESB building?'

Well, I didn't yesterday but do today, she thought.

'Yes!'

'Would you rent the shop?'

'Yes! What do you want it for?'

'A laundry. Could I see it this evening?'

'Give me a half hour and I will meet you there.'

When she got off the phone, she said to her son, 'Never ever doubt your gut, Jarlath, no matter how mad people might think you are. Only you know your journey in this life, only you can hear your guides.'

He smiled but said nothing.

An hour later the place was rented, a two-year lease signed and enough income to pay the mortgage she needed. Two days later, the bank approved the loan. Six months later, she got a call from the tenant to say she wanted to break the lease and move on to a bigger space. All was still in the order of things; this lady came into Mary's life at exactly the right time and now it was the right time for her to exit.

Mary was dumbfounded knowing it wouldn't be easy to get another tenant. The other option was to bring this tenant to court for breaking the lease, which wasn't given a moment's thought. Instead, she sat down in a meditation and asked, *What do I do now?*

Sell the building, we whispered.

Calling her auctioneer who had valued all the properties for her when separating she asked, 'Seamus, would the old ESB office sell?'

'Do you own it? Did you get it in the separation? Is your name on the deeds?'

'Yes, yes and yes.'

'Okay, have your solicitor send me proof of ownership and come to see me tomorrow morning. I have a buyer for you.'

Astonished, Mary put the phone down and sat back in her chair. In less than an hour, her tenant had told her she was leaving, we had told her to sell and the auctioneer had told her he had a buyer. A coincidence? No! it was the right time for everyone, the tenant needed a bigger place, a solicitor needed a premises to buy and Mary needed to move on.

The following morning, she was sitting in Seamus's office when a fax confirming her ownership of the property came in.

'How much do you want for the building?' he asked.

Having already done her homework and knew the boom that had just started had pushed up the price in the previous six months, she believed it was now worth €40,000 more than she paid for it. She opened her mouth to say this and was surprised when the words, 'What do you think it's worth?' came out of her mouth.

He named an amount that was €20,000 more than she was planning to ask.

'Okay,' she said and walked out of his office, stunned.

The next day the auctioneer called to say he had a bid for the asking price.

'Does the bidder have the money in place?' Mary asked.

'Yes, she does.'

'Then sell it to her.' 'No, not yet. I will call a few people that I think might be interested too. We may get more.'

'Seamus,' Mary replied calmly. 'Call whoever you want but

close it on Monday evening if no-one else is bidding. I want to sell. She wants to buy and I'm happy with the price.'

Getting off the phone, she called her son and told him.

'That's great, Mam. Maybe you will get more.'

'I don't want any more, Jarlath. I have got €20,000 more than I expected and €60,000 more than I had six months ago. And my gut has told me to let it go, so I will let it go.'

All went through even though she heard through the grapevine that the purchaser had a bigger bid on a building in worse condition, which didn't bother her. A month later she paid off the bank and was financially secure for the first time in years.

CHAPTER 16

Before the separation was finalised, Mary had got a grant in the North and was in the process of renovating the house in Belfast as she was buying Marty out of the old ESB building. All worked out perfectly apart from a hiccup with the bank when they lost the deeds of the old ESB building and of course blamed everyone else. This left her borrowing money from her parents, her brother and maxing out her credit cards until she had no choice but to face them head-on for the mistake they had made. After an apology and compensation, she moved on with her life, staying with the same bank.

'Why would you stay with that bank?' her son asked.

'They are all the same, Jarlath. When something is sorted you have to let it go and move on, it only weighs you down if you carry it.' (Wise words that she may have followed through with this time but not with everything she did!)

'That's me finished building,' she said to a friend when the renovation was finished on the Belfast property. 'I won't ever build again.'

'It is in your blood,' he replied. 'You will continue to do what you love, and you love building.'

'I did love building as I used it to avoid my past, and the renovations in Belfast were forced on me. If I hadn't taken the grant, the building would have to have been updated without it. I am finished. I can't risk the pressure it puts me under and I don't need the drama anymore.'

So, with all her finances in order we guided her to help her neighbour, now friend, Mary Ellen in Mayo who was selling more of her land.

'Why don't you get planning permission for a site on the fork of the road?' Mary asked her. 'It is beautiful there overlooking the mountains. It won't cost that much to apply for permission, and if you get it, it would be worth a lot more than selling it as a field.'

'I wouldn't have a clue how to,' Mary Ellen replied.

'Don't worry, I will help you,' Mary answered.

After working together, the planning permission was obtained and the site was put up for sale.

With the auctioneer's sign glaring at her, her friends and family, as they walked into the mountains repeatedly asked, 'Why don't you buy that site?'

'No way,' she replied every time. 'I have had enough of building.'

Then one day as she walked past the sign alone, we whispered, *Buy the site.* She knew immediately it was us, and for the first time ever, questioned us in the purchase of a property asking through her thoughts, *What would I want it for?*

You never needed to know before.

I am alone now. I would have to take all the responsibility on myself, my mother will kill me and this is the first time I have had money in the bank, she replied through her thoughts.

We repeated, *Buy the site.*

She kept looking back at it as she walked on into the mountains, looking for a sign, for something on the site that had changed, but there were none. Nothing on the site had changed, but Mary had. She was stronger and this was going to be the rebuilding of herself. A building with a strong foundation, an opportunity for us to bring her back from the fear of moving forward.

Taking the binoculars out of her rucksack at the top of the mountain, she studied the site knowing in her heart that this was something that was meant to be, even if she didn't understand why. *Why would I need another project, why would I sacrifice everything I have gained financially?* were her thoughts on the way back before walking onto the site. She then wandered into the old granary which had been there for over a hundred years and looked like the gate lodge to the mountains which was supposed to be knocked down to facilitate the planning permission, something she didn't agree with but as it was not her site, it had been none of her business. But that day, it felt so right, the same feeling she got when buying every property.

That night and the following morning, she meditated on it, and we continued to say, *Buy the site.*

The following day she returned to Mary Ellen and made the deal, using most of the money she had left over from the sale of the last building.

'Why would you spend most of your savings on that site, Mam?' Jarlath asked.

'I have no idea, Jarlath.'

'When will you know?'

'I have no idea … Maybe it is just my job just to get retention on the granary. I never did believe that it should be knocked. That granary is part of the community, Jarlath, part of the mountain, built by local people more than a hundred years ago.'

'What kind of way is that to run a business?' says he who had just started a degree in business.

'It's the way I have always done it and the way that works for me, Jarlath,' neglecting to say what she was thinking, *That is why I never wanted to go to college to study business. I have always been guided and have a knowing when things are right.*

She applied for and got the retention on the granary. After clearing it out and renovating it, the savings were all gone, the paperwork was then filed to the relief of both her mother and herself. Having done as asked, she needed a break.

*   *   *

About a year later, we whispered one morning, *Check your planning permission on the site.* (She ignored us as she believed that she had another four years to build or sell.) The next day we repeated, *Check your planning permission.* Again, we were ignored. When we repeated it the third morning she jumped out of bed and headed to the filing cabinet.

It says five years, she thought, smiling.

Turn the page, we whispered. She did this and discovered that the planning permission was from the date it was given, not the date the site was bought, something we neglected to tell her at the time. (She was guided on a need-to-know basis and had been told what she needed to know at the time!)

To her horror she realised that nearly four and half years were up. She realised immediately that the site would have to be sold, the house built to the roof within the following six months or try to get an extension on the planning permission. She called the architect who had bought the rest of the land from Mary Ellen.

'What are the chances of me getting an extension on the planning permission next door to you, Mark?'

'Very low,' he replied. 'They've got very strict. You could take a chance, but I wouldn't.'

Mary knew at that moment that we had left her with no choice: the house needed to be built to the roof within six months or the planning permission would be lost. There was no other way. It couldn't be sold as the buyer would be left with the same issue as her, with even less time to sort it. She was snookered. She had to build.

'Where are you going to get the money?' Jarlath enquired as Roisín walked out of the kitchen. Her daughter had no interest in anything other than media, which she was now studying at university.

'The economy is booming. I have a good track record and credit rating, Jarlath. I will mortgage and start working and pay it off when I sell the cottage and be mortgage free. There will be no problem.'

The bank agreed, and we did not contradict her illusion that she was going to sell the cottage, which was now worth a small fortune. There was no point in bursting her bubble, her illusion would keep her motivated.

'What's the new business plan?' Jarlath asked.

'Set up a centre for people who are traumatised; for people like me who have nowhere to go when they need to take time for themselves. A place where people can meditate, not medicate.'

'Right! And you think you will make a lot of money doing that?'

'I don't need to make a lot of money, Jarlath. I will still be able to afford to pay for you and Roisín to finish your education and start making a lot of money, if that is what you want. I have been there, done that, and a lot of money didn't make me happy.'

As Christmas rolled in, Mary was making plans to build a big house and start a new life. As everyone else was enjoying the season, she was poring over different materials after deciding to build an energy-efficient, A-rated house with no idea how, but without any doubt that we would be guiding her every step of the way. By the time the holidays were over she had decided to build with ICF (insulated concrete formwork) which would leave her with an airtight house that she had planned to ventilate mechanically.

Over the next six months, she flowed with us as her brothers came onboard to use materials most of them had never heard of before but they had it to the roof in time to secure her planning permission, but there was an enormous problem. Mary had built the house that she believed should be in this scenic location, not the permission that had been granted, because when she first approached Mark about overseeing the work with her, he suggested a change. 'I would build a property that looked like an old schoolhouse with an extension,' she'd said at the time. So, he drew a different plan which she loved.

'This is exactly what I always had in mind, Mark, but we still don't have the time to change them.'

'Build it, Mary. Let me worry about the county council. It is right.'

So, they started building with a plan that hadn't been sanctioned.

The first major hurdle they had to overcome on the journey to the roof was the framework.

The first factory which had just opened to make ICF in Ireland had a problem with a machine and couldn't meet her time line, so she simply asked the owner if he could recommend someone who was importing it. Two minutes later she was talking to a man in Cork called Jarlath, which she took as a sign from us. (By this time of her life she was very aware of our signs and always smiled when we sent the obvious ones, like a man with the same name as her son, a name she had only encountered a few times before in her lifetime.) He told her where she could see a construction of this build – an address which he believed was close to her, in fact, it was only a few hundred yards from where she was living. She laughed out loud at our second confirmation.

This Jarlath was on the ball and had the ICF blocks delivered the following week with the bonus of two Polish men to help them get started. Then, after getting a local farmer to bring the insulated blocks up the narrow road where the lorry couldn't go, her brother Brendy and the two men got to work. Two weeks later when the Polish men left, Brendy was able to show her other brothers how to finish the construction. Whilst they were doing their work, we lead Mary online to windows which she brought in from Austria. They were both airtight and triple-glazed and not available from any supplier in the country at that time, unless a fortune was paid for them.

'Where do you find all these things?' her older brother Noel asked one day, as they worked together.

'I just send it from my mind out into the universe, like you do on a computer. Only I don't need Google!'

She knew he didn't understand but he certainly knew it worked as *the proof of the pudding was in the eating* (another saying of her mother's). A few months after they had started, he was ordering what he needed for the roof and she watched with amazement as Noel, Brendy and Kevin worked together, getting the roof finished before the six months were up.

All was well until she got a letter from the county council stating the obvious – her building was not in compliance with planning. Her parents were there when she received this bombshell.

'Oh my God, what are you going to do now? They will make you take it down,' said her mother.

'No, they won't. I will figure out what to do,' Mary replied. Neglecting to mention the millions they said they would charge if she didn't close the site immediately. She wasn't in the slightest bit worried, knowing we were behind all this.

The next morning, we were asked, *What now?*

Call the county council.

'The engineer is out,' the lady told her. 'Can I help you?'

'I got a letter to say there was something wrong with my building. Would you mind telling me what that is?' she asked innocently.

After giving her name and address the lady said, 'Let me check.' After a few clicks on the computer, the lady said, 'It is not on the right level with the road, but there are other issues too. You had better talk to the engineer, give me your number and I will have him call you.'

She called Brendy on the way down when she couldn't reach Mark.

'Shite! I never thought they would come out this early to check. In fact, they rarely check anything this side of the border,' he said.

'Leave it with me, just keep working.'

Driving on to the site an hour later, the engineer called and said, 'You got our letter.'

'Yes.'

'The site is above road level and contrary to planning.'

'It is not!' she replied sharply, then lowered her voice and continued. 'I had to spend €8,000 on stones to get it to the level where the county council requested, and believe me, I didn't do that without carefully checking that I really needed to.'

'Let me check the map.'

Mary's heart didn't miss a beat as she knew she was completely connected to us and to this other soul.

'You are right, you did have to raise it, but the roof is not in compliance.'

She opened her mouth and allowed us to speak through her using his name as she did, 'Colin, could I explain.'

'Go ahead,' he said.

'The original plan was for a bungalow, and I was never happy with it. I never thought it would look right in this scenic area, but when I bought the site, my major concern was for the old granary, which was to be gutted, so I got retention on that. When we had no choice but to start the build six months ago, we didn't have time to go back to have the plans changed, so the architect changed the plans to make it look like an old schoolhouse. This, we believe, is more in keeping with the area, so we changed the roof even though it meant I would lose floor space.'

Finishing up, we knew she had reached this man at the level needed.

'I think I know what you mean, and if it is what I think, I will have no problem with it. I have never seen it but will be out in the next few days. In the meantime, get your architect to draw up plans and get them to me.'

'He has already drawn them. We will send them in today.'

Mark called just as she put the phone down. 'I will bring the plans in today to their offices, Mary, in case we don't get this engineer again.'

Walking onto the site, her brothers stopped their work as she shouted up to them. 'I will make the breakfast. I have it sorted.'

Later at the kitchen table, Brendy said, 'You were lucky. I never thought they would come out.'

Luck had nothing to do with it, she was thinking as she smiled.

Mark called later that evening and said, 'I am outside the county council offices and it's all sorted. The engineer even apologised because he would have to charge a fee of €500. But I won't charge you anything as it was my idea, and if I do say so myself, one of the best ideas I ever had.'

'I agree, Mark. And it is the best €500 I will ever spend.'

All was well. In less than twenty-four hours we had put her in a position where the planning permission was sorted.

Nothing can stop me now, she thought, not knowing what was about to happen.

With the roof finished, the windows and doors installed, the house was sealed just before a recession hit the entire world and the banks refused to give her any more money.

As 2008 drew to a close, she accepted that it was now impossible to sell the cottage as the value of her properties fell by over 60% overnight.

Walking the mountain a few days later she called Jarlath and told him.

'That's not fair, Mam!'

'It's life, Jarlath.'

'What are you going to do now?'

'I have no idea, but I will be guided. My life has just changed

direction again! I have my health and it really is my wealth.'
Thinking: *Especially my mental health.*

This was the month before she wrote her first book. This new
venture would bring her to another place where she would work
totally at one with us, as she had always done on a building site.
The only difference was that this new project could be done alone,
and the only cost was her time.

CHAPTER 17

On the 13th of November 2008, Mary was driving Roisín around Dublin on her twenty-first birthday looking for DCU (Dublin City University) where her daughter had decided to do her masters. Out of the blue her daughter asked, 'What is your definition of a recession, Mammy?'

'It is when the waitress has a degree and counts her blessings that she has a job,' she had replied, thinking of all the young Irish women with degrees who had worked as waitresses in New York City twenty-five years before.

In 2009, when Roisín started her masters in multimedia in Dublin, Jarlath continued his business degree in Galway, and Mary was experiencing the worst recession of her lifetime.

The first recession she was aware of was in 1980, when she went to America to work. Her aunt Lucy, who lived in Connecticut, had advised her not to come over as there were no jobs, but she ignored her and instead followed our direction. In New York City she first worked for a nursing agency, making herself indispensable by being both reliable and flexible. 'No problem' was her mantra, no matter where she was asked to work, sometime with little or no notice.

Returning to a recession in 1985, Mary and Marty had left NYC booming, again, following our guidance, finally convincing

Marty it was a good idea even though the young Irish were going in the opposite direction in droves. Within weeks of coming home, she had printed and sold thousands of T-shirts that she had designed for Barry McGuigan's world title boxing championship, which he won in May of that year. The same year she had used their hard-earned cash to buy properties to rent in a property market that had been decimated. As the recession continued, she kept adding to their property portfolio until they hit a boom again.

At the beginning of 2009, Mary was facing another recession, one that had hit the entire world, but as she was immersed in her book, she had no time for any fears. Aware that recession was just another word used to put fear in people and had ignored them in the past and learned so much from them, she knew that her children had lessons to learn from this one; lessons which started immediately as she no longer had any spare cash to give them, creating two more stories for her column.

The first one was about Jarlath calling her one Saturday afternoon to ask, 'Where are you, Mam?'

'In Marita's.'

'Would you have two euros? ... I have three – if you could give me two more, I can get five euro of diesel to get me to work. I get paid tonight and can pay you back tomorrow.'

'Okay, Ja,' Mary replied, delighted at how fast her son's mind had adapted to the recession.

A few minutes later he was at Marita's door and she handed him five euros. As he handed over the three euros he had in his hand, she said, 'It's okay, Jarlath, I can't afford much but I will just about manage this.'

'Thank you very much, Mam. I really appreciate it.'

We watched her smile as she closed the door of her friend's house, thinking, *This is a young man that wouldn't have thanked me for twenty euros a year ago.*

The other story was when Roisín called later in the year and said, 'Mam, I went for an interview for a waitressing job today and they wanted me full-time and I can't do it because I have so much work to do for my masters. My friends have even given me numbers of places I might get a part-time job, but I don't even have the time to send in my CV. What am I going to do?'

'If you don't have the time to do something, Roisín, then you are not meant to do it.'

'But I need to get money somewhere. I have got a loan, but it may not last and how will I pay it back?'

'Take a breath and continue studying, Roisín. You have only another six months left and we will manage somehow. We always do. I have an overdraft and will use it if necessary. You don't want to have to repeat this year, and as you said you have already gone for an interview.'

'But that was only one interview.'

'You only need one job.'

'Okay, Mam. Thanks.'

Later in the year, just after finishing her masters, she called again one Friday morning to ask her mother's advice. 'Mam, I have only €100 in my account left over from my student loan and I want to volunteer at the documentary film festival in Donegal. If I spend this money to get there and for accommodation, I will have nothing on Monday morning and I will have to sign on the dole, and I don't want to sign on the dole. What do you think I should do?'

'You know what you need to do, Roisín. I may be your mother, but you have a journey and I don't know what it is. Follow your gut ... What do you want to do?'

'I want to go.'

'Then go.'

'But I will have no money on Monday morning.'

'And if you stay in Dublin, how much money will you have Monday morning?'

'None ... Thanks, Mam.'

On the Sunday night she called her mother again and said excitedly, 'Mam, you will never guess what happened ... I was getting on the bus this evening to go back to Dublin and my friend asked me what are you going to do now? I said I have only €20 and I have no choice but to go on the dole. I fell asleep and when I woke, I had a text message that said: *Roisín, you came in looking for a job as a waitress a few months ago and you couldn't do full-time. Can you do full-time now?* I replied *yes* and I am starting tomorrow. Can you believe that?'

'Yes, Rois, I can. If you do the right thing, the right thing happens. You did the right thing for you and now the right thing has happened for you. This is the only job you were interviewed for and the only one you need, and it will give you time to volunteer for media jobs in Dublin.'

'That's right, Mam, and if I am lucky ... this waitress will have a masters!'

They both laughed. Putting down the phone, Mary looked up and said, *Thank you.* Knowing that both her children were learning their lessons well.

Mary was a very grateful person; she found simple things every day to be grateful for, especially now in her financial crisis. A euro where she didn't know she had one, a bargain where she could save money on the essentials, and we heard her repeatedly tell her children, 'Always say thank you. The universe loves a grateful person.'

'The other waitresses say I say thank you too much,' Roisín told her in the kitchen one evening a few months later.

'You can never say thank you too much, Rois. In fact, they say if you have only one breath left you should use it to say thank you.'

'Thank you, Mam!' Roisín replied with a grin.

For the rest of the year, Mary continued writing and editing as Roisín worked in a city centre restaurant using her wages and tips to pay off her student loan, pay her rent and keep herself saving enough money to sustain her for the following year in NYC where she had got a visa to work in media for that year. Mary had no question that her daughter was heading in the right direction as she watched everything flow for her. Jarlath always had a job, had always earnt his own money outside the home from when he was twelve working in the local shop, a time when Roisín was employed by her mother in-house helping with the extended family. He was now doing well at college after failing a couple of first term exams.

When he diplomatically told her at the beginning of 2009 that he would have to repeat two exams in the summer, she asked why.

'Because I failed two at Christmas … because the lecturers didn't care whether I went to class or not.'

'Why would they care, Jarlath, when I don't? Haven't I told you since you started primary school that you do your homework for yourself and not for me or anyone else. And haven't I always told you that I will love you whether you go to college or not?' Then she asked, 'What happens if you fail the exams in the summer?'

'I will have to repeat the year.'

Mary hesitated for a moment, looked her son in the eye and said, 'Jarlath, there is very little chance that I would pay for you to do your first year twice even if I could afford to. There is no chance that your father will. So, you have a choice, do your work and get your exams or get a job.' He did his work and never failed another exam!

When Mary left her daughter to meet her friends at Dublin airport in March 2012, she felt so sad but knew it was the right thing for Roisín. Driving down the motorway afterwards, she turned on the news to hear that the politician who had tried to get her editor to remove her from the paper had been removed as party leader. By the time she reached home, she had a column written in her head. An hour later it was on her laptop. A column called, 'Time to say goodbye', finishing it by saying: *Today, as my daughter started her dream, Tom has ended his nightmare, and to both of them, I wish the best of luck. It is time to say goodbye.*

In the spring of 2012, Mary received the cheque from the sale of the house in Belfast and paid off all her debts. After being broke for over three years, she had no hesitation spending the money on everything and anything but herself. Spending money on herself was something she would learn to do in the future.

One Saturday in April, before she was to start phase three of the building (phase two being when she convinced the banks to give her €10,000 more of her mortgage in the middle of the recession, to put in the kitchen and a floor in the living area!) she picked up her friend Michael on the way to meet people from their group who had travelled from all over the country, who supported each other with mental health issues.

As they walked across the road to the yoga room where the meeting was taking place, she was thinking the house would be finished in time for their next annual weekend get-together. She had spent the last get-together in Leitrim, the weekend after her book launch. Entering the room, everyone greeted them. Happy with her lot, she chatted away, not realising that this day someone was going to come into her life and shake it to its very core. (These two people had chosen each other before they had journeyed into this life, his arrival taking place ten years before hers!)

As he entered the room later with Timothy (another member), Mary felt an immediate attraction to him. (How else were we to get people together! 'Love at first sight', humans called it, but actually it was a soul recognition.) When he opened his mouth to introduce himself to the group, she was smitten. His voice was beautiful, like that of a radio presenter. Cool, calm and collected. (Something he certainly was not, but he was a good actor!)

When he walked outside at lunchtime with a mutual friend, she followed and was introduced to another Gerry, from another city. When he started smoking, she walked on to join another friend and we heard her thoughts. *I would never go out with a smoker.* We smiled at her innocence, believing that he was going to be that easy to dismiss.

Later that night, as she lay in the guestroom in Michael's house, she texted another member who had travelled in the same car as him.

What is Gerry like? Mary asked.

Lovely gentleman, Margie replied. *Why, are you interested in him?*

I haven't the time to be interested in anyone. I have a house to finish in the next four months and we are starting tomorrow morning.

Driving home from Michael's house the following morning, she thought of Gerry. An hour later, she met her brother Noel at the new house. They started working immediately, and for the following three and half months, Gerry's name never crossed her mind.

CHAPTER 18

N ow that you understand why Mary was in her element in the middle of a building site, (avoiding herself) we will give you a bird's-eye view of how things work when humans work with us. We will show you in minute detail how easy things flow when you are at one with your guides. Nothing is a problem as we are all connected and can get you anything you want when we reach out to other guides – if you are on the right road. If you are on the wrong road and walking *against the tide,* life becomes chaotic. This doesn't mean that you can't force issues. You certainly can, and Mary was an expert at this, but everything will eventually get back on track as no human can sustain the force that is required to go against your life plan without destroying oneself in the process.

Now that Mary was connected to her source, there was no time for any other thought. Only where to get the men and materials needed to finish the house on time. This building was the biggest and most expensive project she had ever undertaken and would be the last one if she learnt her lessons.

As the kitchen/living area was the only room in the house with a finished floor, the other 3,500 square foot needed to be completed by Noel before any other tradesman could get into the house to work. The type of flooring used was one of the biggest decisions Mary was going to have to make as this was going to eat a huge hole in her budget.

The first price quote was €42 a square yard, and there was no way this could be afforded, but we knew from experience if we asked, she would buy it. The second flooring she liked brought the price down to €22 a square yard, but it still didn't feel right (it wasn't). As there was nothing else worth looking at, she waited to see what happened next. Then, out of the blue, her brother Peter called and asked how she was getting on. When she told him her dilemma, he, who wasn't a carpenter, said, 'You can't put any floor down without a subfloor.'

'I can't afford a subfloor,' she replied.

'You can't afford to do without it, a floor needs a base to support it.'

It wasn't like him to put his nose into issues like these and it annoyed her, but she headed to the local builders' suppliers to see what they thought.

The yardman agreed with her brother, pointing out the 8x4 sheets needed, and then calculated that ninety-six sheets would be required.

Before looking at them, Mary had calculated that this was going to cost €2,000 before the flooring could even be started, but seeing them and loving them asked, 'Could I not use these for the main floor as they are far too nice to cover?'

'No! They are only used for attics, but you could get it tongued and grooved.'

'Oh, that would be great,' she replied, following him further into the shed thinking, *This could be a finished job,* but unfortunately the tongued and groove sheet was not remotely like the one she loved and were much more expensive. Knowing there was no choice, the 8x4 sheets were ordered, before Mary went home deflated.

That weekend, she cleared and hoovered the house where the floors were going down. On the Monday morning, Noel arrived at the same time as forty of the ninety-six sheets, and together they carried them into the house.

With four sheets brought up the makeshift stairs, Noel started on the first bedroom and Mary headed to town to get more supplies from the hardware and grocery shops. Arriving home later, she went straight up the stairs to look at what he had done.

'Oh my God, that flooring is just beautiful. We are not going to be covering that floor no matter what anyone else does with it. I'm heading back to the hardware to get varnish for it.'

'Well … I suppose I am going to have to lay it for a finished look,' replied Noel, smiling.

'Please,' Mary said as she ran to the car to get back to hardware before it closed, thinking along the way: *I can finish this job for €2,000 and it will be beautiful, but it needs to be varnished right away before it gets dirty. I can't believe people are not using this as their finished floor!* Then, going straight to the office she asked for advice.

'We get them from a Northern supplier,' the man told her. 'Do you want me to call him and ask him to find out what varnish to use?'

'Yes please,' she replied, whilst thinking: *I need to know now. I need to do this tonight.*

Then a man at the back of the office raised his head from the computer and said, 'That flooring is made in Tipperary.'

'Do you have a number for the factory?' Mary asked.

A few minutes later an Englishman answered the number she had been given and she asked what varnish was already on the sheets so that she could apply a few more coats.

'None,' he replied. 'That is the effect that we get from compressing the woodchips.'

'Then what varnish could I use to give it a better seal?' she enquired as she headed to the paint department.

'I will check and call you back.'

Mary was asking the same question of the girl at the paint counter when her phone rang.

'Oil,' he said.

'Oil-based varnish,' she repeated out loud whilst the girl behind the counter shook her head.

'Water based,' the assistant whispered.

'Thank you,' Mary replied into the phone and hung up.

'Water based,' the assistant repeated. 'All the painters use it. Come, and I will show you, it is much harder wearing, dries quicker and can be recoated in two hours.'

Fifteen minutes later, Mary was back in the car with the water-based varnish, a roller, a tray and smiling from ear to ear. The answer for her floor covering was loud and clear. For the next two weeks she hoovered and then varnished the floors as soon as Noel finished the rooms. Two hours later she varnished again and before going to bed at night they got a third coat. It was simple, it was easy to do because it was right. Two weeks later, Noel left. As he was going out the door, he turned and said, 'I never want to see an 8x4 sheet of anything again!'

Over that weekend, Mary hoovered her beautiful floors yet again and gave them all another coat, realising as she did that not only had she got exactly what she wanted, but it was finished at €7 a square yard – including the varnish!

On the Sunday night, another bedroom was made ready in the cottage for her nephew Packie (the plumber), who was arriving the following morning with the radiators. He had called her a few weeks before to say that a local manufacturer of radiators was selling out the old style. 'They are better than the new ones and can be bought for a song,' he said.

'Get them. They are the ones I was looking for. The new ones would make the house look too modern. I want all the modern conveniences of a new house, but I want the house to look like it has always been here. I will need a big cylinder too, Packie, and I know they are expensive. Could you tell me the type needed and I will check them out?'

'No need,' he replied. 'I'm taking one out of our Kevin's tonight and he will be delighted to sell it.'

Packie arrived the following morning and got to work. As her brother started the doorframes, his son started the plumbing and Mary started painting a white basecoat on every wall and ceiling in the house. All was well; but the next big cost was worrying her as twenty-three internal doors were needed and we had told her to get fire doors. These were €180 each – and that was before handles!

Mary tried to blank this, aware that when the time was right, they would appear from somewhere, but she was human and worrying seemed to be a way of life for them.

Heading to get her car serviced in the town she had left the previous summer, Mary spotted an old friend in her garden. As she was having problems with her hip at the time she decided to talk to this woman about special insoles for her shoes. She had gotten them from this lady before for Jarlath and knew how expensive they were, but her hip needed support.

'I will leave the car in the garage and walk back to you,' she shouted out the window, and fifteen minutes later, they were sitting down to a cup of tea.

'How are you getting on with the house?' her friend Mary F asked. (Every family in this country seemed to have a child called Mary!)

'Just finished the floors, and the plumbing is underway as I paint. Noel is putting up frames for the internal fire doors which is the next job, but I don't want to think about it today as they are so expensive.'

'Why don't you look on DoneDeal?'

'I need twenty-three of them and no-one is going to have that many.'

Her friend had already picked up the laptop, and within a few minutes had given her four numbers of people advertising fire doors.

Mary took the piece of paper and slipped it in her pocket as she said, 'I need to get insoles for my shoes as my right hip is killing me.'

'Why don't you try a pair from the chemist for €20 first?' her friend said. 'They might work, if not, come back to me.'

Delighted with this information, we watched as the two Marys caught up on all the local news before she went home to her new county.

The next morning she heard us whisper, *Check out the numbers for the fire doors.*

'They are all gone,' the man told her after calling the first number. There was no answer to the second number and the third gave her the measurements of the few doors he had but they were all the wrong size. As she was about to call the last number the phone rang.

'I had a missed call from this number?' the man said.

'Do you have fire doors for sale?'

'Yes. What are you looking for?'

'Twenty-three four-panel, half-hour pre-painted fire doors,' she answered, smiling, believing that this was an impossible task, even for us.

'I have twenty-six of them, but I need three for myself,' he replied.

'How much?' '€40 each but let me check and I will call you back. I think we might have dropped the price.'

€40 is a steal, she thought, and as he was checking it out on DoneDeal so was she. It said thirty-five each ONO (or nearest offer).

The man called back and said, '€35 each.'

'I will take them all,' she replied, thinking, *There is no way I am going to haggle with anyone at that price.* 'Please don't give them to anyone else. I can be there tomorrow to pick them up.' (Even though she had no idea where they were or how she was going to pick them up.)

'Don't worry,' he laughed. 'I am going on holidays tomorrow for ten days and won't be selling to anyone else.'

'I can give you a deposit,' Mary then said.

'No need. I will call you when I get back.'

She ran to tell Noel.

'Brilliant! We can go in my van, where are they?'

'I forgot to ask.'

'Galway,' the man informed her. *Only an hour away. Who could make this up?*

Two weeks later they went with the cash to pick up the twenty-three brand-new fire doors. 'I bought them to do a job before the crash,' the contractor explained. 'I have a few more,' he continued as he pointed out a small door.

'Would that do the bedroom in the wee apartment?' she asked Noel, who took the tape from his pocket.

'Aye.'

'€20,' the man said. 'And I have one more half-hour door if you want it as I realised that I only need two.' Mary heard us whisper, *Take it.* Which she did.

As they headed home, she spoke out loud as if to herself, 'That last door will do for the house in Castlerea. Those doors need to be changed before I sell the house.' (A decision she had made recently without our input.) 'The one heading downstairs to the boiler room is a fire door and I will need to get seven more. I'm going to see Raymond in the salvage yard in Enniskillen to see if he has any Belfast brick for the fireplace, so I will check if he has old four-panelled pitched pine doors that will match.'

'Right!' said Noel. 'I will start hanging the doors and you better start looking for handles for them.'

'I know, I have already started. They are all so expensive and I haven't seen one that I like. Don't know what I will do.'

'I'm sure you'll find them somewhere and at the right price,' he replied, grinning.

'I'm sure I will,' she replied, stepping out of the van, only realising at that moment that there had been no pain in her hip since the insoles were inserted ten days before!

CHAPTER 19

A few days later, Mary headed into the salvage yard. As Raymond wasn't about, she walked around thinking about all the recycled slates and doors bought from him for the cottage twelve years before. Also the recycled maple flooring for kitchen/living/dining room in the new house. This maple flooring had been taken out of the town hall in Ballina, brought to Enniskillen and then taken back home to Mayo. She loved to know where everything came from and always asked. Continuing walking through the yard after finding the Belfast brick needed for the fireplace, she made her way to the next shed. As there were no doors to be seen, she was about to leave when her eye was drawn to a stack of wood.

'Looking for beds?' a man asked from behind her, breaking into her thoughts and making her jump.

'No! But I will need beds.'

'€20 each, and they come with headboards and mattresses.'

'Teak?'

'Yes.'

'From where?'

'Stranmillis College in Belfast.'

We watched as she checked out the beautiful, handcrafted

bed frames, then turned up her nose at the second-hand mattress and the cheap headboards.

'Let me think about it.'

Walking into the last shed looking for doors, Raymond arrived in behind her.

'Beds, Mary?' he asked.

'Maybe, but bricks and doors for now.'

His phone rang and as he stepped out to take the call, Mary continued to look around and finally found what she was looking for. Taking out her tape to measure them, she found that they were a little large but knew they could be easily cut back, and the ones with frosted glass could be used for the bathroom and toilet or maybe the living room.

As Raymond returned, he asked, 'What do you think of those doors?'

'Great! Where did they come from?'

'I shouldn't tell you,' he replied, laughing. 'Your brother will probably not hang them for you if I do.'

'Why?'

'They are from the police station in Leak.' To which, Mary laughed out loud. 'They have working handles too,' he continued as he showed her how the spring still worked perfectly.

'How much?'

'€30 each.'

'Pitched pine?'

'Yes.'

'Okay. I will take the two with glass and five more plain ones.'

'What about the beds?'

Seven doors, a hundred Belfast bricks and fifteen beds, but I don't want the mattresses nor the headboards.'

'Take the mattresses and headboards and I will deliver everything to your house for free, burn them if you don't want them.'"

'A deal,' she said, knowing that if everyone was so insistent that the mattresses and headboards be brought to the house then they must have a purpose. Her plan was to furnish the whole place with second-hand furniture, but that didn't include mattresses or the ugliest headboards she had ever seen.

Raymond wrote everything down and gave the price, which would be paid on delivery. Delighted that she now had doors for the house in Castlerea and beds for every room in the new house, she headed home, but within minutes pulled the car into the side of the road as we put another thought in her mind.

Calling Raymond, she asked, 'The knobs of those old doors, are they brass?'

'No. They are copper which is unusual. Do you like them?'

'Love them. Would you sell me the knobs of the doors that I didn't buy?'

'I will. How many do you want?'

'I have already got seven on the doors I bought so I would need another … seventeen.'

He checked and called her back. 'I have another eighteen.'

'I will take them all. How much do you want for them?' Knowing that whatever price he charged they would be less than the €30 paid for the doors.

'€10 each.'

'Great. Add it to what I owe you.'

Putting down the phone, she said out loud, 'Oh my God, why couldn't all my life be like this?'

We repeated as we always had, *It could be if you …* but she had already blanked us before we had finished the sentence and we wondered if we would ever get an opportunity to bring this way of living into her relationships.

Arriving home later, she filled Noel in about the doors.

Laughing, he said, 'Tell everyone that they came out of our local police station.'

Walking around the house together later, she asked, 'What do you think of the white walls and ceilings, Noel?'

'I wouldn't change them. They look great as they are.'

'Just what I was thinking. Thank God for that. I am sick of painting and need to get on to other things and only have four weeks left to finish. That is, furniture, curtains, mattresses and bedding ...' *The headboards can be done without for now.*

Having already checked out furniture in a second-hand shop in Ballina, Mary went directly to town when we told her it was time to buy and left after half an hour in the shop, with all she needed and more, knowing she could take anything back that wasn't right. (Had she listened more carefully there would be nothing going back!)

Later that evening, she checked what was already in the house before deciding where the new furniture was going to be placed. The dining room table had come from her friend Henk, a table that had lain in his shed for nearly thirty years after he had got it off his sister when she was changing her furniture in Holland. It was a beautiful handcrafted pine table that was made without one screw and the six high-backed pine chairs purchased that day would be perfect around it. Henk had also given her a light that had hung over the table in Holland, but her electrician had told her it couldn't be hung here, so it lay in the corner of the dining area. The material on the Dutch sofa bought that day would match not only the table, but also blend in with the colour of the Belfast brick for the fireplace. Two high chairs that had been bought a few years before were taken out of their boxes and sat at the countertop. A huge armchair sat on one side of the fireplace, and like every piece of furniture that came to live with her, it too had a story. It had belonged to her son's friend's father. Charlie had bought a suite of furniture and hadn't room for the second armchair in the living room, so put it in his son's bedroom which left him with little space.

'Mary, will you please take the armchair out of my bedroom?' he asked.

She went to see it and said, 'It's so big, where would it fit in my house, Nathan?'

Looking at her with surprise, he asked, 'Mary, if it doesn't fit in that big house of yours, where *is* it going to fit?'

She bought it off him. At the other side of the fireplace sat a rocking chair that her friend Georgina had given her when moving house. It too was pine.

The following morning the furniture arrived, and all was put in place, making her realise immediately that another dining room table was needed as this big room still looked empty, and another table would be required for the crowd arriving in a few weeks, so planned to go back to the second-hand shop the following day to see what she had overlooked. Then Noel came into the sitting room with the phone in his hand and said, 'Vera has asked me to dump her kitchen table this weekend as she has got a new one, do you want it?'

'Yes, please. Has it got chairs with it?'

'Yes, but they are not in great shape.'

'Please bring them too. They will have to do.'

Finishing up painting that week, a member of the group came to check out how the house was progressing. When leaving, he said, 'Mary, if you feed and keep me, I will come help you finish up.'

She stared at Barry, who was impeccably dressed, wondering if he had ever done a day's work in his life. Whilst this was going through her mind he said, 'I had a look at those beds in the big room and the headboards could do with a sprucing up.'

'Sprucing up! I was going to burn them, but if you can spruce them up anyway, Barry, that would be wonderful.'

'Okay, I will be back tomorrow with my staple gun and foam from the factory. Do you have any material to cover them?'

'No, but I will have by tomorrow.' And as he was leaving, she followed him out and went in to the town and found a sale in the curtain centre. Walking around, we guided her to the corner of the shop where there was a roll of mustard velvet material reduced from €50 a yard to €10. *Must be for me*, she thought as she felt the quality of the material blocking her immediate thought which was, *I hate that colour.*

'I will give you what's left for €5 a yard,' the assistant said. 'If you take what is left on the roll.'

'How much is left on it?'

Mary didn't really need to know but she needed to think. Mustard was not a colour she would have chosen but she would accept if we chose it for her.

There was ten yards in it, and at €50, it was bought knowing it had a use somewhere.

With this roll under her arm, and also material bought for most of the bedroom windows, she went home happy. Throwing the mustard material on a bedroom floor later that evening, she smiled. It was perfect for the headboards as it brought out all the tones in the woodchip floor.

When the first headboard was finished, Mary couldn't believe how quickly she had dismissed the headboards, the material and Barry's talents, exclaiming, 'My God, Barry, that is beautiful.'

He grinned like a Cheshire cat, delighted to be back doing something he had loved before he had sold the factory that made both headboards and mattresses.

'What about mattresses?' he asked that night at dinner.

'I was going to ask you for help to find the right ones.'

'I will design them for you and ask the new owner of the factory to make them for you. I will design the perfect mattress … not too hard, not too soft.'

'At what price?' Mary asked, as the money was dwindling.

'Leave that to me, I will get you a good deal.'

With Barry's expensive taste, she wondered what he would consider a good deal but said nothing.

The next day the blinds for the windows were started, which she knew from experience were the cheapest way to cover windows. Sewing, she thought of all that had to be done, and time was running out – then Dara called.

'Can we put the weekend off to the second weekend in September, Mary, as the first doesn't suit a lot of the group?'

'Perfect,' she replied with relief. Lost in her thoughts about what to do next, Barry came in.

'Have you got a price for the mattresses?' she asked nervously.

'Not yet,' he replied. 'But I was thinking now that I have finished the headboards, I could put some foam on those dining room chairs and cover them with the same mustard material.'

'That would be brilliant, Barry. Those chairs are too hard, and the mustard will match in with the sofa and everything else in the living room.'

Noel arrived back on Monday with the table and chairs. The table was in good shape and fitted neatly under the front windows which looked out at the mountains. He then took in the chairs and showed her the damage.

'Can't you glue them together and use a few screws?' she asked.

'I can,' he said, as Barry looked on. 'I will then cover the seats with the same material to match the other dining chairs.'

'Thank you, Barry, and do you think we would we have enough left to cover the last bedroom window with a blind?' He went off with his tape and came back with a smile and a 'yes'.

'Well, that must be one of the best €50 I have ever spent,' she said to the two men as the entire house was being pulled together with the mustard colour she hadn't liked.

177

CHAPTER 20

The following Monday morning, Noel arrived with the stairs he had designed and had a local man near his home make. With Barry's help, the simple, elegant stairs were put in place. When installed, Mary stood at the top of them with the two men looking down on the hall floor below. They all stared in amazement at how the teak staircase drew out the teak woodchips on the flooring below. Not a word was said but we could read her thoughts. *No designer could have got it better; they were made for each other, coming from the two sides of the border to be together!*

The living/dining room was now finished except for the blinds, which Mary decided would have to be carefully chosen as it was the main room in the house for now. This material would have to complement the fireplace, the sofa and all the wood in the room. This wouldn't be found in a sale – we guided her to a book of expensive samples. With no need for blinds in the dining areas as only the birds and wild goats had a view in, there were only two windows left to cover. After that it would be time to furnish the bedrooms, bedside lockers, wardrobes and lights, which had to be sourced – and she was getting tired of it all.

Knowing that a little distraction was needed, we whispered that there was a man coming into her life and listened to her immediate thoughts. *New house, new life and now a new man.*

This sounded good to her, but she did ponder, *I'm not interested in anyone even though I am surrounded by men and not all of them are family. Maybe this is the time for me to settle for someone comfortable.* Only one man in her group of friends fit into this category, a man she liked but wasn't really attracted to. We watched with interest as she tried to take control of the situation, knowing that this is where Mary had the most to learn. In relationships she still did not understand that all happened naturally when the time was right, with a person who would be both her teacher and student. Even though controlling had never worked before, this didn't deter her. Her greatest relationship challenge was on its way and it wasn't the man she had in mind.

With this distraction, she perked up and continued to work at the speed needed to finish on time.

'Any word on mattresses yet, Barry?' she asked again.

'No. Anything else for me to do?'

'What else can you do apart from upholstering?'

'Well … I used to be an electrician.'

'Really?' Mary replied as she walked over to the dining room table, picked up the light that Henk had given her and asked, 'What are the chances that this light could be hung over this table?'

He looked at it and replied, 'No problem.'

'Really! The electrician said it couldn't be done.'

'Of course, it can. All it needs is a few adjustments.'

Watching in amazement, Barry made the adjustments, put the light up and switched it on. She wanted to hug him but thought it best not to, knowing something in her had opened up and didn't want to give him the wrong idea. He arrived again the following day, this time with a price for the mattresses.

'€100 each,' he said.

'That is great, Barry. Order twelve.'

'Okay, but why twelve if you have fifteen frames?'

'I don't know why I got fifteen frames, but I am sure I will when the time is right.'

Grinning, he headed off but came back a few minutes later, and she knew by his face that there was a problem.

'Those frames are only two and a half foot wide. A small single. A standard single three-foot mattress won't fit on it.'

Following him as cool as a cucumber, wondering how we would solve this problem as she had no doubt these were the right bed frames.

'But … can't a three-foot mattress fit on the top?' she asked.

'Yes, but we will need to build up the centre. How are we going to do that?'

Noel stopped as he passed and said, 'What about 2x1s, there are a few lying around which you could try?'

'That would work, but I could get the smaller mattresses,' replied Barry.

'No! We need standard beds. Now I know why I got them so cheap. They were made for students.'

As he started to work, Mary watched him and said, 'Barry, I have no double beds. Would it be possible to push two of those beds together and make a king when needed?'

'No problem. I will get a few hooks that connect them when I'm in the factory paying for the mattresses.'

'Great! Thanks!' Mary replied and walked away smiling, her thoughts already on the next part of her project.

The headboards are finished, the beds are being upgraded, the blinds are up and the walls are painted – it is time to look for quilts, pillows, sheets, pillowcases and quilt covers. As she had already found a local factory outlet on the internet, she rushed there straightaway, ordering the material for the living room windows on the way, deciding that if all the bedding was the same it would make life so much easier. Cream was the colour in her mind, easy to keep clean and maybe with a little print, but cream and a little print and enough for twelve beds she knew was a tall order – but she also knew nothing was impossible.

'What are you looking for?' asked the owner.

'Bedding for a guest house.'

'White,' he stated.

'White?' she replied aghast. 'White …' she repeated, thinking, *How the hell would you keep white sheets clean?*

'It's what all the hotels use.'

Ignoring what he said but taking his advice on quilts and pillows, she took samples of cream and white sheets home wondering what the hell the white one was for.

Needing a woman's advice, she crossed the road and asked her friend MaryEllen.

'What colour of sheets would you use if you were in my shoes?'

MaryEllen looked at her as if to say *I would never be in your shoes*, but replied, 'I always use white sheets.'

'White sheets. How the hell do you keep them clean?'

Turning, her friend put her hand under the sink, pulled out a bottle of Parazone and replied, 'There is no stain that this can't take out.'

'Okay, thanks. I get it.' Then she spoke to us, *I don't use Parazone, but the sheets can be boiled in the washing machine.*

That evening, all the sheets, pillowcases and quilt covers were ordered in white. Knowing the rooms were going to look very bland, the following day she was back in town looking for throws for the beds to match the blinds in each room. As this proved to be an impossible task, she decided to buy narrow throws found in another sale and cover them with the scraps of curtain material leftover from the windows of each bedroom. Very little material was left, but enough to bring a splash of colour to every room. Finishing the last room, Mary looked from the door at the mustard headboards, the throw matching the blind and thought with satisfaction, *That is perfect.*

With all the major work finished it was time to go to Ikea

in Dublin to get the last bits and pieces. It wasn't a store Mary would usually be found in as she would prefer to pick up individual second-hand pieces, but they had things that could be bought in bulk and would be easy to match. Their catalogue had already been checked out, cheap and cheerful bedside lockers, lights and paper lampshades had been found, and she was hoping to pick up enough matching crockery too. But after a day in the store, she left without a dish or a cup, not realising that we already had all this sorted – she hadn't been listening. We would have to put it in front of her again as she was blinded with her own idea of matching delft.

When her brothers went home that weekend, she asked the man, who ticked a few boxes in what she would want in a partner, to come help do something (that she could have done alone) and invited him to stay for dinner. Just when they were finishing up, he got a call from a member of his family and had to leave. We watched as the relief flowed through her. When he left, we knew it was time to introduce her to the man she had already chosen before she wasted any more time trying to control the uncontrollable and for her to realise that we would never bring anyone into any part of her life that wasn't meant to be there.

As it was now time to send out a message to the group to say all was ready for the weekend (even if it wasn't), her attention turned to this. Composing her message, she sent it out to the entire group of about sixty people. The usual people were in first to get one of the limited spaces, and then she got a message that shocked her. No, that is not true, it wasn't the message that shocked her, it was her response to it. It came from Gerry, the man she had met in Athlone five months previously and had completely forgotten about. It was beautifully written but basically said that he had heard from Timothy (who had visited in the summer) that the place was beautiful and that he was looking forward to seeing it. She finished her reply by saying: *Looking forward to seeing you.* Her heart thumped as she knew she had stepped over a line that she rarely crossed, in fact, had never crossed before! *He will probably not notice,* she thought, *but if he does this will be interesting.* Whilst waiting for a response, she got back to basics, like figuring out what her guests were going to eat of and drink out off. She had some delft but not enough for the group that were coming and none of it matching. It was then she got a call from her friend Georgina who said, 'Remember I told you about the boxes of delft and glasses that I had taken out of the house of the old man across the road who died last year? Well, Michael has told me to get rid of them.' Finishing by saying … 'Pick them up or he will dump them.'

Dump them, Mary was thinking but said, 'Okay, I will be in Castlerea before the end of the week and I will pick them up.'

Sitting down after dinner a week later with Barry and four of her brothers, she opened the boxes to find beautiful old delft and glasses, but again very few of them matching.

'They're lovely,' Brendy said.

'They will have to do,' she replied and took them to the sink to wash them.

Her architect Mark came in the next evening to have a look at what had been done as he hadn't been around since she had started the final phase.

'Love the floors,' he said as soon as he came through the door.

'Cheapest I could get,' Mary replied. 'But I love them too.'

'They are the latest thing in interior design.'

'Really?' she answered, thinking he was joking.

'Really, they are also putting them on walls and ceilings and sometimes on all three.'

'God, I wouldn't like them everywhere but delighted to hear that I'm up to date on this.'

He walked around and loved what she had done.

When they got to the kitchen she said in despair, 'Couldn't get the dishes I wanted. There is barely a plate or cup matching in the place.'

'Latest fad,' Mark replied. 'Have nothing matching.'

'You are joking this time!'

'No! That is the latest fad. Very practical, I think. You can break anything and replace it with just another cup or plate that you like.'

Later she told this to MaryEllen.

'I know,' her friend replied. 'My cousin's daughter borrowed delft from all her family and friends so that none of the dishes would be matching in the hotel for her wedding.'

'I can't believe it. She was trying to get mismatches whilst I was looking for them all to match!'

The night before everyone arrived for the weekend, Barry, Packie, Noel and everybody available were sweeping floors, cleaning windows and making up beds. The last three bedframes were put in the big room upstairs which was to be used for meditation, yoga and tai chi, with three of the fifteen old mattresses on top. These mattresses that had already been aired in the sun were covered with matching quilt covers found in a sale bin for €5 each. The matching pillowcases were used to cover cheap pillows then put at the backs of the three bedframes to make them look like sofas. The rest of the mattresses were stacked two on top of each other, making up the rest of the sofas which lined the walls of the room with the rest of the pillows used for the backs of them. Nothing was wasted!

The next morning when Henk arrived to do the cooking, Mary was at the back door painting a partition that had just been finished.

CHAPTER 21

As requests for rooms came in, Mary had tried to control things. She had her heart set on having Gerry in the cottage with her even though we asked her to let it go and allow people to choose where they stayed as they arrived. This would give us an opportunity to show her how things worked when she completely surrendered in her relationships. Finally, but reluctantly, she let go.

The big house was nearly full that afternoon when Henk said, 'We need to go to Tesco to get more supplies.'

Mary didn't want to go, she wanted to be there when Gerry arrived, but had no choice as they needed more food. Watching, we wondered how this woman could completely surrender to us when writing or on a building site, but not an inch in her personal life!

Walking through the aisles of Tesco, a few people called looking for directions and then Timothy called to say he and Gerry were lost. As she gave the directions, we whispered, *You will meet them at the junction*, before flashing the junction in question into her mind, then watched as she tried to push Henk faster around Tesco wanting to get to the junction as soon as possible.

And what are you going to do when you get there. Wait? we whispered, but we were ignored again. The flow of the summer had stopped dead. We were back to square one.

On the way back she didn't hear a word Henk was saying, thinking, *If by any chance, we meet at the junction in question then there will be no doubt Gerry is the man coming into my life.* As they approached the junction, a white van was coming from the other direction. Not knowing what they were driving, Mary slowed down and watched the van do the same. There they were, right on schedule. Waving at them to follow her, she drove the last mile home as her heart thumped in her chest.

Parking her car at the cottage she got out and gave Timothy and Gerry a huge hug, then showed them to the last available bedrooms which were in the cottage. She followed Henk to the big house with the biggest grin we had ever seen on her face.

Everyone was seated at the two dining room tables when Timothy and Gerry arrived for dinner – which she was serving. Timothy took the last seat at one of the tables, leaving Gerry no choice but to take the high stool at the countertop in front of her. When she'd finished her work, the only seat available to her was the one beside him! And so began a weekend of chat, and by the end of it, there was no doubt in her mind that this was the man sent to her, as everything had fallen into place without any of her interference, and the attraction was strong. We now hoped she would trust us with this relationship, but we wouldn't be taking any bets on it!

Mary had known immediately when she met Marty that they were to marry, and even though she had no intentions of ever marrying again, she already knew that Gerry and her had a journey together. (How long this journey would take would depend on how much she interfered!)

And even though she saw a lost lonely soul, she was smitten. No-one before had mirrored her deepest wounds, and that is what he was, her mirror. He could (if allowed) fast-track her healing. We had done our job getting them together, now all we could do was watch to see what happened next.

He declined to come on the last walk the group had planned

on the Sunday before leaving. Disappointed, she hugged him and wished him well.

First thing the following morning, she was on the phone to Michael to discuss the weekend and how it went. This was the Michael who a friend insisted she meet so brought him to her book launch. After reading her book, Michael persuaded her to go to the weekend the group met in Leitrim and after that they became great friends and he was always on the other side of the phone for her.

'I met someone lovely at the weekend,' she said when he answered the phone.

'Gerry?'

'How do you know?'

'I would have to be blind not to notice.'

'Was it that obvious?'

'You were like two peas in a pod, and you could see the energy between you.'

'I am going to contact him and ask if we could talk some more,' she then stated. 'The group did decide we should get phone numbers and talk to each other about our experiences, and I didn't get his number.'

'Let him contact you,' Michael suggested.

'He won't. I know he won't. He had said he doesn't want any more relationships, but I would be happy to be his friend.'

'Would you? ... Give him a few days and see what happens.'

'I will give him a day and if he hasn't contacted me, I will contact him.' This was said in a tone that was not up for discussion.

Going about that day not expecting or getting a message from Gerry, we watched her nervously send an email the following day asking him to send her his number if he wanted to talk some more. She checked her messages that evening to find a short reply that said: *I would like to talk to you some more too. Call me when you are free as you are a lot busier than I am. G*

Her heart was pounding as she wrote back with an honesty

which had continued since writing her book: *Busy day. Exhausted. Will call you when I get a chance tomorrow.*

The next day after lunch, she made time to call and then spent two hours on the phone. He talked and listened, and the call would have lasted longer, only she had to get back to work. That night, before going to sleep, they were chatting again, then every day and sometimes twice a day for hours at a time after that, as she spoke openly and honestly about her life. It was like the confessional box as she didn't have to look at his face for his reactions – but he didn't judge or give her penance. Telling him about how we guided her in the building and the decorating of her new house, he said, 'You have such faith. I wish I had your faith.'

'How could I not? I am given everything I need and more. Everybody is.'

'I'm not.'

'Yes, you are, you just don't recognise it. When you recognise and acknowledge what you are given, then you are given even more. I always say a silent thank you for everything I get, even the simplest of things. A spool of thread where I looked for it, a tea bag when I thought they were all finished. I thank the universe for everything, and even taught my children that when you are grateful for the small things the big things will appear, if they are for your highest good.'

In time, their conversations got more intimate, and she wanted so much to meet him, but he lived a long drive away which she didn't have the time to make. Then, one night, he mentioned that he was thinking of moving back to Dublin and she immediately started making plans to meet him there as there was a train from the local town.

The same night he said, 'I won't be able to talk to you tomorrow as I have to go to visit my daughter.'

In a meditation the following morning, we asked her to ask him to come down and help her run her business. Shocked with our request, she immediately called Michael.

'What a great idea,' he said.

'I don't think so. He will be living in the big house and me in the cottage. We will be neighbours and I won't be able to go out with him.'

'Why not? Can't you have the best of both worlds?'

'It wouldn't work, but if the world wants him to come here, I won't stop him. But I can't see it going any further.'

As he was out of touch for the day, she let it sit. The next morning there was a text saying he missed talking to her and to call him when free.

Before asking him, Mary explained that she had been looking for someone to help run the place. She told him how Henk had found her an American lady but it hadn't worked out. Only then did she mention what we had asked of her.

'Yes!' he replied. 'I would love to.'

'But don't you have to think about?'

'No, I don't. I would like to do it.'

It was then she told him directly that if he was living next door and working with her it couldn't go any further.

'Why?'

After repeating what she had said to Michael, Gerry replied, 'Let me come down to see what happens.'

'Okay'

'When?'

'I don't know. When are you free?'

'Anytime. I can come tomorrow and stay a few days.'

She agreed and later asked him if he would bring her back with him to visit a friend who lived close to his home as she needed to get away from all the work.

'No problem, but you can stay with me. I have a spare room.'

She hesitated, but only for a moment, and then said, 'Okay, I can visit my friend from your house.'

Getting into bed that night, Mary wondered what she had gotten herself into. Gerry had had a lot of what people considered failed relationships – that is, relationships where people were left hurt (including himself). Unlike him, Mary didn't see any of her relationships as failures, especially the one with her ex-husband. Accepting that Marty would always be in her life, knowing that their bond could never be broken as he was the father of her children and would be the grandfather of her grandchildren if any souls had chosen either Roisín or Jarlath as parents!

CHAPTER 22

When Gerry arrived the following day, Mary watched him from the window of the cottage. As he walked across the narrow road to the door, we knew that if she chose this man to be part of her journey, he would trigger all her deep-seated wounds and rage – that is if she allowed him to stay long enough.

For the following few days, she changed her mind many times. When they were alone, she thought *yes*, when they were in company, she thought *no*. By Friday, no decision had been made. When her brother and another guest left Friday evening, Mary sat on the stone wall at the side of the house wondering what she was going to do.

Gerry came around the corner and asked, 'Well … What are we doing tonight? Going to my house or staying here?'

Without a thought, she put out her arms and spoke from her heart. 'I don't care where I am tonight as long as you are with me.'

And he smiled. After dinner they sat in front of the stove and he said, 'You have been so honest with me about your relationships, I feel I need to tell you about all mine.'

Listening as he told her about a litany of failed relationships (failed because he was still hanging onto them), she heard nothing as her decision had been made. After spending the night together, they headed to his cottage the following day. On the Monday night Mary took the train home, crying all the way as he already mirrored her most vulnerable places, opening wounds that had been festering for a lifetime. As the train passed through the town where she had lived with her husband and children, she wanted to get off and go back to the life she knew. A life where she'd used everything possible to avoid these wounds.

Calling him later that night he asked, 'Are you alright?'

'I will be.'

'Will I still come down next week?'

'Yes. When you are ready.'

Her pain intensified but the focus was put on Gerry until one night, she saw a rage in him that frightened her. Leaving the cottage, she called Dara.

'Are you afraid of him?' Dara asked.

'I am afraid of his rage.'

'But it is not his rage, Mary,' he replied. 'It is a reflection of your own.'

'No way!' she replied, raising her voice. 'I am not that angry.'

'If you weren't, Mary, you wouldn't see it in him. He is a reflection of you.'

Cutting Dara off the phone, she sat back and reflected on what he had just said, reminding her of a dream she'd had recently and the words we had spoken to her in it. *You look in the mirror and try and to change the reflection. Change yourself and the reflection will change.*

Calling Dara back she said, 'Are you telling me that if I deal with the rage in me that I will not be triggered by the anger or rage in Gerry or anyone else?'

'Yes.'

'Okay. Thank you, Dara, then I guess it is time for me to put the focus on myself.'

We couldn't believe it; she had just spoken the words that we had waited her lifetime to hear.

Later that night when the rage rose in her, she slipped out of bed and went downstairs to the sitting room. He found her there under a quilt in the big armchair, crying.

'What's wrong?' he asked gently.

'I have such a rage in me, and I don't know what to do with it.'

'Come back to bed. You don't have to do this.'

'Yes, I do. The alternative is to be triggered by everyone else's anger and rages, and I don't want that anymore.'

Gerry knew there was no way he was going to change her mind. When leaving the room, he turned and said, 'I know what you are doing … I wish I had your strength to face my rage but I don't. I am not going to do it … Not in this lifetime, anyway.'

When he left, Mary asked us for help, and we reminded her of the rage that rose years before. A rage so strong that she believed that breaking every window in the family home would only take the steam of it and knowing if she did, they would take her away in a straitjacket. That night she had begged us for help, then completely surrendered, allowing the rage to exit in what she later described as a convulsion; the only words she had to describe how her body took over and shook naturally, like animals did when faced with both fear and trauma, not needing to hide it to be accepted. That night after the convulsion she went back to bed and slept. This night we whispered, *It is part of you. Engage with it. Go to where it is.*

Letting go and falling into a dark painful place, Mary went deeper into her wound than ever before, remembering Dara's words from before: *You don't need to know what it is or where it came from, Mary, just stay with the pain until it passes.*

Twisting as the pain exploded in her body, finally falling asleep in the armchair and waking up exhausted, knowing in her heart that something huge had cleared without any idea what it was and no longer needing to know.

'Standing in front of Gerry is like standing in front of a machine gun,' she told her sisters one night in their parents' house.

'Then, what are you doing with him?' asked her sister Lucy, who was sitting cross-legged on the floor in front of her.

'Because I like him, and he is the best teacher I've ever had. He is only rising what is already there. He is the trigger; the explosives are in my body, only I can defuse them.'

We were delighted for her as not only had she understood what was happening, but she was open about it. Even though she was still blaming Gerry when things got too much for her, asking him to leave again and again, missing him before he had been gone an hour, missing her reflection. We often thought how much easier this world she lived in would be if they could all understand that they were all teachers and students, to take nothing personal, understanding that nothing could damage their soul.

They had great times together too, as Gerry was a very intelligent and entertaining man. They both loved movies and watched them together in perfect peace when neither felt that they had to defend themselves. The very first night they did this, she watched as a beautiful energy from their souls joined at a place where most people never reached, and their silences were truly golden. Lost in a movie or asleep, they were totally at one with each other, illusions they lived and defended disappearing in this silence.

This relationship, which was to continue over the following five years, was very intense, very rocky and was off as much as it was on. Knowing that when she had the strength to face all that he mirrored, he would have the choice to either move to that place with her or move on alone without her, as the relationship would have been impossible otherwise. Time would tell, they were both on their own journeys with their own lessons, and his business was none of either hers or ours. He had his own guides.

* * *

As 2012 was drawing to a close, Jarlath was making plans to go to Australia in the New Year, Roisín was continuing to enjoy her year in New York and Mary continued to write in the paper every week and take guests in distress into her house.

Some of the stories she wrote were told to her by Gerry. Stories about his life and also stories told by the people who came to stay, traumatised people who never had a voice and continued to tell stories about her own life both past and present. In January 2013, she wrote about her son leaving and how it broke her heart and called it 'The leave-taking'. For the following week she sat in the armchair staring out the window, feeling the pain of all the mothers who had let their children go. Even though Jarlath wasn't going to war and she had a date for his return, it brought up more losses in her own life that had not been dealt with.

Roisín returned a few weeks later, and this time got a paying job at the documentary film festival in Donegal, so Mary, Gerry and two friends decided to go.

'There is a documentary I think you should see,' Roisín said one night on the phone.

'What is it called?'

'A day after peace.'

'Have you seen it?'

'No, but I think you would like it, Mammy.'

'Okay. We will see you tomorrow when we arrive.'

Two days later she sat to watch the documentary with Gerry beside her, crying throughout most of it as it triggered so much of her own past.

'What is it that you don't understand about people fighting back when they feel that they have no other choice?' her thirteen-year-old self spoke through her to the producer.

She got an intellectual answer, one that was bullshit to the child in her who had made that choice.

Afterwards, she went to speak to the moderator because he had mentioned he had written a play about conflict resolution.

'We are doing the play in Donegal town tomorrow night,' he

said, after Mary had told him that she had written a book about how the conflict had affected her. 'I would love if you could come.'

'Can't make tomorrow night. I have to get home,' she replied.

'Then Friday night in Derry?'

Walking away, she said, 'Maybe.' Even though she had no intentions of going as it was a seven-hour return journey, but we knew she would be going, as there was someone going to be there to change her direction again.

'Mam, would you drop off the banner we borrowed from Derry City Council on your way home?' Roisín asked the following morning.

'But we are not going home until the evening and the council will be closed.'

'Ahhh … how will I get it back? I have to take the bus to Dublin, and I promised I would have it back for a reception they have on Monday.'

'I might go to Derry Friday,' Mary said without thinking, and before finishing the sentence knew that she needed to be there.

On the way home she told Michael, who said he would like to go with her as he had never been in Derry and would be delighted to drive her, as Gerry had a friend staying.

'Great,' she replied, thrilled that not only would she have company but she didn't have to drive.

On the Friday, Gerry decided he was coming too so they drove the long journey early and dropped off the banner. Then they went up the coast of Antrim before returning for the play. Afterwards, the writer of the play introduced Mary as an author of a book on trauma. Later, when heading for the door to leave, a man approached her saying, 'You are Mary Lynch and you wrote a book.'

'Yes.'

'My granny's maiden name was Lynch. Could I buy your book?'

'Sure.'

He followed her out, bought the book and said as he was leaving, 'I am a slow reader but I will read it.'

'Let me know what you think,' she replied, getting into the car. 'There is an email address at the back.'

The following day, feeling very vulnerable and emotional, Mary tried to write her column about the documentary – but no words would come. After writing for the paper for two and a half years, she knew in her heart that it was over. Emailing Denzil to say that there would be no column that week she tried one more time to no avail; the flow had stopped.

A few days later she had an email from John saying: *I finished your book! I know I said I was a slow reader, but I couldn't put it down. It was like I was reading about a distant cousin. Could you get back to me sometime? I would like to come to stay at your centre for a couple of nights.*

She wrote back immediately saying: *You are welcome anytime, John.*

He arrived the following week on a hot April evening, and she took him for a walk around the circle before dinner, as she was emotionally and physically exhausted and was trying to stay awake.

As they walked, they talked about their childhoods and he told her what the book had brought up in him then stopped in the middle of the road for a minute before saying, 'Can I ask you a question?'

'Sure.'

'I read about all the businesses you have run in your life and I believe you are a good businesswoman. I have a business that I was thinking of starting and wondered if I could run it by you as everyone else thinks I'm mad.'

'Go ahead.'

He told her what he had in mind and finished by saying, 'I would need a man to work with me on this.'

'I think it's a great idea,' she replied. 'But you will never know unless you try, and you will need someone to work with you.'

Mary had started dinner when Gerry came in and she said to John, 'Tell Gerry about your idea.'

He did and again finished saying, 'I need a man to help me with this.'

'You do need someone to help, but it doesn't have to be a man,' Mary stated.

'Would you crawl through attics and lift manholes?' he asked.

'Do it all the time,' she replied.

Gerry laughed and said, 'Tell me more.'

They talked for hours over dinner, and before going to bed they had made plans for the three of them to try this business out. Later in bed, she said to Gerry, 'Do you really think you and I could work together?' Thinking of all the problems they already had.

'Of course, we can. This is different,' he replied. But as they fell asleep, she was not convinced.

The next day was another hot one. As they sat on the steps of the big house John said, 'I never slept a wink last night.'

'Why?' Mary asked, surprised, as people were always telling her how comfortable the beds and rooms were.

'Well … I was thinking that I may have got you involved in something that might not work.'

'Don't worry about that,' she replied immediately. 'It has already worked for me … I didn't sleep well either. I have finally crossed the border in my mind. It's time for me to go home to the North to work there for the first time in over thirty-five years. Whether it is with you or not doesn't matter, John.'

We listened in horror as we realised that a part of Mary still believed that others forced her from her home in the late seventies; now she believed she needed to force her way back. Knowing how everything worked when she was on the right road, everything down to the material for the throws on the bed, she was now going to have to face how things worked when she was on the wrong one. She was now going to truly understand the saying: *When one is on the right road, everything gets easier. When you are on the wrong road it just gets harder.*

Before John left that day, the three of them had committed to trying this new business after the summer, as John was busy at that time, Gerry was heading to France for a month and Mary was working on the family home in Castlerea. (Getting it ready for sale, she believed!)

Driving out of Roscommon town a few months later, John called and asked, 'How's your work coming along?'

'I'm finished for now, and Gerry is back. What about you?'

'I will be down next weekend if that's okay? I am ready to start.'

He arrived the following weekend and before he left, they had a plan. Gerry would set up the company and do the office work; Mary, the sales; and John the silent partner as he continued his work in construction.

That first week, Gerry and Mary worked together like never before and she thought, *Maybe he is right. Maybe we will be able to work together at this.* But her ego had completely taken over, and Gerry and her were at loggerheads from the first day on the road. She pushed on as if this was not a problem even though it was taking all her strength to keep going. With a lot of hard work things started to move, they got clients and got paid, but she was exhausted.

Before long, Gerry and she were barely speaking. Mary decided to say nothing to John until she had no choice, as he was the one who decided he needed a man in the business, and there was nothing we could do but watch to see what happened next.

CHAPTER 23

B y June 2014, Mary was under so much stress that she decided to treat herself to a massage for her birthday – something she had done regularly until the recession left her with no spare cash. With Gerry away again (something he now did when he'd had too much of their bickering), she went to stay with her friend Anne in Westport, giving us an opportunity to introduce a man into her life that could help.

'You have to get rid of that man,' Anne said as they discussed Gerry the night before her appointment.

'Why? Gerry is not my problem; he is just the one that triggers my issues. I don't need to change my teacher. I need to learn my lessons.'

Wow! we thought. *She understands.*

The following morning as she lay on Joe's massage table, she twisted in pain as he worked on her back.

'It is not a massage you need, Mary,' he whispered. 'It is shen therapy. I will finish this session with shen if that is okay with you.'

'Okay,' she whispered back, knowing what shen therapy was even though it was one of the few therapies that she had never tried. As he worked on her, she could feel something move. When finished, he said, 'You need another treatment as soon as possible,

200

Mary. I have a free hour this afternoon if you want to come back. You can pay me at another time if you don't have the money.'

She really didn't have the money as it was all going back into the business but knew she badly needed help and already knew that Joe was that person and also that we would find the money for her if she was doing the right thing.

Back with him a few hours later, Mary started a process of clearing what Gerry had helped to raise in her body, but it was a slow, difficult process, as letting go of anything didn't seem to be easy for humans – even if it was not serving them well. The wounds from Mary's childhood were what identified her, letting them go to move into the unknown was never encouraged, but the alternative was worse. She was heading for another breakdown, this time we hoped for a breakthrough without the breakdown.

At this point, Mary was carrying the business on her own proving she could do what John believed he needed a man for.

'Gerry has to go,' John said when she told him what was happening. 'We need to see a solicitor to see how to sort this out.'

Martin, a friend who she had met after he too had read her book, said, 'What did I tell you, Mary? Partners are for dancing. Go out on your own.'

After an hour with the solicitor, she knew Martin was right. She couldn't work with either of these two men (the fact was, it was difficult to work with anyone because this was not part of her journey). So, she left John with the opportunity to continue with what he initially suggested, planning to forge ahead with what she had expanded into, but he declined and walked away, leaving her alone. Before long, Gerry was back helping, which as usual, only worked for a while. By this time Jarlath had decided he was staying in Australia. Hoping he would change his mind and come home if she built up the business, Mary pushed on and started sliding down a very slippery slope.

Then, her mother asked her to go to the states to check out

how her aunt was doing, giving her the break she needed, which brought her back to her senses.

Two weeks later, Mary asked Gerry to leave again. She told her sister, 'I have nothing more to learn from him, and as everything has gone against Jarlath getting a visa to stay in Perth, he's coming home.' She redoubled her efforts to keep a business afloat that was not meant for neither her or her son, believing in her heart that Jarlath belonged in Ireland. She was right about that, but it was none of her business as he was an adult and had his own guides.

As we watched her heading downhill again, we knew that the fastest way to bring her to her senses this time would involve Gerry, so we whispered to her to call him and ask him to come back.

No, no, no, she replied.

Knowing we had to do something drastic to get her attention, we left her incapacitated with vertigo.

When Roisín entered the room later, her mother was staring out the window unable to move.

'What will I do, Mammy? Will I call the doctor?'

'No, help me to the bedroom at the bottom of the stairs. I need to be in bed beside a toilet. I have vertigo.'

'How do you know what it is?"

'I have had it before, and it's not something you forget in a hurry.'

With the help of a guest staying, they got her to bed where Mary cancelled all her appointments north of the border for the following few days.

'I won't go back tomorrow,' Roisín said. 'The referendum is in two days and there is nothing more I can do. They have enough people canvassing.'

'No. You go back as planned tomorrow, Rois. You want to be in Dublin when gay marriage is passed by the people in the first country in the world. I will be fine. I need to rest.'

Rest was all Mary could do as she stared at the cciling, unable to move her head as her stomach churned and her head spun, still ignoring our plea to call Gerry. The following day, a friend took her to vote. The process of dressing, getting to the car and to a polling station two miles away took hours – like a drunk woman, her friend had to hold her arm as he walked her into the local primary school to vote.

Feeling much better the next morning, Mary made her way to the kitchen alone.

Call Gerry, we whispered again.

I will text him, she answered through her thoughts.

Call him! we repeated.

He picked up his phone on the first ring and was delighted to hear from her, asking immediately if he could come see her. She said yes but put the meeting off until the end of the week.

He moved back into the house, and the changes the months of his absence had made on her were so obvious.

Mary didn't need his drama anymore and wondered why he was back believing all was well in her business, as she was now working with some of the biggest companies in the country – but they were slow to pay. In fact, some took her advice and didn't pay.

By the time her birthday came around again, she was coping so much better with the help of Joe and the knowledge that Jarlath was on his way home, convincing herself that things were eventually falling into place.

Mary may seem to have let go of helping people with their emotional issues, but in reality, all that had changed was that she working like a lunatic in a business to avoid her own problems.

Sitting in her car in Enniskillen on her fifty-sixth birthday, Mary was taking stock of her life as she always did this time of the year, believing that Gerry was back to confirm her progress. *Things are good,* she thought, smiling as the sun streamed through the windscreen of her car, warming her entire body. The sound of her phone ringing brought her back to reality with a jolt. It was a number she didn't recognise, but she answered.

'Hi,' a woman said. 'My name is Jane and I read your book. Michael gave it to me and your number and he said I could call you.'

'Yes,' Mary replied. 'He mentioned you might call. How are you?'

Jane opened her mouth and started to talk and didn't stop for about ten minutes as she blamed her husband for all her woes. When she had finally finished, Mary said sharply, 'Your problems have nothing to do with your husband. You have got to take it all back to yourself. You can't hand over your power to someone else, which is what you do when you blame another. Let him go and start dealing with your own wounds.' (She was also talking to herself, of course, as humans usually were when giving advice to another!)

The woman listened and then said, 'Can I come to see you tomorrow?'

Mary hesitated for a moment before saying, 'Okay, but I don't want to hear another word about your husband.'

'Okay, I will see you tomorrow.'

When Jane hung up, we watched as Mary pulled down the sun visor, looked into the mirror on the back of it and spoke directly to us.

'You said I didn't have to do this anymore. You said if I helped myself, that would be all I needed to do. That people would learn from my actions not my words … What the hell was that all about? I could do without another person blaming someone else, especially on my birthday.'

We didn't reply even though we wanted to whisper, *This woman is your birthday present. She will bring you to a place where you will not need to help anyone else, a place where there will be lots of help for you if you choose to take it.*

CHAPTER 24

Jane arrived the following day, and Mary took her for a walk so they could have some exercise and fresh air. Jane started where she'd left off, complaining about her husband and what he had done to her, how she still loved him and wanted him back. Mary was smart enough not to say anything as she recognised that this was a compulsive behaviour used to avoid her own issues. Switching off from the woman's voice for a moment, we heard Mary's thoughts loud and clear: *I understand what you are trying to say to me, exactly what I am saying to this woman. We both need help.*

As Jane went on and on about her husband, Mary realised she was describing a man very like Gerry.

'Is your husband an alcoholic?'

'Yes.'

'And where did you say you went for help?'

'Al-anon.'

'When are you going again?'

'Monday night.'

'Can I come with you?'

'Yes,' Jane answered.

The following Monday night, Mary went to the meeting. When it came for her to speak, she said, 'I believe I have been affected by someone's alcoholism even though he hasn't drunk in all the years I have known him. But I am not here to blame him. I am here to figure out why I was attracted to his behaviour, as he is definitely mirroring something in me.'

Leaving the meeting that night, Mary was aware not only that she was in the right place, but why Gerry was back in her life. Avoiding him or complaining about him was not the solution; accepting him and letting him go with love was.

Driving home, we reminded her of the man who had approached her after the launch of her book and said, 'As I turned each page of your book, I thought this is the page in which she will admit that she is an alcoholic.'

'Why would you think that? I couldn't drink to save my life,' Mary had replied.

'Because you are working the twelve steps.'

'What are the twelve steps?'

'The steps we follow for recovery.'

She had stood on the street that day with no idea what the man was talking about, but now she realised she had been trying to reinvent the wheel. All she needed to do now was to show up for herself and work the steps with the help of others.

The following week she attended a meeting at a different venue and again expressed her thoughts. 'I have never been affected by anyone's drinking. I have no doubt Gerry never had a drink since I met him and this feels like the right place for me to be, but another part of me feels like I don't belong here.'

After the meeting, a woman approached her and said, 'We have a co-dependence twelve-step meeting here on a Thursday night. I think it might interest you.'

Mary had read a few books on co-dependence and had even written a column in the paper called 'Co-dependent no more' after reading a book of the same name, deluding herself into believing that the book had taught her all she needed to know.

Sitting at that first meeting and hearing the words, 'The only requirement for membership of CoDA is a desire for healing and loving relationships,' she knew immediately that this was the right twelve-step program for her.

When walking to her car that night, we whispered to her, *This will help with every relationship in your life. The most important one being the one with us, yourself, then your adult children.*

Jarlath arrived home two months later and started working with her and Gerry, and from the start, it was a disaster.

By Christmas 2015, Mary could take no more and once again asked Gerry to leave, thinking that Jarlath and herself could build the company together, but Jarlath was wise enough to move on with another company, aware that this was not his path.

Struggling on alone, her last remaining extended family member John died a few months later. This death was not only felt on a deeply personal level, as he had been part of her family for over twenty-five years, but it also left her without the income she got for his care. She was now without any guaranteed income, as she was entitled to no benefits from the government on either side of the border.

At this time, Mary also heard the devastating news that her cousin Diedre, who'd recovered from breast cancer, had relapsed and was dying. Overcome with fear, this too was blanked, but thankfully she continued to meditate and go to meetings.

By her fifty-seventh birthday, Mary was marching to the rapid beat of her own drum, trying to control the uncontrollable, doing everything possible to avoid facing her purpose on this earth and we were beginning to wonder if she would ever break through.

As she was in the habit of taking stock of her life twice a year – at the beginning of January and again six months later in June – she sat alone on her birthday in 2016 wondering how she would get out of the hole she was in. Wondering if the meeting she had a few days later, seeking financial support for a product she had helped design, could save her failing business but knew in her heart that she was finally snookered. If this didn't work, she had no idea what to do next.

The following Thursday, Mary sat in a huge empty office waiting for the two men who held her future in their hands. An hour later she left the building knowing that it was over, she had 'run out of road' as her mother would say.

Walking into her parents' house later that afternoon, her mother greeted her in the kitchen with the statement. We just voted before asking, where were you?

At a meeting she replied, but said no more as she had never mentioned to her parents how serious her business and financial problems were.

Later, as they watched the news together, there was nothing on it, only Brexit. Would Britain leave the EU? She, like most people, believed that there would be a protest vote, but believed that the majority of people in Great Britain didn't want to go it alone.

At six the following morning, Mary rose to the silence of the house and did her meditation, before glancing at the news headlines to read that most of the people in the UK had voted to leave the EU. She knew from her lifetime experience that this change of direction was going to have enormous implications for the people of Ireland, especially her family and neighbours who were border people. The man-made border which had created so many issues in the past, as it divided the country in two, was now the frontier between the UK and the EU, and the problems were going to increase and affect a lot more people.

As her siblings filtered in and out of the house to discuss what had happened, she sat and listened but said nothing. It was like a death that no-one expected, and even her brother, the politician, could shed no light on what came next.

Sitting amongst them, wondering what all this would mean to her, she heard us whisper, *Pack your bags. Go home. You will not be working here anymore.*

She rose from the sofa, walked to the bedroom where she slept in her parents' house when working north of the border and packed her bags, said her goodbyes, got into her car and headed west in a daze, taking the wrong road which left her in a traffic jam in Enniskillen on that eventful Friday evening. As she crossed the border later her phone rang.

'What the hell is going on?' her son asked. (The company he had joined had just opened a number of stores in the UK and this was going to be devastating for them.)

'I guess this is like a divorce, Jarlath,' she replied without thinking. 'We will call the EU Daddy and the UK Mammy. The problem here is that the mother had a few children before she married. We will call these children England, Scotland, Wales and north-east of Ireland. Even though the heart of the mother is in London, and in her heart, she wants to stay in the marriage, the majority in England has voted to leave. Wales has voted to leave too. Scotland and the six counties want the marriage to continue, but when all the votes were added together the majority in the UK are in favour of the divorce. Wales is happy with the decision. Scotland can't leave without another vote or permission from the mother, which she is not going to give. Northern Ireland has an attachment to the father that no-one can deny, and we will call this attachment the Border. I have no idea what is going to happen next. All I know is I am going home and not going back there to work. I am too old for all this, Jarlath, and God only knows how long it will take to sort it out.'

Later, as she drove across the mountains to where she lived, Mary knew she had finally no choice but to surrender to what would be, feeling like she was going home. To what, she had no idea. Even though this feeling of home had flitted across her consciousness many times in her life, this time it felt different. The fact was that after all the running she had done, Mary had finally nowhere else to go but home. Home to herself. Home to that place that no-one could ever take from her, a place she had been avoiding for a long time, as in this place there were things she didn't want to face.

After a bath, she went to bed and woke with the question, *What now?*

Airbnb your house, we answered.

She hesitated, but only for a moment. If she had surrendered to what was going to be, Mary knew she had no choice but to follow this voice that had guided her in the most devastating and distressing times of her life and always in business. A part of her believed that we had abandoned her in her latest business venture in the North, but in her heart, she knew that she had just stopped listening.

Airbnb in her home was the last thing Mary wanted to do. Strangers in her home were never pleasant as a child, as they had always been wearing uniforms and carrying guns.

We watched as she rose from the bed, opened up her laptop and started to load pictures of the rooms she could rent out. By the time she pressed send, she was both hungry and exhausted. By the time she had eaten, her first booking had come in.

The first couple to arrive were German. Mary welcomed them the following day then headed to her bedroom and locked the door. The next morning, as she sat with them over a cup of tea, she heard and understood that she was being protected. Locking her bedroom door was a wise thing to do, but she had nothing to fear.

*   *   *

She grounded herself in the moment and was learning to live in the now. What came after the summer when there would be no more guests or income, she didn't dare think about. She was in the void, the place most people avoided until they had no choice but to go there. From here, Mary had to face the choice of moving into a new way of living, taking up where she had left off seven years before or going down the slippery slope of insanity that she had been on since.

PART 3

THE JOURNEY CONTINUES...

CHAPTER 1

For the rest of the summer of 2016, Mary continued to do Airbnb, welcoming guests to both her home and cottage as if they were family and enjoyed every minute of it.

Then, one day in early autumn when things were very quiet, she got a request that she had been dreading; a request for a room for two men wanting to come to stay that very night. She checked the profile of the man who had booked for some reassurance but got none.

'No!' she said out loud. 'No, I cannot take them into my home.'

You must, we whispered.

But the cottage is rented and there is no-one else here with me tonight and even if there was, I wouldn't want to take them. Please don't ask me to do this.

Take them in. It will be okay, we replied.

Her heart thumped in her chest as she pressed 'Accept'.

These men were from the same part of the country as she had been born, but from the other side of the divide. They had been brought up in a completely different culture and religion than her. Looking at the profile picture, she tried to convince herself that they didn't look like terrorists as anger, hurt and bitterness rose like bile in her throat and all the critics of her columns in the paper flashed before her. One in particular by the organiser of a local community group (but from the same area as these men) that sent a scathing letter to the paper regarding a column she had written. The editor had forwarded the letter to her at the time and she replied, 'Do you think I should call this man directly, Denzil?'

'Yes.'

'I believe you had a problem with my column last week?' Mary said when he took the call.

'Yes! I had a lot of people calling my office to complain about it.' He then raised his voice and said, 'Have you any idea what it was like to be a Protestant living in this county where they were in the minority? Lying in bed every night in fear of men coming to their homes with balaclavas and guns, afraid for their lives of terrorists.?'

We watched as Mary took a deep breath and replied, 'I am sure it was not easy … Can you imagine what it was like to be a Catholic in the same county? A person who was in the majority but had no rights? Unable to find employment because of your religion, unable to buy a property because you had no job, unable to vote because to do so you needed property? Even if you were lucky enough to have property and vote, you still couldn't change anything as the government used gerrymandering to reach into the next county where the majority was Protestant, guaranteeing the status quo … Can you imagine what it was like to lie in bed at night knowing that men in uniforms and blackened faces carrying legal guns could enter your home at any time, with the backing of the government to do whatever they wanted with the knowledge that they would never be brought to justice for their reign of terror? State terrorists!' she stopped, took another breath and asked into a silent phone, 'Are you still there?'

'Yes.'

'Thank you for listening.'

'Thank you for calling,' he replied politely.

Staring at her silent phone, Mary wondered how she could have spoken so calmly about the foundation of her life. Spoken facts that could not be or were not refuted.

The doorbell rang, breaking through her thoughts. She rose slowly from the armchair and walked down the long corridor to invite two men into her home for the night as if she were going to the gallows. Through the glass in the door, she saw two giants with tattoos all over their arms. As they followed her up the hallway, she could feel a cold sweat run down her back.

In the kitchen, with her back to her planned emergency exit, she offered them a cup of tea.

'Where are you from?' one of them asked, recognising her accent.

Taking a deep breath, Mary told them the truth knowing it only took a second for them to figure out by her name and her place of birth what religion she was. After a pregnant pause, the same man asked, 'What took you to this part of the country?'

For a second, she thought about taking her book out and saying, *Read this and you will know what I am doing here, how I was forced out of my home by the security forces*, but instead repeated her standard answer, 'A man!' and smiled.

The two men smiled back, and within minutes, all talk went back to the other side of the border. For the following two hours she stood on the opposite side of the countertop as they discussed as much of their individual but shared pasts as they could divulge to each other until one of them exclaimed, 'Oh my God, look at the time. We better get to town and get something to eat in the chipper before it closes. Thanks for the tea. We will see you in the morning.'

As soon as they left, Mary flopped into the big armchair and wondered how the hell she had got through that conversation, knowing in her heart that she had prejudged these men before giving them a chance to speak. This was the sign we were waiting for. She was ready to move on.

Lying in bed staring at the ceiling later, she realised that away from their differences, these men and herself had met at a place where they could agree about how much all their lives had improved since the peace agreement.

The next morning when they arrived in the kitchen, she offered them breakfast even though it wasn't included in the price of their accommodation. Afterwards, when leaving, one of them put out his arms for a hug and she walked into them and hugged him back. As they stood at the door, he said, 'If we are ever back in this part of the country, we will definitely stay here.'

Mary smiled and told him they would be very welcome before reaching into the bookshelf and handing him a copy of her book.

Back in her armchair a few minutes later, processing the past twenty-four hours, she couldn't believe that something that had been dreaded all summer had happened without a hitch when she totally let go and trusted us.

As the October nights drew in and the change of time was looming, Mary heard us when we whispered that it was time to go and see her cousin Deirdre's husband, Brian. Deirdre had passed away in August, but she hadn't been able to make the funeral nor the months mind, due to work commitments (nor was she meant to!).

Arrangements were made to visit Brian the following Monday night, knowing but not understanding why now was the right time.

Driving the two-and-a-half-hour journey in lashing rain she arrived at her parents' house at seven and after a cup of tea announced that she was going out again to see Brian.

'You can't go out again on a night like this,' her mother protested.

'If I don't go now, I may never get there,' she replied.

'But there is no need for you to go. We were all there at the funeral and the months mind.'

But Mary wasn't listening, determined to do as she was asked.

After getting lost on the narrow border roads a couple of times, she finally reached the house on the southern side and had just sat down for a chat when the doorbell rang and in walked the local priest who took over the entire conversation, as Mary looked around wondering why she was there. Half an hour later, as the priest got up to leave, Brian rose too and went with him to the door. Left alone in the quaint sitting room of the old rectory, Mary walked around looking at all the pictures of her cousin on the walls. Even though they were the same age and born into the same townland, they had gone to different primary schools and entered secondary school in different years, leaving them no real chance to get to know each other. But Mary had always had a real fondness for Deirdre and her sisters. When Brian returned from the door saying he was tired, she jumped at the chance to leave, still wondering why on earth she was there in the first place.

Walking into her parents' kitchen the following morning, Mary was still exhausted from driving but with the intention of heading home straightaway. As she was making her morning tea, her mother said, 'Surely you are not going home this morning? Stay another night.' And in that moment, she was under no doubt that we were speaking through her mother as these were not words her mother would usually say.

'Okay.'

'Great. You can watch Brian's documentary about the pitchfork murders on the TV tonight with us.'

'Really! I didn't know he made documentaries.'

'Did he not tell you?'

'I never got to talk to him, the local priest came in and we barely got to speak a word.'

'He has already written a book about the murders and helped with the documentary, and as it is the forty-fourth anniversary today, they are showing the documentary on TV,' her mother said, then added, 'Now that you are staying, I will treat you and Dad to lunch, it will save us cooking.'

Immediately, Mary knew not only where they would be eating but what she was meant to do afterwards, so without a thought said, 'When we've finished lunch can we go to the farm where Michael and Andy were murdered?'

'Yes,' her mother replied.

Walking her parents' dog later, Mary remembered that night forty-four years before, when the world as she knew it utterly collapsed after a devastating year. *The Irish Times* had reported at the time: *The murder of two Catholics has caused widespread fear in the scattered farmhouses of the bitterly divided Fermanagh. The savagery of the killings also aroused particular horror, even though 1972 has already had a shocking toll of violent deaths.*

*   *   *

As they walked into the restaurant, Mary knew what would be on the menu. Plain, simple food that they had been reared on. Roast beef, roast potatoes, peas and gravy – her mother ordered for both herself and Mary's father. 'What will you have, Mary?'

'The same.'

After they had cleared their plates, her mother asked, 'Would you mind reading the desserts from the notice board as I didn't bring my glasses?'

'Jelly and ice cream. Apple tart and custard or sherry trifle,' she smiled as she spoke as these were the only desserts she ever had in her childhood.

'Sherry trifle for me, jelly and ice cream for your father and whatever you want.'

Mary, who rarely ate meat and never dessert, replied, 'I'm okay. I don't want anything.' But when the two large desserts arrived with three spoons, her father pushed his between them and she started eating as if she didn't have a choice but enjoyed every mouthful. Then she ate half her mother's sherry trifle too, chatting away to her parents, aware of the uncanny situation they were in. It was as if they were all on a stage, and she was in the audience watching at the same time. It was like their whole world had slipped back in time.

Driving up the narrow lane to the farm later, her father spoke about the day his cousin and friend met their end in the most violent way. He continued to speak as they drove on to the street between the house and the shed with Mary hoping that there would be no-one to ask what they were doing there but knowing if there was, they would understand. This was unlike the night in question when the army and police stopped the neighbours from getting to the house to save their friends.

They sat in the car undisturbed and left the farmyard a few minutes later without getting out of the car, knowing it wasn't necessary.

Later that night, they watched the documentary together and went to bed early, and by the next morning after breakfast, she was back on the road home.

CHAPTER 2

Crossing the border, Mary felt a presence in the car, and even though there was no physical body there, she knew Deirdre was with her, realising immediately that it wasn't Brian she had went to visit – for some reason Dierdre had been waiting there for her and was coming back with her. None of this made her feel uncomfortable as Deirdre was family, and if she needed help, Mary was happy to do anything to assist.

Closing her eyes to start her meditation that evening, she found herself back at the scene of the murders with the two men screaming. Deirdre arrived and said, *Take care of Michael in the shed. I will go and find Andy,* and within a minute Deirdre was back in the barn with Andy. Then, other neighbours started to come in, people from both sides of the community. The first to appear was a neighbour who had been murdered a few nights before Michael and Andy. He too was a farmer, but also a part-time member of the security forces. We watched Mary hesitate for a moment before relaxing and allowing him in. As others arrived, she knew by how they greeted each other which side of the divide they were from. The barn expanded to accommodate them all but the bitterly divided community moved to opposite sides of the barn, divided in death as they had been in life. By the time the meditation was over the barn was full and the silence was deafening.

Picking up the phone she called Michael.

'So, do you think it is like the last time in 2009?' he asked.

'Yes, and I know I said I would never do this again, but these people were our friends, our neighbours and our relations. I cannot refuse them. It should be sorted in a week like before, and this time I have a better idea of what is happening, plus, Deirdre is with me.'

That evening, Mary went into her meditation again; there hadn't been a single movement from morning, nor was there a sound. We reminded her of Henk's advice from before, so she asked for help as there was nothing more either she or Deidre could do.

Her request was heard through her thoughts. Mary assumed that the help would come from the white brotherhood, but instead it was the energy from seven years before, which arrived and surrounded the barn. As this energy was made up of enemies in this life, Mary believed that it would have a huge influence in the reconciliation of the people of this small area. But this was not to happen, even when the white brotherhood came to help. They weren't ready, it wasn't yet the time, other circumstances had to change first.

Mary watched day after day as the division within the barn remained and in time forgot they were there as she got on with her life. A life that had hit a wall as she lived on the savings from the summer, trying to ignore the fact that there was no more income and her savings were dwindling rapidly. She was snookered again, this time burying her head in the sand finally understanding why others didn't open letters, afraid of their contents.

Mary needed an income and stability and needed it fast if she was to continue the work she had resumed, but as her guides, we had to wait until asked.

At the end of November, her interest-only mortgage came to

an end. After negotiating with the bank for seven years, they were now looking for full mortgage payments each month, and Mary couldn't afford it, or even the interest on it anymore, and knew the bank were unlikely to give her another extension.

We guided her to watch a program on the laptop called *The Moneyless Man*, a story about a man who lived with no income, and Mary decided to visit him. Now grasping at straws, aware that big changes were coming into her life, we whispered, *You need to be open to everything, attached to nothing!* Which, of course, was the only way to live.

The following day a bill arrived that needed to be paid, forcing her to finally check her bank balance. Petrified, Michael was asked to stay on the line as she stood quivering at the cash machine.

€268 it showed. Her heart sank, her body started to shake and her stomach got sick.

'What am I going to do, Michael?'

'You will always have a room in my house, Mary, if you need it, and you could sign on the dole.'

'Thanks, Michael, but I have about seventeen rooms that I can sleep in but I have no money to live on and can't eat the buildings, and I am not entitled to the dole as I am self-employed. Can I come up to you today? I want to go to see a man that I watched a program about and he lives closer to you than me.'

'You know you're very welcome here anytime,' he replied.

Driving through the town where she had reared her children, Mary looked at all the people she knew walking the streets and felt like a complete failure, blaming herself for something that she didn't have any control over, wondering what she going to say to her children who were struggling to make their own way in the world, aware that she could borrow from her brother again if necessary but would never do this without an income. Consciously aware that she could live on her overdraft but that was only kicking the can down the road. *Something huge has got to change,* Mary thought.

And that is you! we whispered.

Driving into the town where Michael lived, we heard a fleeting thought run through her mind: *I would be better off dead. The children would be better off without me.* Something a friend once said and she hadn't understood at the time.

Michael hugged her when he opened his door and took her into the kitchen for tea. 'You are in no fit condition to drive any further,' he said. 'If you stay over, I will drive you tomorrow morning.'

'Fine.'

'I will make us dinner.'

'Okay. I will do a meditation.'

As Mary walked to the bedroom with a hot water bottle under her arm, not only was her body frozen, so too was her mind. After putting everything on hold for five months, it had come crashing in on top of her. *I can't even afford to eat,* she thought in the chair beside Anna's bed (Michael's mother), these two women who met only for five minutes in this life but long enough to make a connection. Mary had no doubt that this woman had guided her to connect with her son when she passed on, a connection that enhanced both their lives.

After dinner she sat with Michael watching television but seeing nothing. Going to bed early, Mary fell asleep immediately but woke a few hours later in the dark, lying rigid and petrified, asking out loud through her tears for help.

We whispered again but still she couldn't hear. Nothing was getting through her wall of fear. Then we heard her thoughts.

What will I do, Anna?

Sell the big house, Anna replied as we spoke through her.

Okay. I will put the big house up for sale. Ten minutes later Mary was asleep.

After breakfast, they drove to find the moneyless man and finally did after making a lot of enquiries and left knowing it wasn't her journey to live without money, but that she could live with a lot less than she had in the past.

Back home the following day, the auctioneer was called, and with the sale of the house in motion, Mary started to use her overdraft as she dealt with all the people that had passed on that were now coming to her for help. Some moved on immediately, others hung around awhile believing it wasn't their time or dealing with fears and traumas they had encountered in their lives. The souls with unresolved issues, she placed in a room adjoining her healing room until they were comfortable to move on, visiting them in her meditations as she listened to their fears, continually reassuring them that where they were going, they would not be judged.

* * *

In November, five months after Brexit, we all watched as a multimillionaire businessman became president of the USA, aware that she was not the only one going through major changes: the entire planet was. Conscious that sometimes the pendulum had to swing completely in another direction (as it had in her life) before finding balance, she had become acutely aware that she was living in a world that really needed balance if it was to survive.

The group of people segregated from each other in the barn on the border, were now five weeks without any movement. Worrying that she might be carrying them for the rest of her life, Mary finally asked for help on the ground. So, we guided her to a woman who was a psychic.

'Do you ever have people who have died come to you looking for help to move on?' she asked one dark winter's evening.

'No.'

'Do you know anyone who does?'

'Yes.'

'Who?'

'A man who lives outside Dublin,' the woman replied.

'Would you please contact him for me and ask if I could call him? I can't do this alone anymore, and I have a group of people too traumatised to move on and I feel like I am going mad.'

Mary had expected a call back in a few days, but a week passed. And then another week, and still no word. Then finally in December, there was a message with a name and number which was called immediately, but Mary knew by the ring tone that he was out of the country so left a message saying who she was and what she wanted. The call wasn't returned. A week later, she called again with no return call.

Coming up to Christmas, Mary was desperate, so Gerry was contacted again. She had told him what had happened in 2009 and had allowed him to distract her from it all. In fact, she was delighted with the distraction and now needed it again. As they hadn't spoken in nearly a year, he was happy to hear from her. After catching up with what was going on in their lives, he said he would love to meet up. Her reply was eager, expecting it would be soon and, *The sooner the better,* she thought.

It was a week before he contacted her again, asking if they could meet up that day or the following one. Having other commitments, Mary considered breaking them, but only for a moment. Then he continued by saying, 'I will be gone for the Christmas period and won't see you till January if I don't see you today or tomorrow.'

She replied, 'Have a lovely Christmas. I will see you in January.' Getting off the phone, Mary was delighted with how far she had come. How much the twelve-step meetings were helping her as this distraction was no longer required. Michael was always there to listen but she now wanted someone who understood.

Sitting in a meditation that evening, she said out loud, 'I need help. You have to send someone who understands this stuff. I need to know I am not the only one if I am going to continue this work. Please, I need help with these people and I need to know that I'm not crazy.' Exhausted, she went to bed at eight and slept as soon as her head hit the pillow waking early to a message that had been sent at nine the previous night.

CHAPTER 3

*H*i Mary, I feel it is time for me to visit you if you have a room. Call me.

It was from a therapist who she had never met but had been in touch with a few times on Facebook. Her friend Marie had forwarded his message when he had been looking for a place to stay in Ireland, as he wanted to get out of London.

Yes, I have room, she texted. *When were you planning on coming and how long did you plan on staying?*

He called her. 'I'm in Dublin and I was planning on coming today and staying a week if you have the room?'

'Perfect,' she replied, after quickly calculating that he would be gone the day before her parents arrived for Christmas. They met at the train station at six that evening, and for the following week talked about the things they saw and understood. When he left on the 23rd, she felt like a new woman and was confident that the group of people in the barn would move on when the time was right.

Then, in a meditation, Mary found herself catapulted into the home of a celebrity who was both rich and famous, someone that had just died. Being rich and famous was considered the ultimate success in the world she lived in. In this world these people were watched twenty-four seven and were an open target for the ego, as they went from highs to low as people's admiration and their criticism ruled their lives. This was someone she had no connection with or any admiration or criticism of, and so she wondered, *What the hell does he want from me?* as she faced him. A man who people believed had everything in life had an expectation of her!

Reading her mind, he said, *I had nothing. You are the one who has everything because your needs are basic. You understand life like I never did. I was unhappy all my life trying to be something I wasn't. Be who you are. Keep being who you are.*

Mary offered no assistance, thinking of the seventy people who were still sitting in a barn on the border that she couldn't help. Five years later, when she finally heard the word psychopomp, she spoke to a lady in the States doing the same work. When Mary told her this story, the woman informed her that the very same person came to her friend that same day, who had no time to help him but guided him to another friend who helped him move on! *My God,* Mary thought with relief, *these lost souls will go to another if I'm not available.*

Her parents, brother, sister, niece, son and daughter all came for Christmas that year, and two days later they were gone.

Then Kai called again and said he needed to come back for another week. This time they both went on a vegetable juice fast and meditated a lot. When he left, she felt cleansed, cleared and was ready for anything – including Gerry. Then, eleven weeks from the day Mary had crossed the border to see Brian, she went into her usual morning meditation and found herself back in the barn on the border, wondering why nothing had changed. Then suddenly, all the souls inside the barn came together in a flash and joined up with the energy that had been waiting patiently outside. As she sat in shock, the energy moved slowly along the border, picking up other lost, distressed souls along the way (and there were many of them!). From the border, it moved north, but stayed within the six counties of occupied Ulster. As it moved, not

227

only did it gain momentum but also strength from the many other souls who were joining along the way. Within fifteen minutes, it had become a solid energy sitting over the six counties, stopping at the border of Cavan Monaghan and Donegal and the coast of North Antrim and Derry.

Michael was called and told before she added, 'Something huge is going to happen in the North today, Michael.'

'What do you think that is?'

'I have no idea, but I have never witnessed anything like this before, and it certainly wasn't me keeping them in the barn for eleven weeks, nor me that moved them on today. I will keep an eye on the news to see what happens.'

Driving into town later, she switched on the radio as the newscaster read, 'Martin McGuinness has resigned as deputy first minister in the North today.'

Mary immediately called Michael and told him.

'Do you think that is it?'

'I have no idea. I can't imagine that is going to make any big change. Can you?'

'You know better than me, Mary.'

'I know nothing, Michael. I just watch what happens. I can't see what difference him resigning will make?'

Later that week, her mother showed her the picture which had been on the front page of *The Irish News* the day of the resignation. A full-page picture of Martin McGuinness walking out of Stormont and her brother (who was now an MLA) walking behind him.

As she drove home the following day, Michael was called again to tell him the latest development.

'Do you think that has any meaning?' he asked.

'I don't know, but of all the MLAs walking out the day he resigned, how come it is our Sean that is pictured with him? Maybe it is a sign. Mam, of course, has the picture already framed and sitting on the fireplace. You know, Michael, there are more pictures of Martin McGuinness in our sitting room than any one of us. I think she considers him another son, as if seven wasn't enough!'

'Have you ever met him?' Michael asked.

'Martin McGuiness? No, but I do have his autograph on the picture I drew of him and Gerry Adams hanging in my house.'

She mentioned this to Gerry (who was back in her life but not in her house) later when he called. 'Don't have anything to do with that,' he said. 'It is not good for you.'

She ignored him.

The following morning, Mary heard us when we told her as we often had before, *Turn off your phone, go on a fast and have a day in silence.* She had written a column about one of these days, which she named 'Silence is golden'.

When we suggested she take a walk in the mountains, she put on her boots and went. Coming back, a man walked beside her (in spirit). Knowing immediately who he was, she completely ignored him, as he was a well-known Northern politician that had passed away, and deep down, she still blamed him for so much. He was from the other side of the divide, and even though she doubted that he ever fired a shot in his lifetime, she had no doubt he caused the deaths of a lot of people as he incited hatred in his speeches against Catholics.

Michael was updated on what was happening but Gerry was told nothing.

The following day, Sunday 22nd of January 2017, we asked her to contact Vincent again (the man that the psychic had told her about).

Feeling like she was now begging, she sent a text message explaining who she was and saying that it was nice to know that someone else was helping others move on. She had no expectations but got a reply immediately: *Call me anytime.*

She stared at the message for a moment in surprise, before

answering with the words we gave her: *I will call you at seven o'clock this evening.*

After introducing herself later, Vincent asked, 'What is happening with you? What do you see?'

'I wouldn't know where to begin.'

'Start at the beginning.'

For the next hour, she told her story and finished by saying, 'You would never guess who walked beside me in the mountains yesterday.'

'Who?'

'The Most Reverend Ian Paisley.'

'I have had dealings with him too,' he replied and then told her his story.

She listened and they continued the conversation until ten o'clock, before she said, 'I had better go. I am exhausted. I will talk to you again soon.'

Walking towards the hall door, Mary turned off the lights in the living room and the hall and at the top of the stairs as she always did. From there, she went into the bathroom and into bed where she fell asleep instantly, waking a few hours later in her sitting room in front of Martin McGuinness. Shocked, she stared at him. He didn't open his mouth, but she could read his thoughts as he stared back.

Who the hell are you?

I'm Mary Lynch, she replied without uttering a word, then continued, *Sean Lynch's sister.*

He stared back at her, puzzled. *What the hell am I doing here?* was the next thought in his mind.

I have no idea, was the next in hers.

Do you want to stay? she asked, something that would have been asked of anyone who had arrived.

I can't stay here! he replied sharply.

With that, she woke up and could not believe that what had just happened was not real. Looking towards the hall door, the first thing she noticed was that the light on the landing was on; getting out of bed and going down the stairs, she found that the lights in the hall downstairs and the sitting room were on too!

It was six o'clock in the morning and too soon to call anyone so Mary sat down to do a meditation, to ground herself thinking, *Was I really that tired last night that I didn't switch off any lights?* She found herself in a room with Martin McGuinness again. His face was stern and beside him stood Ian Paisley. Again, nothing was said but she heard Martin McGuinness' thoughts loud and clear.

Wherever I go, he goes too, nodding his head towards Paisley.

She didn't reply but continued with her meditation in their company, even though she never acknowledged Paisley.

When finished, she texted both Vincent and Michael asking them to call her when they were free.

Vincent called immediately. 'What is it they used to call them pair?' he asked when told what had happened.

'I can't remember.'

'Wonder what they are doing with you now?' he said, as if it was the most natural thing in the world to happen.

'I have no idea but it's strange as they were joint first ministers at one time. Now they are back together for some reason, even though one is dead and one is alive.'

'Ask them.'

'I will not. Martin McGuinness is not very approachable, and I am not talking to Paisley … It looks as if they have work to do together. Whatever it is, it is none of my business. Henk once told me that all I needed to do was create a space and allow things to happen. Maybe that is all I need to do as I have no idea how to stop this.'

With all this going on, Mary was still trying to negotiate with the banks for another interest-only loan, even though she had agreed to sell, backtracking again, deciding to hang on to the new house and sell the original family home instead – which was never going to happen as it was not in the order of things. It was going to delay everything for now but we had no choice but to step back and allow her to do what she wanted.

As the huge number of forms were being completed for the bank, Mary continued to glimpse at the space where the two Northern leaders were and the energy that sat over the six occupied counties of Ulster when she meditated. From Google, she found that these two men had the nickname 'The Chuckle Brothers' as they always seemed to be sharing jokes and laughing. Two men who were enemies for the majority of their lives until they eventually got together and made a deal to form a government where they were equal as leaders, even though Martin McGuinness was called the deputy leader.

Then, one evening, she watched as the energy crossed the border into the Republic of Ireland, moving from Derry to Donegal and down through the country, picking up hundreds of thousands of souls that had been stuck over the centuries – some she recognised as men who had been politicians and leaders of the recent governments south of the border. Neil Blaney in Donegal was the first she recognised, then Albert Reynolds in Longford and finishing with Jack Lynch in Cork (a man her father considered a traitor, to both their name and the country!). It moved slowly, as souls seemed to be coming from every boreen to join it, and for sanity's sake she continued to report all of this to Michael, her sister and Vincent.

CHAPTER 4

Within weeks of Martin McGuiness arriving in her dream, her house, or both, it was obvious to everyone that he was not well.

'Do you think he is going to die?' her sister asked.

'I have no idea. I'm just watching and wasn't he fine a month ago? I'm sure he's not going anywhere.'

One evening as she sat in her meditation watching all the leaders that had passed away (all men!) talking to Martin McGuiness (a conversation she was not privy to) a question ran across her mind. *What am I doing in the middle of this?*

Immediately, Martin McGuinness raised his hand to stop the conversation. *What is it, Mary?* he asked.

Shocked that he could hear her thoughts as he listened to everyone else, she replied, *What do you want from me?*

What we are doing can't be done without you.

Why?

Because you have done this before.

Done what? she wondered as he got back to his meeting without any further explanation, and she continued to meditate and ignore them, as they did her.

In the meantime, the bank refused her request for an extension on her interest-only mortgage but thankfully didn't call in the loan.

A few weeks later, on the 21st of March, Martin McGuiness died.

Her sister called and said, 'Do you realise you are the only one in that room that is still alive?'

'Of course, I do. Maybe I am next!'

'Aren't you afraid?'

'What is the point? I don't have any control over it. I have no idea what is happening, and if I didn't have you, Michael and Vincent, I would probably go mad. Anyway, I have had a glimpse of where we are all going and have no fear of going there.'

The moment she got off the phone, she wondered if she was supposed to go to his funeral and we whispered, *No, it's not necessary.* She didn't know him in this life but a lot of her family did and she had no doubt the family would be well represented. The morning of the funeral, in her meditation, she found herself in the lobby of a hotel in Derry. It was empty except for herself and Martin McGuinness. Having no idea what to say, she remained silent.

But he spoke, 'I want to apologise for being rude to you. I was shocked to find myself in your house. I didn't know what I was doing there.'

'I don't know what I am doing here, what I am doing in the middle of all this?' she replied.

'You can help, but I am not ready yet. I need to stay with my community for a while. I hope that is okay.'

She was gobsmacked! Why was he asking her what she thought? She didn't care what he did but replied politely, 'You do what you need to do for you. I have no idea what is happening, but if I am to create a space for it to happen, I will gladly do that as I have done it before and I know that I am being guided.'

At that he walked across the lobby and gave her a big hug, saying, *I will see you soon.*

It was at a later date that he told her that it was Ian Paisley that took him to her that first night.

Walking across the Ox Mountains later that morning, she called her brother as he drove from Dublin to the funeral.

'What was Martin like?' she asked.

'Well … he was straight, direct and to the point. A lovely man.'

Yes, she thought. *That about describes him. But he is a lot taller than I thought he was.* Although she said nothing else to her brother.

In the meantime, we wanted her to meet Vincent, so got them together in the middle of April. Mary liked Vincent immediately; he had a good, if sometimes impatient, energy. At the end of the day, she knew we wanted her to visit him in his home so followed our guidance and went there. Content that he was an ordinary human being living in an ordinary house with an ordinary lifestyle, she left knowing she wasn't the only one in the world following this guidance. What she didn't know is that we needed them both in the same space for at least twelve hours to cement their energies.

With that sorted, she started working on a new business for her big house, ignoring all the warnings that this was not her direction. One evening in the middle of May 2017, when Michael was staying over, her phone rang.

'Remember I told you that I had been asked to go to Greece to do some work?' Vincent said.

'Yes.'

'Well, I have been told that it has to be this week.'

'So, are you going?'

'Yes, but … the thing is, I have been asked to ask you to come with me.'

'I cannot afford to go,' Mary replied, using the same five words that had become her standard reply to anything that involved money since the recession began.

'Don't worry about money. I will pay your way.'

'If I'm meant to go and you pay my way Vincent, I will pay you back. Leave it with me. I will meditate on it and let you know tomorrow morning.'

Getting off the phone, she said, 'Michael, that was Vincent, he wants me to go to Greece with him this week.'

'Are you going to go?'

'I don't know, but no doubt I will be told if I should, and soon.'

At that she sat down and continued to watch the movie that the phone call had interrupted. We whispered to her to go so Vincent was called but before she got a chance to speak, he said, 'It is not Greece that I have to go to. It is Crete.'

She grinned and replied, 'I have been told to go with you, and I have been told so often by Gerry that I should go to Crete so I'm coming with you.'

'Great. I will go to the travel agent and get prices.'

An hour later he called with the prices.

'No way am I paying that much, Vincent. Leave it with me.'

Gerry was called as he was a seasoned traveller and knew how to do it cheaply. He was delighted to help, especially since she was going to Crete, but he wasn't told why.

Two hours later she called Vincent. 'I have it all booked, everything for half the price you were quoted, but we won't be staying in a five-star hotel. We are going on Thursday, staying in a two-bedroom apartment on the beach and I have a car hired.' She then told him how much had been spent on the credit card number that he had given her.

'Brilliant. You can stay with me the night before and I will drive us to the airport.

'No, I have to stay with my parents, but I will be with you first thing in the morning.'

Mary didn't tell her mother much (and she didn't ask, for a change), only that she was going away for a week with a friend.

Arriving at the airport, Vincent took over as he too was a seasoned traveller. Fifteen hours after she left her parents' house, they picked up the rental car and drove to the apartment building, had dinner, then walked down to the beach.

'Do you feel that energy?' Vincent asked before she could take in her first breath of the sea air.

'I don't feel anything but exhaustion, and the only thing I want to feel is the pillow under my head, Vincent.'

They headed to the apartment and bed. Mary fell asleep in minutes and had no idea how long she had been sleeping when the door of their apartment was kicked open and she was behind the bedroom door when someone looked in and left. Her heart was thumping as she left the apartment and went out into the street with the feeling that the person who had entered her room would be back. The first thing she noticed was the mist and the commotion. People were running around everywhere. Standing still, wondering which was the safest way to go, she saw a soldier approaching and had no doubt that he was British. He called out to her but she turned and ran as fast as her legs could carry her down a back street with the soldier after her. Up and down narrow streets she ran with him hot on her heels. As he closed in on her, she slipped into a house where an old lady was standing dressed all in black.

'I have to hide from them,' she said. 'I know they will go back to the house looking for me and I have had enough of British soldiers to last me a lifetime.'

The old lady looked at her and Mary knew by her blank expression that she knew what was said but didn't understand what she meant.

The door of the apartment closed, waking her up. Vincent had gone out. Drawing her knees up to her chest she cried rocking herself for comfort. About fifteen minutes later, Vincent returned and she ran out to him.

'I just had a dream, Vincent, which I know wasn't a dream,' then told him what it had entailed.

237

'That wasn't a dream. I told you, there are strange energies around here.'

'Can we do a meditation together?' Mary asked as he handed her a drink of water.

As they sat opposite each other and closed their eyes, a man appeared between them looking directly at her. *What the hell do you want?* he screamed in a language she had never heard before but understood as if he had spoken English.

She froze and was unable to utter a sound, then Martin McGuinness appeared at her right shoulder. Paisley arrived at her left, and even though she hadn't developed eyes in the back of her head, she was aware that the British soldier she had seen the night before was at her back.

She is here to help, Martin McGuiness replied calmly.

Help? Help!? the man screamed. *How can she help? There are thousands of us.*

There are hundreds of thousands of us, Martin replied in the same calm voice.

Not another word was spoken as the man disappeared.

'Vincent,' she whispered. He opened his eyes to hear what had just happened.

'We have a lot of work to do here,' he said.

'Like what?'

'This place is so blocked. We have to go to the cemeteries.'

'What cemeteries?'

'The British one first, I was told.'

'Why, what happened here?'

'I have no idea,' he said as he watched her reach for her phone to Google: *War in Crete.*

Battle of Crete, May 20ᵗʰ 1941 appeared on her screen.

'Oh my God! There was a battle here on this island and yesterday was the anniversary ...' 'Seventy-six years ago yesterday ... seventy-six years ago, yesterday, the British arrived here to help!'

She was frozen to the bone as they headed out into the sunshine and down to the beach.

'I will get us breakfast,' Vincent said as she sat on the sand like a zombie feeling the heat, hoping it was strong enough to thaw her.

He had barely been gone a minute when the British soldier sat beside her and said, *He is right. You need to go the cemeteries, and it would be good to start with the commonwealth one.*

She didn't answer him even though he didn't seem to be a threat. He was still there when Vincent returned with food and stayed with her the entire day, asking questions and making small talk. Martin McGuinness joined them and answered the questions that she couldn't (which were most of them), so she just switched off and read her book.

CHAPTER 5

They did very little that first day other than rest, go for a drive and eat. Mary contacted Gerry and asked, 'What do you know about the battle of Crete?'

'The most famous battle of World War II. Did you not learn about it in school?'

'No. I told you before, I was only taught British economic and social history.'

'The Cretans held the Germans at bay and there was a terrible battle there. The Brits were there too.'

When she told him what happened to her, he didn't speak for a moment, then changed the subject. He had switched off. He didn't want to know.

The following morning, we watched as they drove to the first cemetery which lay beside the ocean, administered by the Commonwealth War Graves Commission. *Beautiful spot*, she thought, despite how harrowing it was to look at all the white crosses, each one representing a soldier. Vincent sat on the nearest bench as she walked through the lines of crosses knowing immediately that she had company. It was another British soldier, a different one. She said nothing but he started a conversation. *What do you think you can do and can we trust you?*

Mary felt the question trigger every cell in her body. She was

speechless before replying through her thoughts, *I don't care whether you do or not, it might be more interesting for me to ask, can I trust you?!*
We have been waiting here for years, waiting to be released. Why would we go with you? he then enquired.

I didn't ask you to go anywhere, she replied sharply. *I have no idea what I am doing here and if I had my choice, I would probably leave you all where you are, but it is not my decision.*

Walking on, nervously taking note of the names, ages and countries the young soldiers had come from, she saw the Inniskilling Fusiliers mentioned on a headstone and involuntarily smiled.

You from near Enniskillen? he asked.

Twenty-minute drive, and whilst you were waiting here to be released, I could tell you lots of things that your comrades did to me, my family, neighbours and my country. As these thoughts and her memories were running through her mind, she knew that he saw and heard them. Memories of her childhood forced tears from her eyes and she made no attempt to stop them, keeping Vincent in the corner of her eye as they were the only two people alive in the cemetery.

After walking between every row of crosses, we guided her to what Mary later described to Vincent as a tabernacle, like the one she had stared at in church every Sunday of her childhood. Opening the one that stood in front of her that hot summer's day, she found inside a copy which named every soldier that lay in the graveyard. After opening and looking at the first few pages, she closed it and held it in her arms close to her heart, turning around just in time to see all the souls rise up and join together as one over the graveyard, before disappearing. This included the soldier that had been at her side a moment before. She then slowly made her way back to Vincent who was now in the car, and they drove off without a word being uttered.

'What did you do?' Mary asked when they were back on the motorway.

'I needed to clear what was blocked there. Wasn't too bad but had to be done. What about you?'

She told him what happened, then not another word was spoken about it again until dinner, when they discussed what they would do the next day.

'The German cemetery is next,' he said. 'It needs to be cleared.'

At that very moment, the Cretan soldier (actually, he was a civilian that was forced to defend his island which made him a soldier), that had appeared in their apartment two days before, showed up again and he was not happy.

There is no way we are going anywhere the Germans are, he stated.

With no idea what he was talking about she made no reply.

Early the next morning they headed off in the direction of the German cemetery but couldn't find it, finally having to stop at a garage to ask. Luckily there was one mechanic that could understand and speak a little English, but she got the distinct impression that he was not impressed with where they were going.

Taking his directions, they headed up the back roads and eventually found the cemetery on the side of a steep hill which had an interpreted centre she immediately headed for, believing that Vincent was walking behind, and inside read the stories of different German soldiers buried there, stories told by their families. The one that stood out to her was a young farmer forced to leave the land to join the army and was killed in Crete. Turning around, she expected to find Vincent close by, but there was no sign of him. Leaving the building she tripped and nearly fell, telling Vincent later, 'It was as if I was pushed. Or was it because the energy was so dense and I so nervous that I wasn't watching where I was going?' As there was no-one else around, she walked up the steps to the cemetery, feeling really paranoid, and was delighted to find Vincent sitting on a wall in front of her, staring at all the white crosses in front of him.

As soon as she reached him, he said sharply as if he was in command, 'Come on, this way, to that bench,' as he pointed to a bench under a tree on the left-hand side.

Not one who liked to be ordered around, Mary replied, 'I am going this way and I will meet you at the bench,' and walked in the opposite direction feeling an energy push against her. Labouring her way up the side of the cemetery, she saw a few benches at the top and decided to take a seat on the middle one but didn't make it. She hadn't the energy to force her way past the first bench. It was a very hot afternoon, but Mary knew it wasn't the heat that was stopping her. Very aware that she wasn't welcome in this place, looking to her right she could see Vincent sitting on the bench a few hundred yards from her, although it seemed like a million miles away. It was then she heard a cold, hard voice say, *You are not taking anyone from here. This is where they are staying.*

She blanked her mind and kept her focus on Vincent.

After a short rest, we watched her get up and walk on, slowly feeling the same force against her, finally making it across the top and down the other side to Vincent.

As soon as she sat down, he said, 'They are not going to let these men move on. The energy here is overpowering and I can't move it. It is impossible to move. We need to leave, but we will have to come back.'

Mary didn't reply but was relieved to know that she understood exactly what he was saying, realising as they walked back to the car that she had come to this island with a man that she barely knew – came with our guidance but with no idea what they were to do. Now she understood that even though his work was different from hers, they were definitely singing from the same hymn sheet.

They walked to dinner that night with Vincent making the decision where they went (as he usually did) and she was happy to just follow. Walking down a back street, she saw an old woman dressed all in black through the small window of her home.

'Vincent, she looks like the woman I saw in my vision the other night, but I guess all the wee old women on the island look the same.'

As they sat down outside the restaurant, a woman approached with menus.

'English?' she asked.

'Irish,' Mary replied.

'North or South of the border?'

'I'm from the North. He is from the South,' she answered, shocked that the woman was interested.

During the course of the meal, as the woman came to and from their table, the conversation continued as she told them that one of her best friends was from the North of Ireland and she knew all about the war there.

'And what about the battle here in 1941,' Mary asked, 'did your grandmother ever speak about it?'

'No, not much, but my mother was a child at the time and remembers it well.'

'Where did your mother live on the island?'

'She was born on the next street and still lives in the same house.'

Walking home later Mary asked, 'What are the chances that her mother or her granny was the one in my vision?'

Vincent smiled but didn't answer.

The next day, he said he was told in his meditation that they needed to go back to the German cemetery. Mary wasn't sure she was ready to go back but gladly followed, not wanting to be left alone anywhere on the island.

On the way she told him, 'When I was in my meditation this morning, the Cretan soldier or terrorist – or whatever a society calls a man in his situation – was there again and still insists he is not going anywhere the Germans are. It seems that even though they are all dead, they still see each other as enemies. I told him that he would have to accept that the war is over and if the Germans want to move on, that they too have to be allowed. I explained to him that we all came from the same energy and we would all be going back to that same energy. He then shouted, *I will not bring my people where they are going.*

'I told him that it had nothing to do with me, that I was only doing what I was asked, and in the past, I had no choice but to help people that I believed to be my enemy. He then stated again as if he hadn't heard a word I said, *I will not bring the men, women and children they murdered anywhere near them.*

'I didn't repeat myself, but I knew he could read my mind.' When they reached the cemetery, nothing had changed.

The energy there was so strong Vincent said, 'I don't know if it can be moved.'

Again, as he sat on the bench, Mary walked defiantly (this time knowing that it was the Germans, not Vincent, she was defying) through the cemetery. Looking at the names and ages of the soldiers, her eye caught the name of the young man she had read about in the interpreted centre and could feel his soul and hear his voice.

I never wanted to leave the land. I want to leave here. But as he tried to move, he was stopped.

'Keep trying,' Mary whispered, even though she knew everyone could hear her and also knew it was going to be very difficult for him to move on alone as no-one else was budging, telling Vincent what had occurred when she reached him. 'I have just realised that those who controlled the soldiers in life are still in charge in death. No-one will leave unless they are ordered to. They are all still part of an army unless ... they desert?'

'We only need one to break the spell,' he replied. 'If only one would leave ... Let's get out of here. There is only so much of this anyone can take.'

Vincent loved his food, and as it was lunchtime, they drove to the same restaurant in the mountains that they had walked through the first day. On the way, Mary again pointed out the monument overlooking the sea; the monument to the people of the island that had died in the battle. 'We need to go up there.'

'Later. I am hungry and need to eat. All this takes so much energy.'

After lunch they made their way up to the monument.

'There is no-one here,' is the first thing Mary said when she got out of the car, then added, 'but why would they come here if they are from the island? Wouldn't they go back to their own villages or are they really not coming because we are trying to bring the Germans?'

'That must be why I was asked to drive around the island,' replied Vincent. 'We will do that tomorrow. We will spend the day sightseeing and see what happens.'

After breakfast, they were on the road early; Mary sat looking around as Vincent drove, asking him to stop whenever she saw a graveyard. In it she would just stand and watch any souls still there move on to join all the others that had already joined their leader.

'We will be all day doing this,' Vincent remarked with impatience after stopping for the fifth time.

'No, we won't. As you said, we only have to move a few and the rest will follow. I have done this before with the famine victims at home. After going to a few famine graveyards and watching them move, more followed in time. Oh … that must be what Martin McGuinness meant when he said there were hundreds of thousands of us – he was including those who died in the famine.'

'Why is it always soldiers with you, Mary?' Vincent then asked.

'I don't know. War was all I knew as a child, and soldiers are those who participate in wars and they are probably the people who cause most deaths.'

After a lovely day driving around and eating in beautiful restaurants, Mary went to bed exhausted whilst Vincent went out for a drink to meet the locals after saying, to her relief, that they were taking the next day off.

'Okay, you will find me on the beach if you need me for anything.'

CHAPTER 6

The following day, as Mary sat on her sun lounger with her eyes closed, she expected to get some peace, but instead watched the energy that had originated in Ireland form a long rectangular shape. The Cretan energy did the same, as souls continued to leave the graveyards and join their comrades. This second energy ran in the same direction but did not join the Irish. The British and Commonwealth soldiers had joined together and formed the same shape going in the opposite direction, and to her amazement, the lone German soldier was standing in a rectangle in the opposite direction from the Brits forming the shape of a cross. The same shape she had seen eight years before when the healing energy had started.

The Cretan leader reiterated the fact that he was not allowing his people anywhere near the Germans even if there was only one of them. The British soldier, who she had met in the cemetery, who was the leader of the Commonwealth soldiers, stepped into centre at the same time as Martin McGuinness and Ian Paisley, joining the two sides together as the Cretan and the German soldier stood their ground.

For the rest of the day, Mary lay there reading her book after making one call to her sister to update her with what was happening.

Their last day on the island, all they did was rest and meditate. In her meditations, Mary noticed that another German soldier had broken rank and joined his comrade.

Sitting on the plane later that evening, she thought back to the conversation she'd had with Vincent at the airport a few hours before:

'How come you don't bring people home?' he asked. 'It is what I have always done.'

'I have no idea. It is as if they are creating an energy together that is stronger than being alone. As if it has a purpose.'

'What purpose?'

'I have no idea.'

'Ask.'

'I don't want to know – when I've asked anything in the past it's slowed everything down. I now allow it to take its course and the faster it moves on the sooner I can get back to my own life.'

'I ask lots of questions.'

'I know, but how many answers do you get?'

'Well, I have been told that you and I have a lot of other places to go and work to do.'

'Well, the truth is, Vincent, I can't afford to go anywhere else. I will pay you back for this trip when I get money. In the meantime, I don't want any more debt.'

'Why don't you ask to be given the money if you are to do this work? This energy has access to everything and will get you whatever you need so that you can do what is asked of you.'

'Mmmm ... I can do that. I need a home that is mortgage free and an income until I get my pension.'

'That's not asking for much,' he said.

'A few euros in the bank for a rainy day would be good too,' Mary continued, laughing.

Checking in her meditation later on the plane, she found all the souls from the German graveyard, except their commander, had joined the two comrades, but the cross was not connected.

'I could be carrying all this for months,' she said to Vincent as they headed down the motorway from the airport to his house where she was staying the night.

'Leave it aside, there is nothing else you can do.'

'I know. I already have done that. The only thing I can do now is watch, and I will keep you posted.'

Sleeping soundly that night, Mary woke early, drew her legs in under her body and started her meditation and was immediately catapulted back to the unfinished cross. She heard Martin McGuiness say, *We will achieve nothing unless we all work together*, just before all the energies came together as one. All that had been created in Ireland starting in 2009, all the Cretans, the British, Commonwealth and the Germans too.

'What does that mean?' Vincent asked at breakfast when she told him about her latest vision.

'I have no idea and I don't need to know. I am exhausted. I need to get back home and to the business of making a living.'

CHAPTER 7

B ack in the west, Mary embarked on her latest business idea, but within a week she got a call from Vincent to say that they needed to go to Scotland immediately.

'I can't go.'

'We have to,' Vincent replied. 'We can bring my Jeep and it won't cost you anything.'

'No, I have to pay my way and that Jeep of yours guzzles up diesel. Leave it with me, if we are meant to go it will be easy. If not, I won't be going.'

She looked at both the ferry and flights; both were very expensive with short notice so we guided her to a cheap flight from Derry, plus car rental and accommodation in the places he said they needed to go. Vincent was called and told.

'I will go but only for three nights as I am very busy. We fly out on the 8ᵗʰ of June, the day of Theresa May's snap election.'

'Great,' he replied.

Eleven months after Brexit, they headed for the airport. As they entered the plane in Derry, she knew they had company. Martin McGuinness was there with Paisley hanging back deciding whether or not to come.

Come on, Ian, said Martin, laughing. *There is nothing more you can do. People have made up their minds and aren't going to change them just because you are around. We have work to do. Let's go.*

And with that, he joined them.

An hour later they were picking up the hired car.

'What do you think the election results will be?' Mary asked the young man in the car rental as Vincent looked on, bored with her question.

'I think the Scottish will bring a protest vote as they are not happy leaving Europe. My friends don't agree, but I have voted that way.'

'Interesting,' Mary said to Vincent as they got into the car.

'You know I have no interest in politics,' he replied as they drove up the motorway to the first guest house.

'I haven't either, but I love watching politicians. I once heard someone say a politician thinks of the next election, a statesman thinks of the next generation. We have had very few statesmen.'

'Have we ever had any?' Vincent enquired, raising his eyebrow.

'Yes ... Martin McGuinness.'

'Really ... I thought he was a called a terrorist.'

'He was called a lot of different things by a lot of different people, Vincent. Now he would be considered a statesman by most leaders. Did you watch his funeral? Leaders from all over the world came to show their respect to a man who helped to broker our peace agreement. And by the way, he isn't the only statesman that's been called a terrorist in the past!'

He didn't answer.

Arriving late, they went to bed, but not before seeing the tallyman's prediction, and it wasn't looking good for Theresa May, but it seemed as if Ian and Martin's parties were taking all the seats in the North of Ireland.

They headed up another motorway for the north coast the following day where Vincent had work to do – that is after hearing that Theresa May's snap election had backfired.

Mary said, 'Her days are numbered, Vincent. Now not only

will America be run by a right-wing government, but looks like Boris Johnson is making his way to be the next prime minister.'

Driving on up through the highlands they were laughing about something when everything changed.

'You feel that?' asked Vincent.

'Yes!' she replied, shocked with the intensity of the energy and how quickly it had changed.

'What is it? There is nothing around here. Not a sight of a car, a house or anything.'

She couldn't answer; the energy had taken her breath away. Not unlike when she was in the German cemetery, but there was nothing to be seen in this wilderness. They drove on and over a small hill to be met with the sight of a huge monument surrounded by buses, cars and people.

'What the hell is that?' asked Vincent.

'I have no idea.'

'Let's check it out. The energy here needs to be cleared.'

As they drove in slowly to the car park, Mary stared at the two soldiers on the monument and her blood ran cold.

'What is it?' asked Vincent.

'Looks like a monument to the commandos.'

'Who are they?'

'Killing machines. Assassins.'

'They are soldiers. Aren't they all trained to kill?'

'Not like these. They are special units, trained to kill like they did in Derry on Bloody Sunday and the SAS who shot my brother when they killed Seamus McElwaine.'

'Let's go,' Vincent said as he got out of the car. 'I need to clear something here.'

She followed him even though she didn't want to move. Immediately, there was a young commando beside her. She felt sick.

We need help, he said. *We need to get out of here.* She didn't reply even with a thought, so scared of what he represented, trying her best not to think of anything knowing what these soldiers were capable of when alive. Dead, they had created an energy that no-one but Vincent and her seemed to be able to feel.

We didn't know what we were doing, he continued in the most distressing voice she'd ever heard. Mary did not answer but couldn't stop her memory of the soldier waking her with the point of his gun when she was fourteen years old, the time when she was convinced her family were going to be massacred. Followed by the memory of lying on the floor of her brother's car after the soldiers said that they were all going to be shot before they reached the next corner of the road, then the trigger of a gun being pulled at her head at the age of eighteen when her entire family were threatened with the Shankill Butchers if she ever told what happened to her, all making her want to vomit. She could barely walk but needed to walk away from this commando. He followed her.

We didn't know what we were doing, he repeated. "*We were trained to kill, to do as we were commanded, without question. We need help. Please help us.* Feeling the tears congregate around her eyes, ready to spill at any moment, she scanned the crowd looking for Vincent and found him standing at the other side of the memorial with his head down. Finally making it back in the car where Vincent was waiting, they drove off and neither spoke for nearly an hour, until Vincent pulled over into a park beside a river and said, 'What was that all about?'

'It is a monument built to the commandos in the Second World War, but commandos from all over the world that have passed away since have congregated there and they all want to be released.'

'And have to be,' he replied. 'I cleared as much stuff there as I could, and they are ready to go. You need to move them on.'

'You know these are the people I feared my entire life. Feared as a child that they would come in and kill all my family without fear of conviction. They shot my brother and his friend, murdered

Seamus as he lay on the ground defenceless. They could have arrested them, but this was a shoot-to-kill policy sanctioned by their government and they were sent in to shoot and kill so many people. The commandos at that monument have killed innocent people all over the world. They were called the red berets in the North. In America I think they are called army rangers.

'But they are dead now and need to move on.'

'I know they are, but you have to allow me to say what I have to say and feel what I feel, Vincent. I understand and accept that they were living the life they were meant to live but that doesn't make it any easier for me.'

They walked along by the river for some fresh air and exercise then got back into the car and drove in silence to the place they were staying on their second night in Scotland.

Later at dinner, Vincent asked again, 'What is it about you and soldiers?'

'This is where my trauma originated, and I guess it is what I need to heal from most. I'm always brought to places where I am forced to face my past, a place where I have an opportunity to heal, to grow, to move on.'

'I know nothing about war or history,' he replied.

'Neither do I, only my own. I know your trauma came from an entirely different source but with the same results. Like me, you saw past this life into another, you know that we are all moving back into the same energy that we came from. I know that I am a spiritual being having a human experience, but I still have to deal with that human experience. My tai chi teacher always said, "If you didn't feel it when it was going in, you have to feel it when it is coming out." I numbed all feeling to survive. I now have no choice but to feel them.'

The commando that had followed her woke her in the middle of that night, pleading for help as Mary lay frozen in the bed, unable to reply. The following day, after Vincent had finished the work that he had come to do, they drove back towards the airport. As the flight wasn't until the next day, she had booked them into the only place she could find, a twin-bedded room in a guest house. She really didn't have a problem with this as they were now friends and had no doubt that this, like everything else, happened for a reason.

As they slept, the energy between them strengthened. She was now ready to do what needed to be done, accepting Vincent's energy to help do it. In their meditation together she watched the commando join the energy of the other soldiers, taking his comrades and those who had congregated at the memorial with him. Then, just before the meditation ended, he came back alone and shocked her to the core when he asked if she would help them take everyone they had killed in all the wars and conflicts they had been involved in, and we watched as the tears flowed down her face with both surprise and gratitude.

She didn't say a word, but he had read it from her heart; she was absolutely delighted to help. She sat back and watched as souls from all over the world came home to this energy. This was something Mary had never experienced before and knew that by following our guidance, the right thing happened. Not only was she free, but so were thousands of others. Telling Vincent what had happened as they drove to the airport, she said, 'It is as if this energy is coming together for some reason, it is getting stronger and stronger – there has to be reason.'

'Ask.'

'No! I am being guided one step at a time, and that is all I can handle. One step at a time.'

She then continued by telling him that the only time she had asked what was going to happen was when she was completely overwrought after her younger brother Kevin was arrested two years after he had been released from Long Kesh (also known as the Maze Prison). 'He had already spent most of his twenties in Long Kesh and now he was incarcerated again in Crumlin Road Jail awaiting a trial, guilty until proven innocent! Verballed, the policeman saying that he admitted to the crime. No-one had any hope of him getting out, he was facing twenty-five years in prison even though he had witnesses placing him elsewhere when the incident happened. I simply asked, *Will he get out?* and they replied, *Yes.* For the following two and a half years I was the only person who gave him hope. The solicitors and barristers were fighting the system for his release but no- one held out any hope with the justice system they were dealing with. The day he was released he said to me, "'You were the only one who saw me out, Mary.'"

Vincent didn't answer as they drove on to the airport in silence.

CHAPTER 8

Mary had no problem telling her children the things that were happening to her. Roisín always listened but said nothing. Jarlath once made the remark, 'Don't you think there's lots of work to be done in this country, Mam? Lots of people who may need to move on?'

'Yes, Jarlath, I certainly do, and I have done a lot and I know there is a lot more to do, but I can't do a thing unless I am asked.'

It was now June 2017, and Mary decided to go to Dublin to do some work that she believed needed to be done, not sure if she was being asked or the conversation with Jarlath had prompted her to take matters into her own hands.

By this time, she had watched leaders in the North enter the energy that had been created, and others followed from the Republic but none from the War of Independence, nor the civil war that followed, even though the aftermath of the civil war had seeped into every blade of grass in the country. It was rarely talked about, remaining the elephant in the room as families tried to blank the trauma it had left in their lives.

The night before Vincent picked her up to bring her to the gaol, she stayed with her brother and his partner Caitriona. The following morning Caitriona asked, 'Are you going to Kilmainham Gaol for a reason?'

257

'Yes.'

'To help those that might be stuck there?' she enquired as her and Mary had talked about this before.

'I don't know. It might just be me that wants to go as when things are personal it's so easy to pick it up wrong. I never studied Irish history but I know enough to understand that there are lots of souls still trapped.'

Arriving at the gaol, she and Vincent found a long queue at the entrance waiting to get in and were told that it would be after lunch before they could gain admission. Knowing Vincent wouldn't have the patience to wait, she said, 'What do you think, Vincent? Will we just walk around the building to see if we can feel anything?'

'Okay,' he replied.

They walked up to the traffic lights and turned right at the corner when Vincent realised that the keys of his Jeep were missing.

'Go look for them and I will wait here.'

As soon as he left, Mary put her back to the railing and felt as if she was nailed to the ground, unable to move a muscle, wanting to close her eyes but afraid to, feeling really vulnerable as cars stopped at the pedestrian crossing and the energy from the prison overwhelmed her.

When Vincent returned with his keys, she said, 'Please, just stand there beside me. I need to close my eyes, and I'm afraid I might fall.'

'Okay, sure.'

With her eyes closed, she could see the souls of all those executed in the prison rise (even though they were behind her) then come together over the building. It was fast and intense. Taking Vincent's arm for support, she kept her eyes closed for another while but nothing else happened.

'Let's go. I'm finished. Is there somewhere I could sit down?' she asked as her heart thumped in her chest and her legs were so weak they could barely carry her.

'Yep. Hotel across the road,' he said as he took her by the arm, then went to get her a drink.

Sitting there like a zombie, feeling as weak as a kitten, Mary stared ahead, afraid to move.

After telling Vincent what had happened, he asked, 'Is there anywhere else you need to go?'

'No. I am finished, I'm not able for anything else.'

On the way back to her brother's house he asked her a question again that he had asked her many times before, 'Do you think we are the only ones doing this – there has to be others? We couldn't be the only ones, but I have never met anyone else. Maybe it's just the two of us and we are both mad.'

She smiled but didn't have the strength to answer.

Back in her brother's empty house, Mary sat in a meditation before heading home. In it she could see the one energy over the gaol and expected that they would move to join the others, but not a move was made. An hour later, after a rest and some food, she got into her car and drove slowly out of the capital.

* * *

In the following weeks, Mary blanked everything that had happened the previous few months as she prepared her house for her new business – that is, after she rented the cottage. She had come to the conclusion that she knew better than us even though we were the only ones in possession of the map of her journey, deciding that if she could get three old people to share her big house, she could afford to keep it, which was not going to happen. We watched as she emailed the local radio station presenter with her idea which he thought was great and invited her on to talk about it.

* * *

Her fifty-eighth birthday came and went in a flurry of work on her home, and by July she was ready to start. After the radio interview on the 11th, the calls started to come in and she was delighted. At the same time, renovations had started on the bottom level of her split-level bungalow in Castlerea where her extended family had lived. That is after she finally took our advice and took it off the market, to the relief of her son who was living there with his girlfriend Laura (the children who had met the week that Laura was born!).

Mary was now under the illusion that she could keep all her properties, so asked for and received financial help from her brother again, knowing that the rent from the family home and the cottage would easily pay him back. Believing all was well in her world, she was literally stopped in her tracks the following week when she got a letter from the bank that began *Under Section 37 of The Criminal Justice* [money laundering and terrorist financing] *Act of 2010*. Not able to read another line as her entire past was flashed before her in that moment, she handed it over to her friend Timothy who we had arranged to be with her for this bombshell.

'They can't do that!' he said when he finished reading the rest of the letter out loud.

The bank was demanding information from her regarding her sources of income (and her with none!) because she was deemed to be an immediate family member of a PEP (politically exposed person). Shocked to receive such a letter and under no doubt that if she gave any information she would be opening herself up to them looking into her past income, which had been made in New York in the eighties when both her and her ex-husband were illegal aliens. With no way to prove this income as her boss in NYC was now dead and with no intentions of jeopardising the relationship she had with the father of her children to entertain any bank, she was snookered – again.

'Another huge organisation with the power to destroy me, Timothy,' she said

Or change your direction! we whispered.

By the end of the day, Mary was a nervous wreck, knowing that the threat of closing her bank accounts was real if the information requested was not handed over, so, was left with no choice but to postpone the start of the new business venture until this was sorted, as without the confidence of a fully functioning current account, she couldn't run a business.

As no other member of her family had received such a letter, including the politician in question, Mary was under no doubt that she had been singled out because of an incident in the past when she had got an apology and compensation for the behaviour of a bank official when buying the building of her ex-husband.

Realising this, she asked us for help again, and we were only too glad to be of service as we were aware of a huge change that was coming to the planet she was living on, something that would stop the entire world in its tracks. A change that no-one could foresee, and Mary needed to be free of this latest venture when this change took place.

We reminded her of the words spoken by a woman she had met a few weeks before, as she worked on her friend's organic farm, 'If you ever have any issues with the bank, get in touch with my ex-husband.' And that night she contacted Liam.

'Never heard of such a thing, send me the letter,' he said. 'We need to write to the bank for an explanation.'

So, the letters to and from the bank started and her business idea was put on hold, even though by this time Mary had read the law and understood that in it she was not considered to be an immediate family member of her brother, the politician.

This was not the first time that Mary had faced a system that was there to change her direction. This time they weren't carrying guns and did not have the power to either kill or imprison her, but they did have the power to leave her destitute by selling her properties in a fire sale if she didn't sell them herself.

Thankfully throughout this, Mary continued to meditate which kept her in constant contact with us, and going to CoDA meetings for over two years, was ready to do the twelve steps but never found anyone she trusted. Then one night a lady walked into a meeting, and before she opened her mouth, Mary had felt the connection. After listening to her speak at meetings for a few months, she finally asked if she would be her sponsor.

Knowing that the relationship with Gerry was over, Mary felt the need to finish with him before the first meeting with her sponsor, but again was forcing something that had not yet come to a conclusion. The following week she was back with him.

'I thought you said it was over?' her sponsor said at their next meeting.

'It's nearly over,' she replied like a child as she looked at the puzzled expression on the other woman's face. 'I need it to die its own natural death. I need to let go with love.'

The following week, Gerry, who was now living in the next county, arrived at her home, late as usual. He wasn't in through the door when he had to take yet another call from someone he was in a co-dependent relationship with. The feeling of resentment swept through Mary like a tornado, but instead of reacting, she walked out the door and off to a meeting and returned later to find him gone. 'I wasn't feeling well,' he said when he answered her call. Fifteen minutes later she got a text message that read: *I miss you already, I will miss you so much. I wish it could be so.*

Mary knew instantly that this was the natural ending that she had been waiting for. He had written from his heart, aware that she had moved on, and he couldn't cope with the change in her. He had let her go with love and she accepted it, knowing she would miss him too but also aware that her co-dependent relationship with him was over. He had been a wonderful teacher, but the lessons had been learnt and it was time for her to move on.

A few nights later, as Mary sat alone in her big house, a woman called asking her if she would take her aunt into her home, short-term if necessary. As this was the first of the elderly people who had contacted her in the summer, she replied, 'Yes!'

Liam's letters had forced the bank to withdraw the request for the information they sought, but Mary wasn't happy with the fact that they stated that the request for the same information could by requested again at any time in the future, so had written back questioning this and was waiting on a reply when Philomena moved in, then, decided it was best to go with Liam to a local solicitor for help. As they sat in his office looking for assistance, he uttered the words, 'What do you expect coming from a family like yours?'

She had no doubt what he meant as he ignored the fact that it was his ancestors that had put her family in the position they found themselves in, or the fact that no-one else in her family had received such a letter!

Looking at her stunned face, he tried to backtrack, knowing he was way out of order.

'What are you most afraid of?' he then asked.

'That they will resend the letter and I will be left with no option but to put the elderly people in residence out and have to sell the property.'

He leaned back on his seat and said with arrogance, 'They made a stupid mistake once; they are not likely to make it again.'

Feeling little comfort going home that dark November evening in 2017, no longer surprised with the reaction she got because of her background but delighted that she didn't stoop to his level, she immediately got back to work with her plans, believing the solicitor knew the banks better than she did.

But within weeks, not only did the bank send the same letter again from a different department but also called in her mortgage. When she couldn't believe things could get worse, her aunt in America died. Three blows that left her reeling.

This was her Aunt Lucy who had sent clothes from the States to clothe her and her siblings when they were children. The aunt who had been like a second mother to them when they were in exile in New York. The same aunt that she had gone to help out three years before when the neighbours had alerted the family of her behaviour due to Alzheimer's. At that time, her father had wanted to bring his sister home where he, her only brother and her seventeen nieces and nephews, could take care of her. Instead, the American court decided it was best for her to stay where she was under the guardianship of two conservators who were to look after her, but they didn't. With lots of distressing calls from her aunt's wonderful neighbours, her family had no choice but to go back to court to get Lucy into a nursing home. As the conservators still retained all rights over her, they had not allowed any member of Mary's family to communicate with Lucy either by visiting or even talking to her on the phone, but they were able to see her on the Facebook page of the nursing home and had to be content with the fact that she was safe, no longer wandering the roads at night alone. Now she was dead. This was communicated to the family by the neighbours. When arrangements were being made by Mary's sisters to attend the funeral, the conservators buried her before they could book their tickets!

'What is wrong with those people?' her brother asked in a rage when he called. 'What did they achieve?'

'Control,' Mary replied.

'No! Her estate,' he answered.

'No, I don't believe they have her estate. They tried to change her will when we were there in 2014 but I saw the will. It was all left to Dad.'

'Not that I care about the money, but after all they put us through, I would hate to see them get anything.'

As Christmas rolled in, Mary was feeling totally overwhelmed with all that was happening but strong enough to call her auctioneer and ask him to take the cottage off the market and to put the new house she was living in on, finally surrendering to what was to be. After spending the Christmas with her parents, children, brother, sister and niece, she faced 2018 knowing she may have lost her aunt, her home, her business and her companion, but had connected with us at a level never reached before and gained a sponsor that was guiding her into a new life with a solid foundation.

CHAPTER 9

To Mary's surprise (not ours) the auctioneer valued her home at a much higher price than she had expected; a price that would clear all her debts and leave her with money in the bank. She would be free from all mortgages and with an income from the original family home and its flats in the basement to sustain her, and she was right about her aunt's will. Everything was left to her father, and her parents decided to divide the money from the estate between their twelve children, which wasn't a huge amount of money but it was a huge amount to Mary, who had none. Things were now flowing as she surrendered to her journey.

Her brother offered her the money to pay off her mortgage arrears and free herself from the bank as the money from the inheritance would pay him back, and for a moment we thought she would go back to square one, but instead she replied, 'Thanks, Peter, but I think everything is indicating that I let this place go.'

When her tenants in the cottage decided to move, Mary took the opportunity to get it ready for herself, deciding that if she was going to live there it would be in a comfortable and cosy space. The only thing she could afford at the time was paint, which was what she needed to do first and now had the time to do it.

As spring ran into summer, homes were found for the elderly people living with her and the small cottage got ready for rent, leaving the bigger one for herself, finally learning to put herself first. But not one person came to see the property for sale and the banks started putting more and more pressure on her. Then they started court proceedings.

Feeling desperate, she asked the auctioneer why no-one was viewing.

'It's too big for most people,' John told her.

'What if we cut the price?'

'It won't make any difference. It is still too big for most people, but we only need one buyer and it is worth what we are asking.'

'Okay, John,' she replied, trusting that he knew what he was doing, which he did.

With the painting finished in both cottages and only one guest left in the big house with a date for her move, her sister called one evening and said, 'Mary, I think Mam and Dad need someone with them full-time now as even though they are in good shape, Dad is nearly a hundred and Mam nearly ninety. When is your last guest leaving?'

'The 10th of June, I will then have all the time in the world to help.'

'Great.'

The following day, Geraldine called again. 'I'm in Derry hospital with Mam. She broke her hip last night!'

Two weeks later, her mother was released from hospital the day before Mary's last guest was leaving. The following morning, we watched as Mary took her usual walk up the mountain road with her neighbour.

'What are you going to do now?' Terri asked.

'I will call the auctioneer on my way North today and ask him to rent the wee cottage and I will move to the bigger one if my house ever sells.'

Returning from the walk later, she was surprised to see two men sitting on her sofa and Joan (who had been helping her with the elderly guests) serving them tea. Recognising one of the men as someone who would keep her back talking all day, she glared at Joan.

'Joan says you have a cottage to rent,' said the man she doesn't know.

'Yes,' she replied through gritted teeth. 'It is small.''

'Only need a small place … Can I see it?'

Mary really didn't have the time as Philomena's family were on the way to pick her up, but she heard us whisper, *Show it to him.*

Walking down to the cottage, she explained that the two cottages were connected and that he wouldn't have use of the garden.

'I don't want a garden.'

With no time to negotiate anything, she told them the rent, then added, 'Sorry, I really don't have any more time to chat. Think about it but I will be calling the auctioneer in the next hour to put it up for rent.'

'I will take it,' the man said.

Shocked she replied, 'Fine. I will be back on Thursday and if you are still interested you can call me then.'

'I will be,' he answered. 'I can get you a deposit now if you can wait.'

'Sorry, I can't wait as my parents are expecting me in two hours, but don't worry, it won't be rented before Thursday as no-one else has a key.'

After kissing Philomena goodbye, Mary headed North realising that if the rental came through, she would have enough income to survive. All she needed to do now was to sell her home.

Four days later, Timothy helped Paddy move into the cottage. For the rest of the summer, Mary spent three days every week with her parents caring for them both, leaving her little time to do anything else.

Then one day in August, Vincent called to say they needed to go to Belgium immediately. 'I see a huge war memorial in my meditations, something to do with another war, so you need to come with me. We really need to go, and I can't do it without you. You are the one with a connection to soldiers and there is no use in me going alone.'

'Leave it with me. I will let you know.'

Go with him, we whispered.

The following day she booked two one-way flights to Brussels when Vincent informed her it was Flanders they were going. As he had no idea how long they would be, there were no return flights booked.

'Do you know anything about it?' he asked on the way to the airport.

'About what?'

'Flanders?'

'Something to do with World War I. Don't know anything else and didn't have time to do any research as you were in such a hurry!'

They arrived safely, got the hire car and headed straight to a beautiful small village where she had booked an apartment for three nights. After bed and breakfast, they drove out into the countryside through the flattest land she had ever seen, and there in the middle of working farms, were lots of small cemeteries.

'Stop!' she said to Vincent after they had driven a few miles. He followed her across the road to a cemetery as a tractor worked in the next field. He sat at the entrance as she walked through the crosses of young men slaughtered in a war where there were twenty million deaths and twenty-one million wounded (something Google had told her at the airport).

'Nothing going to budge there,' she said to Vincent when they got back to the car, getting the same feeling in the next three cemeteries on the same long stretch of road.

'Let's go to the place I was told to go,' Vincent said as Mary thought, *What the hell is going on, and if everything is so calm, what are we doing here?*

They finally found Palingbeek Park and followed the crowd

into a forest where there was a huge memorial to all the soldiers that had died in Belgium in WWI. The memorial looked like a huge egg with a lot of little eggs surrounding it. It was only when they got closer that she realised that the little eggs were clay sculptures of bodies hunched down showing the outline of their spine as they held their heads between their legs. There was 600,000 of these, one to represent every victim that had died in Belgium between 1914–1918. The sculpture was called 'Coming World Remember Me', located in a place called The Bluff. The brochure read: *The statues depict a bent human form, which seems to be lost in contemplation. At the same time, the figure also seems to be bracing itself, as though preparing to face a challenge. The pronounced BACKBONE underlines the power of the life force, the determination to carry on, the desire to build and not to destroy.*

This all made perfect sense to Mary, who was honoured to be there, for whatever reason.

'I need to clear the space here for something,' said Vincent, and whilst he took a seat on another bench, she continued to wander around.

In the information centre she read that the monument was built on what was known as 'no man's land', the scene of some of the most terrible fighting of the war and that this was where some of the war's cruellest weapons were used for the first time, such as mustard gas and flamethrowers. The monument had been built in April of that year, very close to the hundredth anniversary which was on the 11th of November, when people representing soldiers from 125 modern-day nations were to meet to acknowledge those who fought in Flanders. She read that the artist Koen Vanmechelen sees the work as a warning against forgetting, saying: 'It is very dangerous that we could easily create a new war if we don't know what war is.'

Reading these words, Mary felt a shiver down her spine, like someone had walked on her grave. The small, egg-like sculptures were made over a period of four years in various workshops by many different people, of many different nationalities, leaving their own mark on them after they were given the name of the person it represented.

Walking through the woods later, she found a section of it was dedicated to the poets that had died during the war, and one of them was Irish.

Meeting Vincent back at the car she asked, 'Can we go to where Francis Ledwidge is buried as he is the only Irish name I can find here?'

He nodded. They drove around for the next hour until finally the GPS led them to an industrial estate. As they drove out to the junction and indicated to turn left, we guided her eye to the right, and there in the middle of a field, an Irish flag flew in the gentle breeze. 'That must be it, Vincent!' Mary said, delighted.

He turned right, then left down a narrow road and found the spot where Francis Ledwidge had been killed. After saying a prayer at his place of death and another at the headstone which bore his name in the adjoining cemetery, they went back to the apartment.

After a meditation together the following morning Vincent said, 'We need to go back to Palingbeek.'

Whilst he sat again on the same bench, clearing the space that so much trauma had blocked, she walked on alone. This time we guided her to a lookout post above the field where thousands of soldiers had met their maker. Standing there, Mary felt the energy change dramatically, then watched as thousands of souls arrived to take their place at the statue that was made to represent them then stood frozen for about fifteen minutes before slowly making her way back to the car in a daze.

'There must have been a mass movement from all the cemeteries in Belgium, Vincent. I watched as they greeted their friends, comrades and victims in this place that was so carefully constructed to represent them.'

'Do you think if they don't leave when we are here, will they leave on the 11th of November? Do we need to come back?'

'We will be told, but right now I need to get out of here. I am exhausted. I need to go home.' It was only when Mary got on the computer to book flights that she realised, since they had cut themselves off from the outside world, Ryanair pilots had gone on strike!

'There has to be two seats on some plane,' Vincent said over her shoulder.

Exhausted too and feeling under huge pressure, she found two seats on a flight early next morning. 'Book them,' Vincent said. It was only when they got back to the apartment after dinner that she realised she had got the dates wrong and had booked flights for the following week, then rechecked everything to find that they had no way of getting home.

With little sleep, they left early next morning and tried in vain to explain their situation to the airline official as thousands sat stranded at the airport.

'We have to get out of here,' Vincent repeated a few times.

Always good in a crisis, Mary checked trains to London, believing that they would have a better chance of getting home from there, but they were all booked out.

Coming back with the bad news to Vincent, he told her that his daughter had called him back to say that they could get a bus from the centre of Brussels to London and that they could return the car close to the bus terminal. Driving through Brussels that Saturday morning, the city was like a dead town. Mary looked in amazement as they passed the parliament building, something she had seen so often on the news but never believed she would ever be near, as Brussels would never be on her bucket list (if she had one).

After dropping off the car, they took a train to the bus station, arriving just in time to get on, sighing with relief as they climbed up the steps as the timetable they had been given was wrong. This relief didn't last long after the realisation that they were arriving in the centre of London at 11pm with nowhere to stay.

As the bus headed for the Channel Tunnel, we reminded her that this was the same journey she took thirty-nine years before when returning from Germany at the age of twenty, so she sat in her seat serenely, knowing that if we could keep her safe when she was travelling alone in 1979, she would be okay in 2018 with company but immediately took out her laptop and started looking for accommodation at a price they could afford in London city centre. The only thing available in their price range was a double room without a window and she wasn't going there – rooms with no windows were cells to her. All the rest were so expensive, but she had no doubt they were on the right road. Why, she didn't need to know, but Vincent did and it wasn't sitting well with him.

Ten hours later they arrived in London on time, but still without accommodation. Vincent asked the newspaper vender at the bus station if he knew of anywhere they could get a room for the night.

'Is it the Ritz you are looking for?' he replied, grinning as he saw Mary's rucksack. 'Out of the station, turn right, there are plenty of guest houses,' he continued.

Mary thanked him as Vincent marched out of the station and started ringing doorbells. Every place was full. At this point Mary would have paid anything for a bed as the alternative was sleeping rough.

Finally, he came out of a guest house smiling and said, 'I have found a place and it's not far from here.' When he mentioned the name, she knew that it was the same one she had found on the internet, but said nothing.

'Is there any chance that you have a room with a window?' she asked when they stood in front of the receptionist.

'Actually, we have,' the lady replied.

'Same price?' Mary enquired with a smile.

'Okay, I will give it to you at the same price.'

Mary smiled again and asked, 'Would it possible to get a twin-bedded room with a window?' Wondering if she would choose a single bed or a window if given a choice.

'No twin-bedded room here,' was the reply, so that was settled.

Entering the bedroom five minutes later, her idea of sleeping on the floor was shattered as she looked at a room that had only space for the double bed. The bathroom was like the toilet on a plane with no space for her there either so off they went to find something to eat.

Later, as they climbed the stairs again in better humour, she said in a flash of inspiration, 'You can sleep at the top of the bed and I will sleep at the bottom.' And this they did, reminding her how often they did this as children when they had visitors staying.

After sleeping the sleep of the dead, they made their way out to find breakfast and a way home. The breakfast was easy, the way home was to take all day until finally, they got a flight to Dublin at €250 a seat! This was money that Mary could ill afford, yet had no choice but to pay it, as no-one knew how long the strike was going to last and the price of seats were going up by the minute.

'We should never have been here,' Vincent said on the train to the airport.

'How could we be here if we were not meant to be? You are never where you are not meant to be,' she replied.

'Give me one reason we were in London?' he asked.

Mary had already been thinking about this in their long silences, not for his benefit but for her own.

'We started in Dublin. We flew to Brussels, bus to London and now we are flying back to Dublin.'

'I know where we have been. Give me one reason why. Just one reason.

'Dublin. Brussels. London. A triangle.'

'So ...?'

'These are the three cities that will negotiate Brexit. These three cities are the crux of the matter of negotiating trade

agreements between the EU and UK. Did you realise that we stayed in a hotel at the back of the houses of parliament last night after driving by the European parliament buildings in Brussels yesterday?'

He didn't answer.

She thought it might be a strange reason but she couldn't come up with any other, until writing this when we reminded her again of the number of deaths and injuries the wars in Europe had caused in the twentieth century alone and how important it was for countries to work together to keep the peace. The border she had grown up beside now divided not only the island of Ireland, but also the UK from the EU and the border her and Vincent moved across every day between their realm and ours helped those who were caught in no man's land.

They sat apart in the airport and arrived in Dublin without another word being uttered. Mary was tired and hungry and just wanted to get home without saying something she might regret, so the journey from the airport to Vincent's house was continued in silence. There, she picked up her car and headed west, doubting if she would hear from Vincent for a while, nor did she want to as her bank account was now seriously in the red and no money due for a while.

Driving home that day, Mary realised that in the middle of the chaos of the past few days, not only had they created a space for thousands of people to come together to heal, but also that in it she had never been more serene in her life, achieved by surrendering and trusting that all was as it was meant to be.

CHAPTER 10

It was now the 12ᵗʰ of August 2018, and Mary had started working on a new plan for her home that not one person had come to view. A plan that we had whispered to her in a meditation. It would involve a little work, cost a little money, but it would put her in a better position for the sale that was coming, even though we had let her dream that maybe she would be able to keep the property. We showed her a vision of the front garden finished and the house divided into apartments that could be rented. The garden really needed to be done as the front of the house still looked like a building site and she was willing to spend the money as a garden would be needed for her new tenants. Before the end of the week, the digger had started its work, that is, after the auctioneer had been called and he had confirmed that apartments would be easy to rent as there was a shortage of accommodation in the county, but he needed to see how the house was going to be divided.

Her brother Noel was knocking down a wall between the kitchen and a bedroom when John arrived the following Monday morning. Showing him her plans, he told her what she could expect to get in rent and she was delighted. Being flexible by nature, she had already started down a different track with the same enthusiasm she brought into everything.

As he was leaving, John turned, hesitating for a moment before asking, 'If you got a buyer, would you still sell?'

'Ahh, yes, but we would need to have someone interested soon as I hope to have the apartments ready in a few weeks.'

'Okay ... it's just that this man keeps ringing and asking about the house.'

'He is probably just someone local being nosy'

'No! He is from Dublin and asking all the right questions and I think he really is interested.'

'Fine, then tell him to come see it soon or forget it,' Mary replied.

'I will. I don't have a number for him, but I know he will call back.'

'You need topsoil,' Kevin (the digger man) said when John left, deleting the previous conversation from her mind. She now had the opportunity to keep her home with the added bonus of paying no tax on the income, as she was entitled to rent out rooms in her home earning up to €14,000 tax free.

'Where would I get topsoil?' we heard her ask Kevin, as she thought of all the times she had looked before.

'What about asking your man who is digging foundations for a house down the road?'

'Brilliant idea. I will go now.'

'How much do you want?' the man on the digger asked.

'Two dumper loads,' Mary replied as she spied the dumpster behind him.

'Okay, I will have it up to you before the end of the day.'

That evening it was delivered, and before Kevin left, the entire garden was levelled and the topsoil on. It looked good but all the stones needed to be picked. When Noel arrived back on Monday, the stones were all picked, and she was cutting the briars in the hedge with grass seed on her mind when a local farmer stopped his tractor and said, 'You are doing a great job, Mary. I know it is very hard work and I wish I could help but I will set the grass seed for you. I have some in the barn and I will do it this evening.'

'What kind of grass seed, Joe?' knowing in her heart that he was talking about seed for the land.

'What I put on my field, but it is also on my garden and it is the only seed strong enough to grow at this time of the year. Trust me, it will work.'

'Okay,' Mary replied doubtfully, but trusted that as everything was flowing, he must have been sent to her. Later that evening, she and Noel watched from the front door as Joe sowed the seed, delighted with how different the house looked with the front garden done, showing off the beautiful wee granary, no longer looking like a building site.

Staring at the bedroom ceiling that night, Mary thought of the thousand euro spent on the garden and knew another few thousand would be needed for the inside work, but her overdraft had come in handy again and she didn't mind using it as by this time her aunt's house had been sold in the States.

The following day the auctioneer called. 'You know the man I told you about last week, the one that was interested in your house?'

'Yes.'

'He wants to see it.'

'When?'

'This weekend?'

'Okay. I hope you told him that I have started to change it into apartments … and tell him that I have Roisín and a crowd of her friends staying for the weekend. They are down for the music festival in Ballina.'

'Okay, I will tell him and see what he says.'

John called later to say they still wanted to view that weekend. On the Friday night, Mary joined her cousin Tony for one of the concerts. After a great night out, she rose the following morning full of the joys of autumn, and when John arrived with the couple to view the house, there were seven people at the breakfast table so the viewing started with the bedrooms which were a mess. Not in the least bit bothered, Mary continued showing the house, answering questions as the auctioneer followed.

Later she said to Michael, 'I am in a unique position. I am the seller and also the person they are bidding against because I don't care what happens. At any other time in the past nine months, I would be at the mercy of the only person who came to see the house. Today I feel under no pressure. I must say my guides have put me in a position that I never believed possible, all I have to do is go with the flow. I watch with interest to see what happens next. Will I stay or will I go? Time will tell.'

On Monday morning as she was heading North to take care of her parents, the auctioneer called with a bid on the house.

'Let me think about it, John,' she replied, as it was more than she had originally thought she would get for the house, but a lot less than the asking price.

The following morning after her meditation, Mary texted John to say that she wanted 20,000 more than she was offered. It would split the difference, which was still 20,000 less than the asking price, finishing the text by saying: *They can take it or leave it. Let me know what they say.*

She had just pressed send when there was a rap on her bedroom window, and when she pulled the curtains, two of her brothers stood there as pale as ghosts.

'Piaras was killed last night in a car accident,' Noel said.

'Piaras who?' Mary asked as her mind had only picked up the face of one Piaras she knew, and he was dead.

'Ruth's Piaras.'

Running up the corridor to let her brothers into the house thinking, *Ruth's baby!* forgetting that Ruth's baby had turned eighteen and had just bought his own car.

'Will you tell Mam and Dad?' Noel asked at the door, as the tears ran down Mary's face. She nodded, knowing her brothers had already spent the night comforting Ruth and her family and were fit for no more.

'Ruth's bonny boy,' her mother said as she sat on the side of the bed getting dressed. Not a woman to cry, she put her head down and whispered, 'Tell Daddy.'

Her father was in the sitting room putting on his shoes when he was told. 'Ahhh ... take care of Ruth.'

This was the man who said when Gary (his other grandson) was killed, 'Gary had his work done.' He had been eighty-two at that time, Gary had been twenty-three but Mary knew her father had always understood death in the way that she was learning to.

Before the day was out, she was headed home to the west to get clothes for the funeral, as she told her mother – but the truth was, Mary needed to be alone after driving to Castlerea to see Jarlath first. He had met his cousin and the rest of the family in the North a month before to celebrate his grandfather's hundredth birthday and now had to return to face his eighteen-year-old cousin's funeral. He was distraught.

'Stay here with us if you want to, Mam,' he said, but she shook her head.

That night, Mary woke in the dark and screamed as if everyone belonging to her had died and in that scream released all her false beliefs of having any control over anyone's life and finally understood what her father had always known. When your time is up, you are going home, no matter what age you are. She had known and accepted this at eighteen years old. She had let go and survived. Piaras was eighteen and dead.

Thinking of the three-hundred-mile journey Roisín had to make from Cork where she was working at the film festival, Mary knew she was powerless over her children's journey, powerless over everything.

After the funeral, she drove home accepting that her days were numbered, finally understanding what powerlessness was.

A week later she accepted the bid on her home which had been increased by €10,000.

CHAPTER 11

With the house sold, Mary was totally at sea, wondering what to do next whilst grieving the loss of the boy with the mop of curly hair who brought so much joy to so many, especially her sister Ruth. Understanding death like never before, she took out her writings of over nine years and started to put them together like the pieces of a jigsaw puzzle.

A few weeks later, her mother called her into the kitchen and asked, 'Will you go to back to America to sort out Aunt Lucy's estate, as that lawyer is dragging his feet?'

Mary's heart sank. She didn't want to go. She hadn't the strength to face it. She hesitated.

'I will pay for your flight and whatever it costs.'

'Thanks, Mam, I appreciate that as I have no money until the house goes through and I will go if there is no-one else.

'There is no-one else who can do it but you, Mary,' her mother replied.

'I can't go until I see someone in Waterford about my issues with the bank. From there I am going to the Cork film festival as I have a room booked for myself and a friend.'

The next day the ticket was booked, the lawyer was called and accommodation arranged with two cousins and her friend Maureen in New Jersey.

Meeting Liam in a car park in Waterford the following week, they faced their last-ditch attempt to get some financial compensation for what the bank had done to her, believing that this was her last hope. After an hour in his office where they discussed everything, the mediator finished by saying, 'I am looking at your age, Mary, and you are nearly ten years older than me. I know what the bank did to you was wrong and you would win your case in court, but this could take five years and you have already dealt with enough stress and have no guarantee that you would be financially compensated. You might only get an apology. If I were in your shoes, I would cut my losses. I would retire with the money I have left after the sale of the house and live on the income of the other house until you get your pension. It may not be what you wanted to hear but you have gone through enough. I would let it go. Do you understand what I am saying?'

She looked him straight in the eye and knew in her heart that we were speaking through him, and even though all the anguish the bank had put her through flashed again before her eyes, she replied, 'Yes.'

The man rose from his seat, put out his hand and shook hands with both her and Liam and wished them well. With a heavy heart Mary drove through the lashing rain to Cork, tailing Liam's car. He was going to the city to stay with a friend after guiding her to her accommodation. That night, after watching a movie at the festival, she went back to her attic room alone as her friend had cancelled, which was the way it was meant to be. Mary needed to be alone for what she was about to face.

In her meditation, her great grandfather Red Tommy was the first person she faced after closing her eyes, then her great-grandmother followed by her grandfathers and grandmothers from both sides of her family. She watched a healing process take place as she had many times before but never within her own family. Before the meditation was over, Gary and Piaras had joined their ancestors. Lying under the quilt afterwards, crying her heart out, wondering when all the healing would be finished, wondering how much more she could take before deciding to call Liam.

He listened and understood as she knew he would, as when we first directed her to him it was not only because he had experience working with the bank.

'I remember having the same thing happen to me in a meditation,' he said. 'Take it easy today, Mary. I can come meet you if you want.'

'No thanks, Liam. I need to be alone. I just needed to tell someone.'

Mary didn't feel alone that day as her ancestors whom she had never met before accompanied her everywhere. The following evening, she drove to Dublin and the next day flew out to Steward Airport where her cousin's wife met her.

As they were driving back to her house, Mary asked, 'What are all the flags flying for?'

'Veteran's day,

Mary's heart sank. *More soldiers*, she thought. *Haven't I done enough?*

Vincent had never contacted her since they arrived back from Flanders, nor she him, but she understood immediately that this was the day she was to arrive in the States, choreographed as always, and whether she liked it or not there was work to be done here – alone, this time.

That night, as Mary drifted off into a mediation, realising that it was the hundredth anniversary of the end of WWI, she watched as every soul congregated at the monument in Palingbeek, Flanders, moving to the energy which had started in Ireland and was now covering all of Europe.

Wondering where all this was going to end, we brought her mind back to the summer of that year when she took a few days off. With no money for accommodation, she had called a friend of a friend, Tony, who had stayed with her for a couple of nights

283

after the death of their mutual friend Gerry B, staying with a friend in Galway on the way before heading down the coast road to a wee village in Clare.

After a good night's sleep, they headed out into the Burren, a place Mary had always wanted to walk, and he knew it like the back of his hand. Within an hour, she had slipped and fell but decided to go on, and on and on for a very long walk. When they reached the car, she could barely put her foot on the ground, so after dinner retired to bed early and in the morning realised how bad her ankle was when she could barely make it down the stairs. Leaving after breakfast, she was aware that she wasn't meant to go home. What was the point? She justified to herself, *I wouldn't be able to make it up the stairs.* But her leg seemed okay to drive so she headed south instead of north.

Her sister who had just retired, had planned to drive the Wild Atlantic Way with Mary, a road that ran along the coast from Donegal to Cork, but nothing came of it. As she had already started this road trip from Galway to Clare, she got back on it and continued down one of the most scenic routes in Ireland, deciding after lunch that she would venture further on down into Kerry, so took the Killimer ferry to Tarbert, arriving at the other side at five o'clock.

With little money to spend on accommodation, she contacted the closest hostel and booked a room, then drove and drove until finally she had to call to say she would be very late as the narrow winding road through the mountains was taking much longer than expected. The first thing Mary noticed when she reached the single bedroom was that there was no phone or internet coverage, which was strange as she had been assured that the connections were good.

Waking up with a heavy heart, she pulled herself up in the bed and went into a meditation to find herself in the company of all her in-laws, her ex-husband's family and their children who had disappeared from her life sixteen years before, after her decision to separate. Even though Mary was still friendly with the women who were separated from her brothers, things were very different in the Republic, where the church had only recently lost control and divorce was now an option. The day she left her marriage, not only had she lost her husband of near twenty years, but all connections with her in-laws that she had loved like family.

For the past sixteen years, she hadn't the time to give this much thought, but alone in a room in a hostel in the middle of nowhere, she started to cry, allowing the tears of this devastating loss to express itself for the first time. For the next hour and a half, she stayed with the terrible grief that ripped through her body, then showered, dressed and moved on after breakfast calling Michael on the way to tell him what had just happened.

'You alright?' he asked when she finally finished speaking.

'I will be now that I have finally acknowledged this huge loss.'

For the rest of the day, Mary was gentle with herself, driving slowly, eating at all the things that gave her comfort and later found a hostel near the yoga centre in West Cork to stay that night. After unpacking and eating, she drove the Beara Peninsula and understood something Gerry had said time and time again: *You can be healed by beauty, Mary.* That evening she was healed by beauty as she drove into the sunset on the narrow winding road with the Atlantic Ocean pulsating on both sides.

Continuing along the Wild Atlantic Way, she made the decision to head back to Clare and stay with Tony again that night. A few hours later, we directed her inland to where Michael Collins had been killed, and without a question, she changed direction. After getting lost a few times, she finally found the place where the man who led the Irish delegation at the peace conference in London, which resulted in the Anglo-Irish treaty of December 1921, had been shot dead. This treaty left the country divided by a border, twenty-six counties which became known as the Free State and the six counties where Mary was born, left under British rule.

Parking her car on the only wide place on the narrow country road, she crossed over and immediately felt his presence at the monument erected there. *Has he been there for the past ninety-seven years?* Mary wondered as she knelt down, blessed herself out of habit and said a prayer. Back in the car, she sat for a moment thinking, *Why was I brought here, why are all my in-laws back in my life, why do I have to do this work? Why can't I be just like everyone else? Why, why, why me?* But as it was getting late and there was no internet coverage, she moved on, bringing her mind back to basic questions – like, *How do I to get back on a main road?* After driving around until she found internet coverage, she then let the GPS take her back to Tony's house in time to fall into bed. Lying there, she could see how the events of the past few days had forced her to a place alone to start another grieving and healing process, this time within herself. It had never occurred to her before now just how much needed to be blocked to survive. Drifting off to sleep, she welcomed back all the souls of her family through marriage. They may never be with her on a human level again but at a level much deeper they were and always would be.

In a meditation early the next day, Mary found herself back in West Cork at the monument where Michael Collins had been killed and watched something move. In the next instant, she was outside Kilmainham Gaol, realising in that moment the reason why not one soul had moved. They were waiting for their friend, and as he moved on, they went with him. Driving home later she had no doubt that they were not only together for the first time in over a hundred years but had joined Martin McGuinness and all the other soldiers from all the other wars that she had helped create a space for healing.

Now, as she fell asleep a few months later, on another continent, Mary was certain that she was in the USA for more reasons than sorting her aunt's estate and headstone. Two days later she drove with another cousin to the lawyer in Connecticut and when all was sorted in his office, they drove to her aunt's grave to choose the headstone to mark her resting place.

Standing beside her grave, Mary thought, *I may not have been able to take you home four years ago, Aunt Lucy, but I will make sure you get home to your family now*, before watching her aunt's soul rise and join her family on the other side of the veil. It was only then that she noticed a soul in a grave beside her aunt's move too – a grave marked with an American flag, a soldier's grave. As there were many flags flying in the cemetery, she looked around to see if there was any other movement, but not another budged. *Okay*, she thought as they headed to the car, *that is my work done*.

The following night she met her friend Maureen for dinner and flew home the following day.

A couple of weeks later, Mary found yet another letter from the bank in her mailbox but was no longer afraid of their letters, so opened it straightaway to find an apology for something she had not been aware of. The letter stated that the court case to get possession of the house was to be stalled immediately and they would pay all solicitor's expenses and compensate her for their mistake. Ecstatic, she called Liam as up until this point, she had been responsible not only for her own solicitor's costs but also the bank's!

'Send me a copy of that letter,' he said. 'I have seen very few apologies from any bank.'

'Well, this is my second one, Liam,' she replied, smiling.

As 2018 came to a close, her cousin Stephen was killed on a motorcycle in Dublin, and that evening she watched him go home to his family on the other side. When her parents and children left after Christmas that year, she was looking forward to a new year, as 2018 had been very difficult one.

CHAPTER 12

Mary started 2019 as she did every year, by taking stock of her life. She would turn sixty this year, and as it was ten years since she had written her first book, she started an account of all that had happened to her since then. We reminded her of the words we whispered to her in 2009, words that were uttered to no-one but her friend Michael. That her book, *The Long Road Home*, was an introduction to who she was, that she would write another book which was much more important. Again, this was blanked and replaced with the narrative that her children needed an account of this other life she led, then put her attention back on the main cottage again. For the first time, she saw early retirement as her only option, even though retirement had never been considered an option before, at any age!

Despite the fact that there were no contracts signed nor deposit paid for the sale of her home, Mary started hanging pictures and moving furniture, feeling that all was well. From writing everything down, she had no doubt that we were orchestrating everything in her life, and by surrendering, she could watch it all with interest instead of anxiety.

Her only alteration to the cottage was to fit a tiny bath in her ensuite, finally allowing herself to have the things that gave her comfort – and the bath was one of her main comforts, that is, after her hot water bottle.

The pictures accumulated over her lifetime were taken out and a collage of all the people that had impacted her life were put in a large frame. All her framed pictures and the drawings she did were brought together – these included pictures of her grandfather and great grandmother that she had taken from the attic of her parents' house weeks before these ancestors appeared in her meditation. Then there was the picture of her great grandfather, Red Tommy, and his family that had hung in her different homes for over thirty years, moving with her every time she flitted. Before the end of January, pictures of family and friends covered most of the cottage's white walls.

As Mary was finally putting herself first, the main bedroom was finally taken for herself, so her antique bed was moved there as everything came together to make her first home alone, a place where she finally felt at peace.

As Roisín was planning on leaving Dublin at the same time, with the idea of setting up a production company in the west, they talked about where she could have an office.

'I could extend the middle of the cottage,' Mary said.

'No,' Roisín replied immediately. 'Could I build a place somewhere on the land? I need an office and a place to sleep when I am at home which won't be that often. I really need all my stuff together. A base. What about old containers?'

'They are small, you would need a few, and I don't believe they would look right in this scenic area. Anyway, I need part of your building to be a storage space as I will have none when I move.'

'What about a steel frame house?' Jarlath said. 'The company I work for make them and they are lovely.'

Mary checked them out as Roisín got excited, but again, it didn't feel right to her and it would still look out of place and needed planning permission. Then one day we whispered, *What about the hay house?* and without hesitation, she called Roisín.

'Oh, Mam, that would be brilliant, but we haven't got a hay house.'

'I know, but there was one here when I bought the land so there has to be a base and some of it still on the ground.'

With Roisín's enthusiasm motivating her, Mary immediately checked out the piece of land that we had encouraged her to buy twenty years before and found the base and some galvanise. More galvanise was needed, so straightaway she started looking for some second-hand on the internet but could find none. Then one day when Timothy was visiting, he asked, 'Have you found any galvanise yet?'

'I have checked. There is none. It's very hard to get.'

'Check again. You need to be checking every day.'

She Googled DoneDeal as he watched over her shoulder and found what was needed not far from her parents' home. The price was right, and as it had already been taken down, it only needed to be picked up, so her friend Martin who had a Jeep was called.

'No problem. I will bring it down for you,' he said after her brother Brendy had checked it out. They then picked up the frame made from railway sleepers and galvanise on one of the worst days of the year and drove it the eighty miles in a storm – after her mother had put a bottle of holy water in his Jeep.

Unloading it the next day, Mary wondered where she would find someone to put it up as no one local could do it. Then Jarlath called and said, 'Micheal puts them up. Ask Daddy.' Micheal was her nephew through marriage who she hadn't seen in over sixteen years.

She called Marty who said, 'I will ask him for you.'

Micheal called her the following day and started the job a week later with his brother Paul helping.

The following Monday, her brother Noel and his buddy PJ arrived to start a project which would be planned as they went along, one step at a time. Roisín needed an office, and she needed a shed, and the hayshed was big enough for both.

'Are you sure you are doing the right thing?' her sister called and asked one evening. 'You are spending the only money you have had in nearly ten years thanks to Aunt Lucy, but the contracts on the house have not been signed and if it doesn't go through you will be left again with nothing.'

'I know it is right. It feels so right, and the money will come. It always does,' Mary replied. 'Life is short, and after all the latest causalities in the family, I'm not wasting any more time. No-one is guaranteed anything and I want to do this for Roisín as Jarlath is talking about buying the house in Castlerea.'

Whilst the men were working on the barn, Mary continued to get the cottage ready for herself. The wooden stairs were bare and she couldn't find what she wanted to cover them. In fact, no-one knew what she was talking about.

'What exactly are you looking for?' Geraldine asked one day on the phone.

'I want covering like we had when we were children growing up in the old house. Remember, it was like lino but non-slip. I have asked in every place that sells floor covering and they say you can't put lino on the stairs as it is dangerous, but it wasn't ordinary lino. Do you remember it?'

'I remember well,' her sister replied. 'It was red and the twelve of us ran up and down it for years and no-one ever slipped, but I have never seen it anywhere since.'

The next time she was up home, we guided her to the attic of her parents' house looking for something else, when she saw a piece of the original lino on the floor. *That's it*, she thought. *That is what I am looking for. I can take this to the shops and show them.* Smiling, she bent to pick it up and there in the corner was a roll of it. Mary ran down the stairs to the kitchen where her mother was making tea, and asked, 'Mam, where did you get the roll of lino that is up in the attic?'

'What lino?'

'The same one as we had on the stairs when we were children.'

'That is the one that we had on the stairs when you were children. Your dad took it with him when Tom was renovating the house. Do you want it?'

'Oh, yes please.'

Mary couldn't believe it, and the next time Noel came down he had it with him. An hour later it was in place, and when they stood at the bottom looking up, she said, 'Oh … if that lino could only talk.'

Noel laughed out loud and replied, 'Can you imagine how many soldiers and police had tramped on it as well as us and it looks as good as new!'

With the work on the barn progressing and her inheritance dwindling, Mary concentrated on living in the moment as she tried to ignore the fact that it was now seven months since she made a deal on the house and still no contracts had been signed. Then one day in the middle of May, the auctioneer called out of the blue. 'Contracts are signed and all the money has been paid over, and the new owners want to move in immediately.'

As the relief swept over her, she said, 'Tell them to call me.'

The buyer called the following day to say that they would like to be in by mid-June.

'What about the 18th?' Mary asked.

'Why the 18th?'

'It's my sixtieth birthday.'

'Okay, the 18th it will be,' he replied.

As the men continued working on the barn, she moved all her personal belongings into the cottage and then called a charity shop to pick up the furniture that the new owners didn't want.

On her sixtieth birthday, Mary and Roisín worked all day cleaning the house. The new owners were to arrive at three, but thankfully didn't as they weren't finished.

At 5:30 Roisín said, 'Mam, come on, let's get out of here. Let me take you out to dinner for your birthday … You need to celebrate.'

When the new owners arrived at six o'clock, Mary and her daughter were on their way to a restaurant to celebrate not only her birthday but also her new home.

Coming home that night she turned her car right for the cottage for the first time in eight years. Left to the big house was a turn she wouldn't be making again. Snuggling into bed later with all her bits and pieces around her, she told her friend that she felt like Maureen O'Hara in *The Quiet Man*. What a birthday present. Mary had finally retired from the madness of the human life she was living, finally ready to embrace her spiritual journey. No longer would she have to take the tourist board, Airbnb, banks or any other organisation into account. She had the place all to herself and was mortgage free. Home alone with only us in residence and an income to sustain her and money in the bank. All the things she had asked for the year before at Chania international airport in Crete.

CHAPTER 13

As Mary was now spending three days every second week with her parents and had her cottage just as she wanted it, we watched her call Henk about the original manuscript that we had dictated to her eleven years before. But he had lost it when he changed computers, so we guided her to where she could find it in her own email.

After editing the first part, she got in touch with Vincent to ask if he would have any objections to her writing about their journey together.

'Not at all,' he had replied, and as they caught up on their time apart, He then said, 'Sorry for my behaviour in Belgium and on the way back. I was exhausted and overwhelmed by it all.'

'I know ... so was I, but you did the bulk of the work. No wonder you were exhausted. I still am overwhelmed by it all and now have to face it all again as I write about it.'

'We do have more places to go and now you have more time and the money and the mortgage-free house that you asked for ...'

'We will see,' Mary replied. 'I don't feel the need to go anywhere else at the moment, but I will go with you if I am asked. I seem to be doing a lot of work in my mediations since I got back from America. I have been watching as soldiers from there and other wars in other countries come together to protect their own countries from more of the same, and I'm thinking God bless them for trying. It's not going to be an easy job in this crazy world we are living in.'

Roisín had returned home from her trip on New Year's Day 2020 and was preparing to go to the Berlin Film Festival as she did at this time every year. Noel and PJ were finishing up the barn. Jarlath and Laura were still in Thailand when Mary and her sister Ruth decided they would go to a retreat in Wales. Ruth needed a break from over a year of grief, and Mary needed a break too. She had gone on her first holiday in eight years the previous September, a trip to Italy, a present from her kids for her big birthday, travelling with her sister Geraldine, her niece Sinead and Roisín, then met up with Jarlath and Laura for the last few nights. They had had a wonderful time, but a retreat from the world was what was needed now.

As they drove up the M1 that January afternoon, heading for the airport in Belfast, Mary told Ruth what Roisín had asked her after their trip to Italy.

'Do you think I'm mad spending all my money on a trip to Australia and New Zealand, Mam, when I could use the money to pay off what I owe you for the barn?'

'No. You may never get an opportunity to do this trip again, and unlike the bank I won't be putting any pressure on you to pay anything back until you are ready. With the house sold, I have more than enough money to do me for now.'

'And Jarlath?' her sister asked. 'Did he ask you for your advice when he and Laura booked their tickets to Thailand?'

'No. He does as he wants, when he wants. Anyway, as long as he is paying his rent, he knows it is none of my business what he does, but had he asked, I would have told him the same. They both do a lot of travelling but they're young and this is the time to do it, like we did.'

Arriving in Wales that night, they both fell into bed exhausted after the long drive from the airport in England. Waking the following morning, Mary checked her phone to find a message from Brendy that read: *How's Dad doing?*

'What happened to Dad?' she asked when he answered his phone.

'He broke his hip yesterday.'

'He is finished,' Ruth said. 'He is strong, but he will never get over this.'

'He is 101, will be 102 this year,' Mary replied. 'We have had him so long. He is a wonderful man, but we will have to let him go sometime.'

Geraldine called and said he was comfortable but probably be in a wheelchair if he ever got out of the hospital.

'We will come home,' Mary said.

'No, that is why I didn't tell you. Stay where you are. Ruth needs the break and Dad is going nowhere.'

By lunchtime they got another message to say that their dad was sitting up comfortably, so they enjoyed the rest of the weekend as best they could and arrived home Sunday night. Mary stayed with their mother, and the following morning at nine, walked into her father's room in the hospital to find it empty. Running to the nurse's station, she was told that he was down getting a scan and when he returned, he lay there weak and vulnerable. Believing that this was the end for him, the thought of staying with him as he moved on did not pose any problem for her – in fact, it would be an honour. Half an hour later her father opened his eyes, pulled himself up in the bed and took his two legs over the edge, he said he wanted to go home. Within a week he was home with his walker and wheelchair.

One morning near the end of January, as Mary sat in her meditation, she watched as the original energy of the soldiers and their casualties from Ireland and two world wars surround the entire globe. It started out very weak as it was stretched to its limits, but then the military and their causalities from all the other countries that were protecting their own rose to join it as she sat there basking in the love of it all. Trying to process what had happened she called no-one, but that evening when her friend Marie called, she said, 'Marie, remember the energy I told you about before, the one that I have been watching for years?'

'Yes.'

'Today I watched it surround the Earth and glow as a light of pure love and peace.'

'What do you think it is? What do you think it means?' Marie asked.

'I have no idea, but something huge is about to change in the world, and whatever it is, it is going to be for the better. Those who have gone before us have come together to support us in whatever is coming.'

Calling Michael and Vincent later to tell them about her latest vision, she then forgot all about it, as her father started experiencing one setback after another, and she was back spending three days every week with her parents. Then in February, Ireland had its first coronavirus case.

With no time to give that much heed, Mary concentrated on her father who had been hospitalised a few times and didn't want to be there. Finally, he got his way just before the hospital closed down and reopened as a coronavirus centre as the virus spread havoc throughout the world.

The local doctor arrived with what looked like a spacesuit on him, bringing enough morphine to kill any pain her father might experience as there was no going back into any hospital.

For the next few weeks, as the country went into complete lockdown, the family home became the hospital with only his five daughters who were taking care of his needs going in, his sons grateful to be able to see him through the bedroom window as everyone tried to come to terms with this new world that they had found themselves in.

There was nothing the girls could do, only keep their father comfortable as he deteriorated, having lost the will to live without his daily routine in his beloved garden.

On the 4th of April, Mary sat by her father's bedside exhausted, knowing he had little time left, wanting to be there to the end but knowing in her heart she needed to go home to rest. After saying her goodbye to her father, she picked up a photograph of her paternal grandparents that had belonged to their Aunt Lucy, as if in a trance, and took it home with her. Arriving back at the cottage, she put the picture on her bedside locker and had dinner with Roisín. Before climbing into bed that night, she knelt at the side of it, held the picture of the grandparents whom she had never met in this life in front of her and said, 'Please take Daddy home to you. He is ready. He cannot bear much more pain.'

Mary woke late and checked her phone to find no message from home, so drew her feet up under her in the bed. In her meditation she brought herself to her father's bedside and said, 'Dad, I always said that you are like an old American Indian and they would simply say, *Today is a good day to die. Dad, today is a good day to die.*' She prayed again to his parents to take him home, then after her meditation checked her phone again. Her brother Sean had a message on the family WhatsApp group that read: *Dad passed away ten minutes ago.*

Lying back into the bed, Mary thanked the God of her understanding for ending her father's pain then got up and packed her bag to go home for the funeral. Before leaving, she put a message on Facebook to tell her friends and relations throughout the world of his passing. Under his picture she wrote*: This beautiful man (my dad) passed away this morning. Born into the pandemic of 1918 and died in this one, but thankfully was affected by neither. May you rest in peace, Dad. I chose the very best when I chose you. Xxx*

There was no wake. He lay there in the company of only his wife and daughters, and the funeral mass was watched by all on the internet because of restrictions. As the family drove behind the hearse with his dog in the car, the neighbours lined the road for a man that they loved and respected as only the family were allowed into the graveyard. Mary knew it was exactly how he would have wanted it: quiet, the way he lived his life. Now he was back with his grandparents, brothers, sisters, mother, father, grandchildren and all the ancestors, everyone who had passed before him.

Mary didn't need to take her father to meet them as he knew the way, had always known the way.

Even though her mother was grieving, things got easier in her parents' house. With no visitors, they got back to some semblance of normality in a world that seemed like it was in a war but with a peace in the air that she hadn't witnessed since a child before The Troubles.

A few months later, in a meditation, she watched as souls of those who had died in the pandemic from every country in the world joined to help send love and light to those dealing with a new world, one that had been brought to a standstill.

Her friend Marie's father hadn't been well at the same time, so they had very little time to talk until one day she called and said, 'You were right, Mary.'

'About what?'

'That there was something huge coming to change the world. Remember you told me in January?'

'I remember it happening, Marie, but I have no memory of telling you. I do remember thinking and saying that it was for the better. Hard to see how this could be for the better, but I suppose things could not go on the way they were going, even a world recession couldn't stop the madness.' Then she added, 'At least this virus isn't prejudiced, it doesn't recognise borders, nationalities, religions, the colour of your skin nor your sexual orientation. It has brought me to understand the real gifts of our world, a world that we have to share with not only the ones in it but those who have gone before us. It taught me that my days are numbered and I have to stop procrastinating and get on with what I came here to do. It has been a great equaliser. Now, that can't be a bad thing.'

Getting off the phone, Mary walked the mountains with her daughter who was locked down in the barn from the day she returned from the Berlin Festival, leaving her no choice but to turn her office into a bedroom and work from there alone for the safety of both her parents and grandparents. As they walked the narrow road to the bog, Roisín asked, 'What do you think of all the conspiracy theories, Mam?'

'I believe they are just another form of control, Rois, manipulated again by those in power. When you learn to trust your inner guides, your gut, or whatever you call it, it doesn't matter what is happening in the world. Everything is and always was as it is meant to be. All you need to ask is, *What do I need to learn from this?* Always bring it back to yourself, it is the only change you can make, and by changing yourself, you can change the world.'

Later, as Mary walked past the big house thinking of all the drama she put herself and others through trying to hold onto something that was meant for someone else, knowing if she had not surrendered that her fate would have been a house full of vulnerable elderly people in the middle of a pandemic with no help from anyone and unable to see her own aged parents. Instead, by surrendering, she got to retire to do what she loved, writing a manuscript that no-one might ever read but one that needed to be written for her own healing. She got to have a home that the bank could never take off her. She got an income to sustain her, but most importantly she got to give back to her parents what they had given to her and to help those who were moving on. Finally accepting her purpose. The one which she had chosen.

Walking on, we heard the prayer from her heart that was written to us every morning in her journal. Thank you, thank you, thank you. I believe, I believe, I believe. I trust, I trust, I trust. I accept, I accept, I accept. I surrender, I surrender, I surrender. I love, I love, I love and before the year was out would add: I forgive, I forgive, I forgive. I flow, I flow, I flow.

Mary had reached a place where people would say she was full of herself and she would ask, who else would I be full of?

EPILOGUE 2020 – 2022

God grant me the serenity to accept the things I cannot change,
the courage to change the things I can and the wisdom to know
the difference.
Grant me patience for the changes that take time.
Appreciation of all that I have.
Tolerance of those with different struggles.
And the strength to get up and try again, one day at a time.

At the end of 2019, I made a decision that I thought I would
never, ever have the strength to make. Picking up the phone in
November, I called the rape crisis centre which I had attended
many times before but not in over ten years.

Driving to the interview on a cold wet miserable winter's day,
which matched my mood, I arrived early and sat outside a cafe
nearby sipping herbal tea, wondering if I was wasting my time
and taxpayers' money and with the reoccurring guilt of taking the
place of someone who needed help more than I did.

I made my way to the discreet door at the side of the building
to sit nervously in a room until a young woman came to get me.
The thought, *what would she know about what I have been through?*
ran through my mind as she sat down opposite me. But leaving
half an hour later, I had no doubt she knew what she was doing,
especially after she said she would get me a counsellor around
my own age as soon as possible, asking what days and times I

was available. My first thought was how I could work around my parents before saying, 'Anytime. I am available anytime.'

'Good,' she replied. 'Then I will have a counsellor for you as quickly as possible.'

I had my first appointment at the beginning of 2020, a few weeks before the country was locked down due to COVID-19 and I thought, *well that's that* (as my mother would say). But the counsellor asked me if I would be interested in Zoom sessions, and I said yes because at this point Pandora's Box had been well and truly opened.

For the following nine months, I revealed the story of that fateful night as the memories unfolded to both the counsellor and myself.

Every Friday, at two o'clock, I opened my laptop before opening my mouth and allowing a frightened teenager to continue her story, that is after the trigger of a gun had been pulled at her head forty-four years earlier. At that time, I had surrendered to my fate without any fear, as my near-death experience left me unconcerned about the body that housed my soul. It was then that the policewoman turned to a form of torture that no sane society could condone. She described in explicit sexual detail what the British soldiers were going to do to me. Details that my virgin mind couldn't comprehend, but leaving me without any doubt that what I was about to experience would scar me physically, mentally and emotionally if I was not lucky enough to die, breaking me in a way that her threats of death hadn't.

After each Friday afternoon session, I would sit frozen in my armchair and stare out the cottage window. The following morning, I would walk with my neighbour but told her nothing, because I was still carrying the shame of what another woman had done to me. By Monday I had processed enough to allow me to proceed through another week as vulnerable as a new-born child waiting in anticipation and dread of what was to come next. I was left with no choice but to go back to the scene of my trauma again and again, to release the pain that was trapped in my body until I finally got to the part where the policeman in the room left and got help. A plain-clothed man then entered the room and spoke to me in a language I understood.

'This should never have happened. If you tell no-one about it, I will make sure it never happens to you again.' Even in my fear and vulnerability, I was aware enough to know what would happen if I survived and told. There would be reprisals but none on the scale of what the police would inflict on our community with the law of the land protecting them.

He then told me that he wouldn't subject me to any more connection to the police, instead he would send me back to the hotel with the soldiers. Unable to speak, I couldn't tell him that the policewoman had said no policeman would ever touch me because I was disgusting and that when the soldiers were finished with me no man would ever want me, if I survived.

I was lead out of the building and put in the back of a Jeep in which soldiers lined the two sides. It was only a ten-minute drive to the hotel, but I never believed I would make it there. The memory of my soul rising from my body in the cell was the vision foremost in my mind at that time, leaving me with an understanding that I was much more than a human being who had had a spiritual experience. So, I spoke to the soldier opposite me without opening my mouth, speaking from my soul to his. *I forgive you for what you are about to do, but if you have any mercy, please kill me first.* Five minutes later, I was thrown off the back of the Jeep at the entrance to the hotel, and before dawn I had blanked everything to survive.

After thirty-six-hour long sessions, I had spoken as much as I could about that night, and by speaking my truth to someone who listened, believed me and did not judge, I had been given the freedom to move on with my future without this baggage from my past.

In order to survive, I had buried the impact of that fateful day in the recess of my mind until June 2017 when the bank had issued two unlawful and unfounded initiations of Section 37 of the Criminal Justice (Money Laundering and Terrorism Financing) Act 2010 against me, which with the help of my friend, Liam, I am still trying to deal with. When no headway could be made, I decided to make a complaint to the ombudsman in 2021. The bank's reaction to my complaint was twofold; first the bank initiated Section 37 against my ninety-three-year-old mother and a third Section 37 against me. This was done despite the fact that my solicitor continually told the bank that Section 37 does not apply to me, and the bank has admitted that there is nothing in my accounts to indicate that I was involved in money laundering or the funding of terrorism, it wrongly claims that it did this as it has a legal obligation to apply Section 37 against the siblings of a politician. Despite this claim, the bank never initiated Section 37 against any of my siblings who also banked with them for years. In an effort to reach a solution, I agreed to the ombudsman appointing a mediator. The bank refused to engage in mediation. The file has now been sent back to the ombudsman for investigation. I was informed that this may take three years as there are so many other complaints ahead of mine!

With a strength that I hadn't had before counselling from the rape crisis centre, I decided I would look for a pension of the British government for psychological damage received in the Troubles, a scheme that had recently been put in place. The first thing that I needed to confirm was that the incident occurred, confirmation that I had never found before but received in a newspaper report in the county library archives in Enniskillen. The second requirement was that I prove that I was at the scene of the incident. An interim of forty-five years left me with no choice but to contact the PSNI (replacement from the RUC) requesting the statement I made to them on the night of the bombing. After months of filing and refiling my request, I was told that they weren't allowed to give out any information for this pension. I applied again saying it was for personal reasons, only to be told that they would look, but a few weeks later I received a letter saying that they could find no statement from me, even though I was the only person who saw the man who planted the bomb. When I realised they had the wrong date of birth on my application form, I called again asking if I should make another application to be was told that it wouldn't make any difference!

Early in 2021, I decided I would join a dating site for the first time in my life – a dating site with a difference. Planet Earth Singles, a site for those spiritually inclined. As there were less than ten men on the site from Ireland, so I had no choice but to communicate with members outside the country, mostly from the USA. Putting up my profile required me to answer a lot of questions, both written and multiple choice, giving me an opportunity to get to know myself in a way I never had before. Having no expectations, I enjoyed the banter for a couple of months until I'd had enough and closed down my profile.

On the morning of the 7th of April 2021, I got a call from my sister to say Brendy had died the night before. Brendy, our fifty-four-year-old brother had moved on in his sleep in the middle of the night without any warning. He had been complaining about his stomach, but it turned out to be his heart. Another funeral, the third in less than three years, left our family heartbroken.

Back in shock and mourning, I tried to come to terms with the latest death, thinking of all the things I wanted to do in my life but hadn't done. It was then that I decided that I would put this book out into the public domain as I no longer cared what anyone thought of me. Immediately, I had a memory of a neighbour I had met recently when walking my parents dog and out of the blue he said. I read your book Mary and liked it. Thanks, I had replied. I think there is another book in you he then stated. Shocked I blurted out, I have started one to which he replied. You should finish it.

I opened up the laptop again and started editing. I also made the decision to ask my mother if I could be buried with my dad and brother in the graveyard that held the bodies of my community. The community I wanted to return my body to, knowing that my soul would meet them all in another place.

In January of 2021, Jarlath had asked me if I would help him get a mortgage to buy the family home from me. I agreed, as this would allow both of us an opportunity to move on with our lives. Me into retirement and him into home ownership, which was difficult to achieve as property had hit an all-time high and mortgages were nearly impossible to secure. This purchase was to take the entire year, but Jarlath started his renovations after the bank sanctioned his loan, so by closing date he was nearly finished. For the Christmas holidays, families were given a window to meet during lockdown, so his father, sister and I were invited for Christmas dinner at the beautiful home he had created with the help of his friends.

January 2022 started with another lockdown, but I did get to a chance to visit my friend Margaret in Cork for a couple of days (a woman I had never met before the pandemic but had become friends on zoom during it). Just before I took the trip, I got another match from Planet Earth Singles (they had kept sending me matches even though I no longer had a profile), and as usual, I checked out where he was from, and low and behold, he was from the North. I read his profile and indeed we did have a lot in common, but his picture looked like he was standing in front of a firing squad. I hesitated for a few days before sending him a friend request and was so proud of myself for doing so, as I had broken a commitment to myself that I would contact no man from north of the border. He was from Belfast, and even though I had no idea which side of the divide he was from, I didn't care. He was a Northerner, and I wasn't going there even for a friendship, so this was just a paper exercise. I needn't have worried as I got no reply.

A couple of weeks later, the cheque came through for the house I'd sold to Jarlath and I lodged it on a Friday.

'Do you have plans for this money?' the cashier asked.

'I have,' I lied as there was no way I was going to invest with a bank and had no intention of explaining why.

Two days later, whilst taking care of my mother, my sister Ruth and I took Spot (Mam's dog) for a walk. On the way we talked about Jarlath's new home and she said, 'He's so lucky. A friend of mine is trying to buy a house and there is none to be got at any price.'

'Really?' I replied. 'I hadn't realised that there was a shortage of housing in the North too.'

'Not a thing to rent either,' she said.

Not that I didn't believe her, but I couldn't help myself checking. She was right, not a thing to rent, so I automatically went onto property sales in the local town and there popped up a terraced house on a street that I knew like the back of my hand. My friend Bernie (the one that knew everything when we were children!) and I had walked up this narrow side street from her home outside the town to the main street heading to secondary school when I stayed in her house.

Curious, I asked my brother about it when he came in for tea.

'Grand wee house,' he said. 'Call Rory, he will know more.'

'Not another house!' my mother said from the kitchen table. 'I thought you would have had enough trouble with the banks.'

'Wouldn't need the bank,' I replied. 'I could buy it with the money I have just got from selling to Jarlath, better than money in the bank, and who knows, I may live there some day!"

'Lot of tragedy on that street,' my other brother said when he joined us in the kitchen later.

Rory informed me that the banks were selling the house and made an appointment for me to see it, so two days later, Noel, Ruth and I met there – on the wettest day of the year. I was surprised that it was in such good condition, but as I looked out the kitchen window, I could see why most people wouldn't want this house. At the back was an old stone building with a roof that was falling in. As building material would need to be brought through the mid terraced house to remedy this, and builders were currently at a premium, it was going to hold up either rental or occupation by the new owner. Running through the lashing rain out the back to this building which I had already fallen in love with, I found it full to the brim with rubbish. Another reason to put others off, but not me.

Driving out of town ten minutes later with the question, *what would I need another house for?* The reply that came immediately said, *what would you want money in the bank for?*

Okay, I will buy if I get it at the right price, I said as a shiver ran down my spine with the thought of returning to my hometown to live. For the next few nights, I had very little sleep until I decided that if I got it, I would rent it out, and if I ever changed my mind to cross the border to live, it would be there for me. That settled me until the day of the auction when I became a nervous wreck. Rory was bidding for me, all I had to do was give him my highest bid, but still I paced the floor in the cottage when the auction started, nervous for fear of getting it – also nervous that I wouldn't, as the week before a local woman who had passed on came into my meditation and asked if I could help those who needed it to move on, especially her son who had passed recently and was finding it difficult. She also told me that the house would be mine at the right price.

I don't want the house if it's not meant for me, I replied, *but I would be honoured to help your son or anyone if they are ready.* I was told to talk to them as they come to me, and over the next few days, I did this on numerous occasions. This I found very difficult. I didn't know them all personally, but I knew who they all were and the lives they had lived before they passed on. Days before the auction I watched as two MPs who worked on the main street of our hometown before passing, come in, also a prominent businessman of the other persuasion and Martin McGuiness and Ian Paisley. Then, Bobby Sands, who had also been our MP before he died on hunger strike and his comrades whose fortieth anniversary it was, came to join them. With the healing continuing in the town, the energy joined forces with all those who had created a healing energy before then moved out the road to Moorlough where a disputed number (up to 2,000) soldiers were killed in 1689 in what was known as The Battle of Newtownbutler.

'Do you want to listen in?' Rory enquired before the auction had started.

'No, go as far as I can afford, and if it's for me, I will get it.'

Ten minutes later he called again and I could hear the auctioneer in the background asking a price way outside my budget.

'Wasn't for me'" I said.

'We got it!' he replied.

'But ... what's that going on in the background?'

'That is the next house up for auction. Actually, we got it for 10,000 less than you would have paid.'

'Great,' I replied, delighted before putting down the phone wondering what its purpose would be apart from renovating the old stone building.

At the beginning of January 2022, as the paperwork was going through for the house, I was very aware that this was the start of the fiftieth anniversary of the year when my life changed irrevocably. I had a choice. I could relive it as the anniversaries arose or I could take the opportunity to let it all go. I had carried this pain too long, so on the 30th of January I went into the house I had just purchased with a 10-litre bucket of white paint, two paint brushes and a roller. It was a Sunday morning, so I tuned into a CoDA Zoom meeting and when it was my time to share, I turned the camera to show the room I was in and said, 'The walls of this room are painted red and the ceiling black as it was a teenager's room. Today is the anniversary of Bloody Sunday and I am going to paint the entire room white. This day fifty years ago my life changed in a way that I believed I could never recover from. Today, it will change again. The black on the ceiling represents my bitterness of what happened that day and the red represents my rage. Today, I must let it go to move on.' I then turned the camera off and listened to others speak their truth. I left the house after three coats of paint had covered the walls, ceiling, doors and skirting boards.

Two days later, I got a reply from the man that I had contacted from Planet Earth Singles, immediately aware from his name that he was from the other side of the divide but, it no longer mattered.

I replied, and in the course of the next few weeks we emailed each other on a regular basis. In his first email Gordon asked me what war I was brought up in as I had mentioned this on my profile. *The same one as you*, I replied. He then stated that he was brought up in a small town in County Down and the conflict hadn't affected his family. *Lucky you*, I thought, even though I didn't believe that there was one soul in the six counties that hadn't been affected as the very air that we breathed was poisoned, and air doesn't discriminate.

A few weeks later, he made a statement that winded me when he wrote: *Actually, I joined the RUC to help defeat the IRA who I thought were the problem, but left shortly after I was trained when I realised they weren't.*

I stared at the email, before replying and telling him my background and didn't hear back from him for a week when he wrote and apologised for his community's treatment of mine (this being the second time this had happened to me, the first being when a lady drove from the north to the west to apologise after reading one of my articles in the paper). After that, we became friends even though we didn't exchange telephone numbers, but I accepted this as emails were all I could deal with at that time.

As I was going to visit my sister outside Belfast, Gordon and I made an arrangement to meet, but I still didn't have a phone number even though I had made a request that we speak before we met. I didn't receive his telephone number until the morning of the meeting but did have an address where he lived, which I had taken from a letter which he had forwarded in an email.

Not wanting my sister to know how nervous I was, I went alone on the train to Belfast that Saturday morning with the arrangement that he would meet me at the station but I had called my friend Liam and gave him Gordons address. 'Be very careful,' he said. 'And call me as soon as you meet him and again when you are finished.'

When I arrived at the meeting place, he wasn't there, so I called Liam again.

'You agreed to meet. That is all you needed to do. Go shopping.' He said.

I was still on the phone to Liam when he pulled up on a bicycle and I recognised him from the one picture I had seen which he later told me was from his driver's licence which certainly hadn't done him justice.

'So sorry I'm late,' he said in a fluster. 'I was doing something and didn't realise the time.'

'It's okay,' I replied. 'I was just about to go shopping. I agreed to meet you and that is more than I thought I would ever be able to do.'

'Do you want to go for a coffee or a walk?' he enquired.

'A walk,' I replied.

We headed for Ormeau Park. A place I didn't know even though my niece lived off it.

From the moment we met, we chatted about all kinds of things. I had already told him about this book which he thought fascinating and insisted that I meet Ciaran, a shaman that he had met for the first time the previous day. At one point when we were walking, I noticed a lot of Union Jacks flying, and a thought crossed my mind, *this man could be leading me to my death*, but thankfully it was only fleeting.

An hour later, we walked out of the park facing the street

where my niece lived and were sitting outside a cafe a few minutes away when my sister called to say she was in the city. When I told her where I was, she said, 'Stay where you are and I will meet you there.'

When she arrived, I introduced her to Gordon. Later, she said, 'That man wouldn't do you any harm. That man couldn't do anyone any harm.' And I knew what she meant.

He emailed the next morning to say that he was going to be busy at work for the next few months but asked if he could meet me near my sister's house that day if I wanted to go for another walk. I did.

After that we were firm friends, and a few weeks later I met Ciaran.

I told him about my life and the things that had happened to me.

'You are doing the work of a shaman,' he said.

'But I was never trained,' I replied.

'Maybe not in this lifetime,' he said. 'But you have been trained.'

I told him of the latest movement that had happened since I took the bus tour of Belfast with my sister and that there were loyalist paramilitaries looking to be moved on, and that I didn't think I was strong enough to do it alone.

'You are not alone,' he replied. 'There are many souls helping you. You have nothing to be afraid of.'

But I was very afraid when I started the following day, going to some of the darkest places in the history of the conflict. Places that scared me so much I shook the entire time I was there, but these people needed help, and I knew I had no choice but to help anyone who asked for it, especially a man who had come for help before and I made a condition at the time that he brought his victims with him. He refused. This time I made no such demands, but as he moved on, he took me to meet them, a place was then created for them all to heal together. All this took weeks of my time and all of my strength.

Then, in a meditation in my cottage, I was brought back to a scene in Belfast where the people were wearing clothes from the 1920s, to a place where there was a stench of death and dying before I realised these people were dying of the Spanish flu, which had happened a hundred years before. From my talk with Ciaran, I decided to set up a bus so they could pass through to the other side in an orderly fashion, and all was going well until a man walked up to me and said, *I'm your grand-uncle.* I was so shocked I froze as he was at least thirty years younger than me! He spoke again before moving on, saying, *that is my sister in the picture on your locker.* I came out of the meditation and looked at the picture of my grandfather and grandmother (who I had never met in this realm) which I had placed on the bedside locker the night before my father died, and I felt a shiver run through me. He was my grandmother's brother who had died in Belfast of the Spanish flu, the same day as his wife in 1919.

He appeared again a few weeks later when I was back in Belfast helping those lost souls who had remained on the streets after the Germans had bombed their city. I cried for the city that had seen so much death and destruction in the previous century, but I was delighted for all those ready to move on. Unblocking this beautiful city, reminding me of what another shaman had told me: blocked souls block energy.

Working with my own people (in the North) brought a healing to me that I didn't believe possible, and I knew before others told me that there was a lightness around me that I never had before. As the year progressed and the fiftieth anniversaries of those who died in the most tragic year of the conflict moved on, I let go of all my fears and opinions and helped all those who asked.

A few months later, I met Gordon again in Belfast and this time we walked to the top of Cave Hill and looked over the city. On the way back, he asked if I wanted to see Stormont, I did and had wanted to for a long time. The parliament building had been opened ten years after the formation of the state, controlled by the unionist population, but had recently closed after Sinn Fein became the biggest party in a hundred years, and the unionist leaders decided that they would not work with them until the protocol was sorted. This protocol was put in place in 2019 to protect the land border between the EU and the UK after its divorce in 2016, leaving the divorce between the North East and Republic of Ireland in 1922 back to haunt everyone again. This closed parliament building also left the prospects of an economic boom in jeopardy (as the six counties now had the opportunity of becoming the Singapore of Europe), for a people that have a hundred years of conflict to heal from. Unionist leader's fears that they were losing control (which they already had) left the distinct possibility that they were going to be forced into a united Ireland sooner rather than later. A place where they would be the minority!

From Stormont, he took me to a loyalist's area where the British flags hung from every house but the murals on the walls were changing. One I read could have been transferred to any republican area!

As I meditated (finally understanding that sometimes I was not meditating but instead going into an altered state of consciousness or journeying, as shamans call it) the following day, a paramilitary from the area I had been in the evening before, presented himself to me and made the statement: *It was all your fault.* I had no doubt it wasn't me personally but my community he was blaming as the fear of moving on with stains on his soul petrified him … Without a thought I replied, *Where you are going there is no blame.* At that, my grand-uncle arrived and they left together. In the days that followed he asked if he could bring his comrades. *If they are ready,* I replied, and each day I watched more and more of them move and meet with republicans, other loyalists and their leaders that had made the journey before them.

Weeks later, when things started to quieten down, I was asked in my meditation to take time in September to travel to where I would be guided in the six counties. Told that I would be drawn to the places I needed to go to reassure those who were waiting to let go and move on, thus allowing their communities to do so too, trusting that their experiences in this life were part of their journey, and they or no-one else would be judged in the next. I did this, driving the perimeters of the six counties as I had walked the perimeters of the graveyards in Crete, this time stopping at some of the scenes of some of the greatest tragedies of the Troubles, including Narrow Water, Warrenpoint, where the eighteen soldiers were killed. There, I visited the rubble where the gate lodge once stood, a place where my tenant was reared, a place he wants his ashes spread when he passes on. I also spent time in both Armagh and Derry, dealing with their most recent conflicts and also those in their past.

On the 24th February 2022, Russia had invaded Ukraine in an ongoing conflict. As the year wore on, this new aspect of the crisis affected the entire world as another of its superpowers started doing what those in power have always done, ignoring the wisdom of Mahatma Gandhi who said, 'Earth provides enough for every man's needs, but not every man's greed.'

Had we faced another crisis where we were going to destroy the planet or had the planet forced us into another crisis which would force us to face ourselves?

Would we continue to destroy the planet that supported us or would the planet that supported us destroy us?

How many more crises do we need before we wake up?

But I knew in my heart all was as it was meant to be as I had finally acknowledged, accepted and surrendered to my purpose on the Earth – a purpose that I had chosen before conception – living in the moment with no idea what will happen next but content in the knowledge that whoever is guiding me (my higher power, angels, the great white brotherhood) and with the support of all those who have gone before me I have nothing to fear. Souls that had now surrounded our planet, waiting to be asked for help. Help that needed to be secured on a personal level as peace can only be found in the self, and from there, move out into the planet, not in reverse as I had been told throughout my life. This brings me full circle to a paragraph I wrote in the first page of my first book, a paragraph that I understand so much better thirteen years later.

As I drove with Roisín, who was sleeping like she was unconscious (she who had partied in Galway with her friends the whole night before), the realisation that I was at home filled every cell in my body. The warmth and love that flowed through me was the most wonderful feeling I ever had.

It was not because I had crossed the border to where I was born, nor the fact that it was so peaceful in the car listening to Lyric FM. It was because I had found a peace that I knew would travel with me wherever I was to journey for the rest of my time on this Earth; a peace that I had been seeking for nearly forty years; a peace that no land, nobody or nothing could give me; a peace that I had finally found in myself.

As 2022 came to a close, Stormont elections loomed as the deadline to form a government had been passed and James Craig (first Prime Minister of Northern Ireland) statement 'All I boast is that we are a Protestant parliament and a Protestant state' no longer applied as Sinn Féin were now the largest party in the Northern Ireland Assembly and the 2021 census reported that Catholics outnumbered protestants for the first time since the partition of the Island. Across the water Britain's Queen Elizabeth 11 (upon her death) had finally given up the reins to her seventy-three-year-old son Charles 111. The British government was facing another new Prime Minister, (the third, in as many months). Scotland were still seeking independence and an increasing number of people in Wales were doing the same. As Ireland was edging closer to being *a Nation once again*, the statement made by Boris Johnson (former Prime Minister) 'Brexit will make Britain Great again' was coming back to bite him and the Conservative Party as the last of their empire dissolved.

It certainly is a long road that has no turn.

The next phase of my work presented itself on 2nd November 2022 (All Souls Day) when I was asked to take the book Lost Lives into my home to give the souls named within its pages an opportunity to heal and move on, thus leaving not only those who had died but also those who were still living with broken hearts the opportunity to heal too.

'We must never forget those who have died or been injured ... but we can best honour them through a fresh start, in which we firmly dedicate ourselves to the achievement of reconciliation, tolerance and mutual trust, and to the protection and vindication of the human rights of all.'

Excerpt from the Good Friday Agreement.

CPSIA information can be obtained
at www.ICGtesting.com
Printed in the USA
LVHW100516081222
734780LV00002B/21